→ I AM
A BULLET
SCENES FROM AN ACCELERATING CULTURE
TEXT BY DEAN KUIPERS AND PHOTOGRAPHS BY DOUG AITKEN

→DESIGN: associates in science   CROWN PUBLISHERS NEW YORK

BIKINI ATOLL, MARCH 1, 1954

Thousandths of a second erase thousands of years of life from the Bikini Atoll in the Marshall Islands, as US hydrogen bomb test Bravo vaporizes entire islands on March 1, 1954. Bravo releases more firepower on the home of 161 evacuated Bikinians than all wars in all of history combined.

03
ikini

BIKINI ATOLL, MARCH 1, 1954

1 **SPEED AS HISTORY:** JOE KITTINGER FALLS AT THE SPEED OF SOUND

2 **SPEED AS DESIRE:** TOKYO YOUTH ENDING THE FUTURE

3 **SPEED AS MEDIA:** URBAN STREET GANGS INVADE RURAL NATIVE AMERICA

4 **SPEED AS CHANCE:** REAL TIME VERSUS GOOD TIME IN LAS VEGAS

5 **SPEED AS ECONOMICS:** GOING ONCE, GOING TWICE, SOLD AT AUCTION

6 **SPEED AS DESTRUCTION:** DEMOLITION DERBY

7 **SPEED AS FANTASY:** BOLLYWOOD DREAMS 900 FILMS A YEAR

8 **SPEED AS IDENTITY:** LONG-HAUL TRUCKERS LOST IN PLACE

9 **SPEED AS VEHICLE:** CHASING IMAGINATION TO A SUPERSONIC LAND SPEED RECORD

BIKINI ATOLL, PRESENT

ACKNOWLEDGMENTS

1 SPEED

AS HISTORY

JOE KITTINGER FALLS AT THE SPEED OF SOUND

"JUST AS THE OLD WORLD MARINERS SUDDENLY GLIMPSED A ROUND EARTH TO BE CIRCUMNAVIGATED AND MAPPED, SO AWAKENED PILGRIMS CATCH HUNGRY FLASHES OF VAST AREAS BEYOND DEATH TO BE CREATED AND DISCOVERED AND CHARTED, OPEN TO ANY-ONE READY TO TAKE A STEP INTO THE UNKNOWN, A STEP AS DRASTIC AND IRRETRIEVABLE AS THE TRANSITION FROM WATER TO LAND. THAT STEP IS FROM WORD INTO SILENCE. FROM TIME INTO SPACE."

↳ WILLIAM S. BURROUGHS

009
history

photo © US Air Force

010

→STANDING ALONE IN THE OPEN GONDOLA OF US AIR FORCE HELIUM BALLOON *EXCELSIOR III*, CAPTAIN JOSEPH W. KITTINGER JR. LOOKS DOWN FROM THE RIM OF SPACE. AT 102,800 FEET, ALMOST 20 MILES UP, HE FLOATS HIGHER THAN ANY OTHER HUMAN HAS GONE WITHOUT JET OR ROCKETSHIP. THE GLARE OF THE SUN IS LIKE SANDPAPER ON THE EYES. THE SIDE OF HIS BODY FACING THE RAW SOLAR HEAT IS BOILING, THE OTHER FREEZING. WITH ONLY A STANDARD-ISSUE AIR FORCE MC-3 PILOT'S PARTIAL-PRESSURE SUIT (RATHER THAN AN ASTRONAUT'S FULL-PRESSURE SUIT) KEEPING HIM FROM EXPLODING INTO THE NEAR VACUUM OF THE UPPER STRATOSPHERE, HIS TOES STICK OUT THE DOOR-WAY WITH 99 PERCENT OF EARTH'S ATMOSPHERE BELOW HIM. HE MUT-TERS, "LORD, TAKE CARE OF ME NOW," THEN DOES WHAT NO ASTRONAUT HAS EVER DONE. HE JUMPS.

KITTINGER HOLDS HIS BREATH AND FEELS…NOTHING. ONLY THE DIS-ORIENTING SENSATION THAT HE IS FLOATING. HE SHOULD BE DROPPING, ACCELERATING AT 32 FEET PER SECOND PER SECOND, BUT EVIDENTLY HE IS NOT. THE NYLON FABRIC OF HIS FLIGHT SUIT ISN'T FLAPPING. HE HOVERS IN A BUBBLE OF UTTER SILENCE AMPLIFYING THE BOOMING OF HIS HEART. HE LOOKS AT HIS WATCH. HE LIES THERE IN THE SKY. THE FEAR PASSES THROUGH HIS MIND AGAIN THAT HE'S GONE TOO HIGH, THAT GRAVITY IS TOO WEAK HERE, THAT SOMEHOW HIS GROUND CREW MISCALCULATED AND NOW HE'S DOOMED TO DRIFT UNTIL HIS TINY AIR SUPPLY DRIPS OUT AND HE SUCCUMBS TO THE BEAUTIFUL ABSOLUTE OF THE COLD. HE NOTES THE BLACK OF SPACE AND THE TRANSITION EARTHWARD THROUGH SHADES OF VIOLET AND BLUE. OVERWHELMED ASTRONAUTS HAVE SPENT HOURS IN DREAMY NEAR-DEMENTIA TRYING TO DESCRIBE THOSE SHADES OF BLUE. WANTING TO SEE THE STARS, KITTINGER STRUGGLES TO FLIP OVER.

"IN EERIE SILENCE, EARTH, SKY, AND DEPARTING BALLOON REVOLVE AROUND ME AS IF I WERE THE CENTER OF THE UNIVERSE," HE WRITES LATER FOR *NATIONAL GEOGRAPHIC*. "I FEEL LIKE A MAN IN SUSPENDED ANIMATION."

HE'S FALLING FASTER THAN ANY OTHER HUMAN IN HISTORY. AFTER 16 SECONDS OF FREE FALL, HE FINALLY FEELS A TINY SHUDDER AT HIS BACK. AN EXPERIMENTAL, SIX-FOOT-WIDE STABILIZATION CHUTE OPENS TO KEEP HIM FROM GOING INTO A LETHAL FLAT SPIN, SLOWING HIM IMPERCEPTIBLY IF AT ALL. "CHUTE OPEN," HE SAYS INTO A MIC, RECORDED BY THE EQUIPMENT PACKAGE STRAPPED TO HIS ASS. TERMINAL VELOC-ITY IS AN ALMOST MEANINGLESS IDEA IN THE ENVIRONMENT ABOVE 63,000 FEET, WHERE THERE IS ONLY A FEW MILLIBARS OF AIR PRESSURE AND NO BREATHABLE OXYGEN. SKY DIVERS FALLING THROUGH THE WARM, THICK TROPOSPHERE (BELOW 40,000 FEET) CAN COUNT ON TOP-PING OUT AT ABOUT 230 MILES PER HOUR. WITHIN SECONDS, KITTINGER HAMMERS THROUGH 90,000 FEET AT A REPORTED 614 MPH, A HUMAN METEOR. IN THE NEXT SEVERAL THOUSAND FEET, HE BECOMES THE FIRST AND ONLY HUMAN TO APPROACH SUPERSONIC SPEEDS WITHOUT THE ASSISTANCE OF AN ENGINE. (AT SEA LEVEL ON A SUMMER DAY, THE SPEED OF SOUND IS AROUND 740 MPH. IN THE COLD OF THE TROPO-PAUSE, IT CAN BE AS LOW AS 660 MPH.) KITTINGER SITS FEET DOWN IN THE "ROCKING CHAIR" POSITION, UNAWARE THAT HIS DESCENT HAS TRANS-FORMED THE HUMAN BODY FROM A TRANSCEIVER OF INFORMATION INTO A CARRIER MEDIUM MOVING BEYOND THE INVISIBLE LIMIT OF SOUND WAVES. HE NEVER FEELS THE VIOLENT RUPTURE IN HUMAN PERCEPTION HIS DESCENT HAS CAUSED. HE'S TOO BUSY TRYING TO KNOW HOW TO FEEL IN THE STRANGE INSENSIBLE CHARACTER OF SPACE. HE SAYS NOTHING. HE FINALLY REMEMBERS TO BREATHE.

A LONG MINUTE FALLS AWAY. THE AIR THICKENS, THE CHUTE BEGINS TO BITE. BELOW 80,000 FEET, HE IS GRIPPED BY A MYSTERIOUS AND PRO-LONGED CHOKING SENSATION, FIGHTING FOR PERHAPS 5,000 FEET SIM-PLY TO REMAIN CONSCIOUS. "CAN'T GET MY…BREATH…" HE WHEEZES. JUST AS MYSTERIOUSLY, THE CHOKING SUDDENLY CEASES ABOVE 70,000 FEET. HE BEGINS TO SLOW. "BEAUTIFUL STABILITY," HE SAYS, REFERRING TO THE EXPERIMENTAL MULTISTAGE PARACHUTE HE IS WEARING. "MULTISTAGE PERFECT." BY 50,000 FEET, FRICTION HAS REDUCED HIS AIRSPEED TO ONLY 250 MPH. HE PASSES THROUGH THE COLDEST AMBIENT TEMPERA-TURE OF THE JUMP, MINUS 98 DEGREES FAHRENHEIT, AT 40,000 FEET. HIS FACEPLATE FOGS UP, THEN CLEARS. AT THREE AND A HALF MINUTES OF FREE FALL, ALREADY (AND STILL) THE LONGEST EVER, HE HURTLES TOWARD A STORM GATHERING ABOVE THE NEW MEXICAN DESERT. HE IS TRAVELING AT SUCH SPEED THAT HE UNCONSCIOUSLY PULLS HIS LEGS UP UNDERNEATH HIM, AS THOUGH EXPECTING THE CLOUDS TO BE SOLID.

HE PUNCHES THROUGH THE UNDERCAST AND AN ANEROID AUTOMAT-ICALLY FIRES THE PINS THAT DEPLOY HIS MAIN CHUTE. "FOUR MINUTES AND THIRTY-SEVEN SECONDS FREE FALL," REMARKS AN ELATED KITTINGER, CHECKING HIS WATCH AS THE RED-AND-WHITE CHUTE BILLOWS

OPEN. "EIGHTEEN THOUSAND FEET. AHHHH BOY!" THE ANXIETY OF THE FREE FALL GRADUALLY DISSIPATES AS HE FALLS TOWARD THE WHITE SANDS TESTING GROUNDS, DAPPLED WITH RAIN FALLEN SINCE HE BOARDED THE BALLOON HOURS EARLIER. HE REMEMBERS THEN THAT THERE ARE PEOPLE WAITING THERE, HIS CREW AND FRIENDS. HE TRIES TO CUT AWAY HIS EQUIPMENT PACK, BUT CANNOT, AND PLOWS INTO A BED OF DESERT GRASS, SAND AND SAGE 27 MILES WEST OF TULAROSA, WEIGHED DOWN BY ABOUT 170 POUNDS OF GEAR. HIS STOPWATCH SAYS HE'S FALLEN FOR 13 MINUTES, 45 SECONDS. AS HIS TEAM POURS OUT OF RESCUE HELICOPTERS, HE SMILES UP AT THEM FROM THE 100-DEGREE DESERT FLOOR AND SAYS, "I'M VERY GLAD TO BE BACK WITH YOU ALL."

THE DATE WAS AUGUST 16, 1960. IN ALMOST 40 YEARS, NO ONE ELSE HAS ATTEMPTED TO JUMP FROM EVEN HALF THAT ALTITUDE. NO ONE ELSE KNOWS WHAT IT'S LIKE TO FLOAT IN THE VACUUM OF THE UPPER STRATOS-PHERE WITH NO VEHICLE AT ALL, TETHERED TO NOTHING BUT NOTHING-NESS, AN AERONAUT FLYING ONLY HIS OWN BODY. IT IS KITTINGER WHO HAS FELT THE FUTURE. AND HE KNEW IT. KITTINGER WANTED TO GO HIGHER.

ACCELERATION IS NO LONGER AN INTANGIBLE FUNCTION OF THE IMAGI-NATION, GENTLY NUDGING THE ORDINARY EVENTS THAT CONSTITUTE HISTORY. RIGHT NOW, ACCELERATION IS HISTORY. IT IS THE EVENT. ACCELERATION IS THE PRIME PHYSICAL, TECHNOLOGICAL AND EVEN SPIR-ITUAL ENGINE OF THIS MOMENT, AND ANY FORESEEABLE FUTURE OTHER THAN NO FUTURE. ACCELERATION IS THE CONSTANT IN THE SPEED OF CHANGE. IT MAY CHANGE FASTER OR SLOWER, BUT IT IS NEVER STATIC. IT NEVER LOOKS BACK.

EXCEPT, PERHAPS, UPON ITS OWN PROFUNDITY. ACCELERATION DESTROYS AS FAST AS IT CREATES. ALFRED NORTH WHITEHEAD WROTE: "THE MAJOR ADVANCES IN CIVILIZATION ARE PROCESSES THAT ALL BUT WRECK THE SOCIETIES IN WHICH THEY OCCUR." THE SUDDENLY PALPABLE CHARACTER OF ACCELERATION IS ONE OF THOSE MAJOR ADVANCES. WRECKAGE IS NOW THE STUFF OF WHICH LIVES ARE MADE. DIFFERENCES BETWEEN PARENTS AND CHILDREN USED TO BE CALLED THE "GENERATION GAP." THAT COMFORTING OLD RELIC ONLY LASTED ABOUT ONE GENERATION. PARENT AND CHILD SPEED UP TOGETHER NOW, AND THE ACCELERATOR TUNES HIS OR HER MIND TO SEE THE GAPS EVERYWHERE AS THEY EMERGE, IN EVERYTHING, ALL THE TIME. MONITORING ACCELERATION IS THE JOB.

FUTURISM, ONCE THE PROVINCE OF PROPHETS AND SOOTHSAYERS AND PHILOSOPHER-SCIENTISTS, IS NOW A BASIC RESUME SKILL.

HOW FAST IS FAST? PERCEIVING ACCELERATION MEANS KNOWING SPEED. BUT THE NUMBERS LIE. THE SCHEDULE BOOK IS NOT THE ACTUAL DAY. THE ACTS THAT DEFINE SPEED ARE SHADOWY HAPPENINGS ON THE SLIPPERY PERIPHERY OF VISION. SPEED IS NOT AN ABSOLUTE: IT IS SIMPLY A PERCEPTUAL EVENT. WHAT YOU SEE IS WHAT YOU GET. THE REAL QUES-TION IS: HOW DO WE *EXPERIENCE* FAST?

WHEN KITTINGER STEPPED OUT OF HIS GONDOLA, HE DIDN'T FEEL WHAT HE EXPECTED TO FEEL. HE HAD BEEN THERE BEFORE, ON A JUMP FROM 76,000 FEET, BUT THIS HEIGHT WAS MUCH MORE EXTREME. HE HAD MORE TIME UP THERE THAN HE THOUGHT. OR, MORE ACCURATELY, HIS PHYSICAL SENSATIONS DIDN'T BLUR TIME THE WAY HE THOUGHT THEY WOULD. AS HE BECAME THE FASTEST-MOVING ENGINELESS HUMAN BEING OF ALL TIME, HIS ENVIRONMENT DENIED HIM INFORMATION. THIS BROUGHT ON A TEMPORARY DISCONNECT, AN INTELLECTUAL DISSONANCE. HIS BRAIN WORKED MANIACALLY TO MATCH THE PHYSICAL REALITY OF FALLING FASTER THAN THE SPEED OF SOUND WITH HIS BODY'S SENSORY INFORMATION, BUT AT THE APEX OF HIS TRUE AIRSPEED THEY CLASHED.

SPEED KILLS. IT IS ITS OWN WORST ENEMY. BY ITS VERY NATURE, A SPEED EVENT RENDERS ITSELF MOOT, REDUNDANT, OUTMODED AS IT IS HAPPENING — BECAUSE THE MODES OF PERCEPTION REQUIRED TO KNOW IT MUST BE CREATED AFTER THE FACT. AND THE FACTS — MOSTLY NUMBERS — ARE CONSTANTLY DESTROYED. AS A SPEED EVENT RATTLES HUMAN SELF-KNOWLEDGE, PERCEPTUAL MODELS MUST BE REBUILT IN ITS WAKE.

TIME, HOWEVER, HEALS. SPEED AND TIME ARE MUTUAL ENEMIES, MATTER AND ANTIMATTER. EINSTEIN'S GENERAL THEORY OF RELATIVITY PROVED THAT SPEED RENDERS TIME RELATIVE, BUT ALSO SHOWED THAT TIME IS IMMUTABLE WITHIN ITS SPEEDING FRAME OF REFERENCE. SPEED IS ABOUT BEATING THE CLOCK, BUT THE CLOCK CAN'T BE BEAT. TIME CANNOT BE DESTROYED AND, LIKE ENERGY, IS CONSERVED. MEANING: YOU DON'T GET IT BACK. SPEED BLURS PERCEPTION, BUT RECONSTRUCTING PERCEPTION ACCORDING TO INCREMENTS OF TIME CLARIFIES THE EVENT ONCE MORE, MAKES IT PERCEIVABLE.

WILLIAM BURROUGHS UNDERSTOOD THE RELATIONSHIP BETWEEN

TIME AND SPEED, OR TIME AND SPACE, AS THE REVERSE OF THE PERCEPTUAL MODEL MENTIONED HERE. HE ARGUED THAT TIME KILLS BECAUSE IT HOLDS US IN OUR BODIES AND MAKES US SLAVES TO GODS. AND THAT SPEED, OR THE LEAP TO PERCEPTION BEYOND ONE GOD AND FIXED MEASUREMENTS, A STATE OF CONSTANT SENSORY AND SPIRITUAL EVOLUTION, IS THE BIG FIX, THE GREAT ESCAPE.

PERHAPS IT'S PRE-MILLENNIAL TENSION, BUT ACCELERATION HAS BEEN THE SUBJECT OF QUITE A BIT OF DISCUSSION LATELY, MUCH OF IT ARGUING PRO OR CON THAT ACCELERATION IS EITHER PROGRESS OR DESTROYING OUR WAY OF LIFE. WHICH IS USELESS. LIFE WILL NEVER MOVE ANY SLOWER. NOSTALGIA LEADS US TO BELIEVE THAT ACCELERATION WILL PLANE OUT, ACHIEVING SOME STATIC FUTURE STATE, BUT PERHAPS THAT STATE WILL BE ONE OF PERMANENT TECHNOLOGICAL AND SENSORY FLUX. CHANGE BEGETS CHANGE.

SPEEDING UP IS WHAT WE DO. IT IS HUMAN NATURE. WE ARE TOOL USERS. WE WILL ALWAYS HUNT FOR A WAY TO DO THINGS FASTER, MORE EFFICIENTLY, WITH LESS EFFORT AND LESS ERROR. DOES IT EVER GAIN US ANYTHING? YES AND NO. QUANTUM LEAPS IN QUALITY OF LIFE COME AT A PRICE: MORE TOOLS WE CAN'T LIVE WITHOUT AND WHICH WE PROBABLY HAVE TO WORK TWICE AS HARD TO BUY.

BUT CONSTANTLY TREADING WATER AT THE SURFACE OF CHANGE HAS CONSEQUENCES. DEEPER HISTORICAL CURRENTS FLOW BENEATH US. WE DON'T SEE THEM AS CLEARLY AS WE SHOULD. SOMETIMES WE DON'T FEEL THEM AT ALL. BUT THE PHYSICS OF SPEED DOES GIVE THEM SOME MEASURE OF PREDICTABILITY. AS SPEED CHANGES PERCEPTION, OUR ABILITY TO KNOW OUR SENSES AND EVEN OUR SENSORY ORGANS ADAPT, AND OUR UNDERSTANDING OF TIME EVOLVES ACCORDINGLY.

FIVE-TIME WORLD LAND SPEED RECORD HOLDER CRAIG BREEDLOVE'S EXPERIENCE ILLUMINATES WHAT A VAST FABRIC TIME MIGHT HAVE BECOME FOR JOE KITTINGER. FILMMAKER AND CRITIC HOLLIS FRAMPTON WROTE IN HIS BOOK *CIRCLES OF CONFUSION*, ABOUT BREEDLOVE'S DISASTROUS 1964 RUN IN THE *SPIRIT OF AMERICA* JET CAR — A RECORD 526 MILE-PER-HOUR BLAST ACROSS UTAH'S BONNEVILLE SALT FLATS. (FRAMPTON, TRUE TO THE TITLE OF HIS BOOK, CONFUSED THE DATES AND SPEEDS IN HIS ACCOUNT). AT THE END OF THE SECOND RUN (SPEED RECORDS ARE MEASURED BY AVERAGING THE CAR'S SPEED OVER A ONE-MILE COURSE IN BOTH DIRECTIONS, WITH THE RUNS TAKING PLACE WITHIN THE SPACE OF ONE HOUR), EVERYTHING WENT WRONG. AS BREEDLOVE BEGAN TO SLOW, A BRAKE EXPLODED AT ABOUT 400 MPH. OVER THE NEXT MILE AND A HALF, BOTH DROGUE CHUTES FAILED AND THE CAR WENT OUT OF CONTROL, SHEARED THROUGH A STRING OF TELEPHONE POLES LIKE A KNIFE, LEFT THE GROUND OVER A SMALL RISE, TURNED UPSIDE DOWN LIKE A WOUNDED JET FIGHTER AND SPLASHED INTO AN 18-FOOT-DEEP SALT BRINE POND. BREEDLOVE, AS IS HIS HABIT, EMERGED UNSCATHED, AND QUIPPED, "FOR MY NEXT TRICK, I'LL SET MYSELF ON FIRE."

AS FRAMPTON TELLS IT, BREEDLOVE "WAS INTERVIEWED IMMEDIATELY AFTER THE WRECK. I HAVE HEARD THE TAPE. IT LASTS AN HOUR AND 35 MINUTES, DURING WHICH TIME BREEDLOVE DELIVERS A CONNECTED ACCOUNT OF WHAT HE THOUGHT AND DID DURING A PERIOD OF ABOUT 8.7 SECONDS...IN THE COURSE OF THE INTERVIEW, BREEDLOVE EVERYWHERE GIVES EVIDENCE OF CONDENSING, OF CURTAILING; NOT WISHING TO BORE ANYONE, HE IS DOING HIS POLITE BEST TO MAKE A LONG STORY SHORT. COMPARED TO THE HISTORICAL INTERVAL HE REFERS TO, HIS ECSTATIC UTTERANCE REPRESENTS, ACCORDING TO MY CALCULATION, A TEMPORAL EXPANSION IN THE RATIO OF SOME 655 TO ONE."

BREEDLOVE'S TRAINING WITH THE JET CAR, A VERSION OF WHICH HE IS STILL RUNNING TODAY, AND THE EXPERIENCE OF NEAR SUPERSONIC SPEEDS HAS CHANGED HIS PERCEPTUAL ABILITIES. HE ONCE REMARKED THAT THE PHYSICAL EFFORT OF A RECORD ATTEMPT IS "LIKE DOING EIGHT HOURS OF WORK IN FORTY SECONDS." PERCEPTUALLY, HE DESCRIBED IT TO ME AS A PROCESS OF UNCONSCIOUS, INSTANTANEOUS ABSORPTION IN MULTIPLE AND CONCURRENT FIELDS. STUFFING AND UNSTUFFING DENSE NETS OF INFORMATION. RESTRUCTURING TIME TO REFLECT THE TRUE NATURE OF THE SPEED.

KITTINGER EXPERIENCED SOMETHING OF A REVERSE EFFECT: HAVING NO REFERENCE POINTS FOR HIS SENSES OTHER THAN A WATCH AND AN ALTIMETER, IT WAS ONLY TIME THAT STRUCTURED HIS EVENT AT ALL. OTHERWISE, FOR A WHILE THERE, IT WASN'T REALLY HAPPENING.

TIME IS NO LONGER AN ABSOLUTE IN THE PERCEIVED WORLD. NOR DISTANCE, NOR LOCATION, NOR RELATIONSHIPS TO OTHER HUMANS, WHICH HAVE ALWAYS BEEN UNDERSTOOD AT LEAST IN PART BY TIME. THE MECHANISTIC NEWTONIAN UNIVERSE, WHICH WAS MADE BY A GOD WHO WOUND IT UP LIKE A SPRING-LOADED TOY AND SET IT RUNNING ON ITS PREDETERMINED, ORDERLY RELATIONSHIP TO THE CLOCK, WAS ALREADY

IN TROUBLE AT THE START OF THE INDUSTRIAL REVOLUTION. NIETZSCHE SAID THAT THIS GOD WAS DEAD. EINSTEIN PUT THE FINAL NAIL IN THAT COFFIN, ARGUING THAT PERCEPTIONS OF A SINGLE EVENT AND THE TIME THAT PASSED COULD DIFFER VASTLY AND STILL BE "CORRECT," DEPENDING ON THE RELATIVE SPEEDS OF THE PERCEIVERS AND THE EVENT.

OR, SEEN ANOTHER WAY, PERCEPTION OF SPEED IS ONE WAY TO DEFINE HOW FAST THE CLOCK IS MOVING. SIX BILLION EARTHLY RESIDENTS HAVE CREATED SIX BILLION DIFFERENTLY ORDERED UNIVERSES. ALL OF THEM CORRECT. WE ARE OUR SPEED.

HOW WOULD ONE ILLUMINATE THAT PRINCIPLE? ONE WOULD HAVE OBSERVERS RECOUNT THEIR VERSIONS SIDE BY SIDE. THAT'S WHAT THIS BOOK IS ABOUT.

THE PERCEPTIONS OF THE SPEEDERS REMAIN. THE HUMAN BEING FEELING, FEARING, AND FREAKING AT THE CENTER OF ANY EVENT RESONATES BEYOND THE DISINTEGRATING EFFECT OF THE NUMBERS. THIS IS WHERE ACCELERATION IS LOCATED, AND THE BREAKTHROUGHS ARE PERHAPS THE EASIEST WAY FOR CONTEMPORARY HISTORY TO BE UNDERSTOOD.

IF, FOR INSTANCE, KITTINGER HAD THROWN A PACKAGE OF CAMERAS OUT OF THE GONDOLA INSTEAD OF HIS OWN BODY, RECORDING ITS OWN DESCENT AS A FILM (HE ACTUALLY WAS FILMED BY 12 DIFFERENT CAMERAS, PLUS HELICOPTER FOOTAGE DURING APPROACH TO LANDING), WOULD WE TRUST THE HAUNTING, TACTILE QUALITY OF THAT NOTHINGNESS? NO, BECAUSE MEDIATION LEAVES SENSORY GAPS, PARTICULARLY WHEN WE NEED TO JUDGE THAT GREAT INTANGIBLE: HUMAN EMOTIONAL RESPONSE. WE NEED HIM TO TELL US ABOUT THE PARTS THE FILM CAN'T RECORD. WHEN YURI GAGARIN BECAME THE FIRST MAN IN SPACE A FEW MONTHS LATER IN APRIL 1961, IT WAS A VASTLY DIFFERENT EVENT THAN WHEN THE DOG LAIKA WENT UP BEFORE HIM. KITTINGER'S GHOSTLY FLOATING SENSATION MUTATES OUR EXPECTATIONS ABOUT THE UPPER ATMOSPHERE BY THE PURITY OF EMOTION WE PROJECT INTO IT. ONLY BECAUSE HIS BODY WAS NOT RIPPED APART BY A SONIC BOOM DO WE KNOW IT'S POSSIBLE TO APPROACH THE SOUND BARRIER RELATIVELY NAKED. HE KNOWS. HE AND HIS MENTOR DR. JOHN PAUL STAPP, WHO USED HIMSELF AS TEST SUBJECT IN EARLY ROCKET SLED TRIALS TO MACH 0.915 AND INCREDIBLE 46.2-G DECELERATIONS. THEY'RE THE ONLY ONES WHO'VE EVER BEEN THERE.

FILMS, PHOTOS, RECORDED INTERVIEWS AND TELEVISION BROADCASTS LET US BE THERE WITH KITTINGER, TOO. IN THE 1960S, MARSHALL MCLUHAN LOOKED AT THE PROLIFERATION OF THESE SIMPLE SIMULATIONS, THE SHARING OF EXPERIENCE, AND RECOGNIZED MEDIA AS AN EXTENSION OF THE HUMAN NERVOUS SYSTEM. HE SAW THE FAVORING OF ANY ONE MEDIUM AS AN EVOLUTIONARY CHANGE IN THE WAY WE PERCEIVE. IT NOT ONLY INCREASES THE TRANSMISSION OF TOTAL SENSORY EXPERIENCE AND EMPATHETIC UNDERSTANDING, BUT WE ADAPT TO IT. THE MEDIUM THAT WAS AND STILL IS EXTENDING THE FASTEST IS ELECTRONIC MEDIA.

PERHAPS EXACTLY *WHAT* WE PERCEIVE ALSO CHANGES THE MEDIUM ITSELF. FOR INSTANCE, RIGHT NOW THE HUMAN USER NEEDS ALL MEDIA TO REFLECT ACCELERATION, OR WE DON'T TRUST IT. WE WANT ELECTRONIC MEDIA TO CATCH UP WITH THE ACTUAL SPEED OF OUR NERVOUS SYSTEMS, JUST LIKE KITTINGER NEEDED HIS SENSES TO CATCH UP WITH THE WEIRDNESS OF HIS UPPER-STRATOSPHERIC EXPERIENCE. THOUGH MANY OF MCLUHAN'S INFERENCES ABOUT THE "INVOLVING" CHARACTER OF HIS ELECTRONIC "GLOBAL VILLAGE" HAVE SHIFTED UNDER HIS NIMBLE FEET (HE WASN'T AROUND TO SEE THE TRULY LONELY, ISOLATED BUSINESS OF ONLINE LIFE, FOR INSTANCE), THE NEURAL NET ANALOGY IS MORE APROPOS TODAY THAN EVER. INSTANTANEOUS TWO-WAY OR INFINITE-WAY COMMUNICATION, WITH EVERYONE, EVERYWHERE, IS NOW ACKNOWLEDGED AS A GIVEN. THE TECHNOLOGY ONLY HAS TO CATCH UP WITH US AND GET FAST. WE'RE ALREADY LOOKING FOR A WAY OUT, TO NOT BE ENSLAVED BY THE NEW TECHNOLOGY WHEN IT ARRIVES.

ACCELERATION IS THE UNIVERSAL DESIRE. WITH EACH ACCELERATION, THE HUMAN TOOLBOX GAINS A PERCEPTUAL ABILITY AND DESTROYS OTHERS. (MAYBE WE NEVER LOSE THEM, BUT JUST PILE UP THE OLD PERCEPTUAL MODELS IN ART MUSEUMS AND ON CAVE WALLS.) WE HAVE A TREMENDOUS EMPATHETIC ABILITY TO SHARE SPEED. KITTINGER FELL AT THE SPEED OF SOUND. THE SPEED OF SOUND IS FASTER THAN THE AIRSPEED OF THE BULLET FROM A STANDARD .45 AUTOMATIC. BECAUSE OF KITTINGER, HUMANS NOW KNOW ONE VERSION OF HOW IT FEELS TO GO THAT FAST.

"I AM A BULLET," SAYS KITTINGER.

"THERE WAS A BIG DIFFERENCE PSYCHOLOGICALLY BETWEEN THE TWO JUMPS," SAYS KITTINGER AS WE SIT AROUND THE KITCHEN TABLE AT HIS UNASSUMING RANCH-STYLE HOME IN A WATERY SUBURB OF ALTAMONTE

SPRINGS, FLORIDA. THE EXCELSIOR PROGRAM WAS A SERIES OF THREE INCREASINGLY HIGHER JUMPS, THE SECOND FROM 76,000 FEET. "BEING A FIGHTER PILOT AND A TEST PILOT, YOU ALWAYS HAVE SOME FALL-BACK POSITION. I FELT THAT IF I'D HAD A FAILURE OF MY PRESSURE SUIT, OF MY FACEPLATE, OF MY REGULATOR, OF ANYTHING WHEN I WAS AT 76,000 FEET, THERE WAS A CHANCE I COULD SURVIVE. BUT OVER 100,000 FEET, I KNEW THAT IF SOMETHING WENT WRONG, I WAS DEAD."

THE FULL SCOPE OF KITTINGER'S BREAKTHROUGH RESONATES HERE IN THE SMOKY HEAT OF A SUMMER WHEN ALL BUT ONE FLORIDA COUNTY ARE ON FIRE, SEEING HIM AS AN ORDINARY MAN. A FRIENDLY, BARREL-CHESTED, RED-HAIRED GRANDFATHER, HE RARELY SPENDS MORE THAN A WEEK AT HOME. HE AND HIS WIFE, SHERRIE, KEEP TO AN AGGRESSIVE SCHEDULE OF APPEARANCES AND BARNSTORM AROUND THE COUNTRY IN HIS 1929 NEW STANDARD BIPLANE. HE IS STILL ENERVATED BY A DISTURBING IDEA BORN OF THAT LONG LOOK INTO THE BLACK OF SPACE.

"AS I STOOD IN THE DOOR OF THE CAPSULE, I KNEW HOW HOSTILE SPACE WAS," HE SAYS. "BEFORE I JUMPED, I SAID [INTO HIS TAPE RECORDER] THAT WE'D NEVER CONQUER SPACE." THESE COMMENTS REFLECT HIS FEAR AT THAT ALTITUDE, BUT HE BELIEVES THEM STILL. DURING THE ASCENT THROUGH 40,000 FEET ON *EXCELSIOR III*, KITTINGER'S RIGHT PRESSURE GLOVE FAILED TO INFLATE, AND HIS HAND EXPANDED TO ALMOST TWICE ITS NORMAL SIZE. HE SAID NOTHING TO THE MEDICAL OFFICER, FEARING THEY'D SCRUB THE MISSION. AT PEAK ALTITUDE, HE WAS IN EXCRUCIATING PAIN WITH BLOOD POOLING IN THAT HAND AS IT SURGED OUTWARD TOWARD THE VACUUM. "IT'S A VERY HOSTILE ENVIRONMENT. MAN IS A ONE-G, 68-DEGREE, ONE-ATMOSPHERE BODY. WE'RE PRETTY FRAGILE, AND WE'RE PRETTY LIMITED IN WHAT WE CAN DO AS A BIOLOGICAL SPECIMEN. WE'LL LEARN HOW TO LIVE IN [SPACE], BUT WE'LL NEVER CONQUER IT. THE NOTHINGNESS IS FRIGHTENING."

WHETHER KITTINGER MEANS WE WILL NEVER ADAPT OUR BODIES TO THE ABSOLUTE CONDITIONS OF SPACE OR, CONVERSELY, WE WILL NEVER BEND IT TO OUR OWN WILL, HIS JUMP DOES IRONICALLY REFLECT THE MILITARIZED CHARACTER OF OUR SPACE PROGRAMS. HE MADE A HOLE IN OUR PERCEPTION OF THAT HOSTILE ENVIRONMENT. A HOLE THAT REMAINS. THE SCIENTISTS AND MILITARY MEN WHO WERE PAYING ATTENTION POURED THROUGH THAT HOLE TO GET A LOOK AROUND. THEY HATCHED A NEW MISSION FOR KITTINGER THAT SHATTERS EVERYTHING WE KNOW ABOUT SPACE TRAVEL. AS SARTRE WROTE: "TO UNDERSTAND IS TO CHANGE, TO GO BEYOND ONESELF."

IN KITTINGER'S CASE, WAY BEYOND. HIS JUMP MADE IT PLAIN, BEFORE GAGARIN OR JOHN GLENN HAD BEEN IN SPACE, THAT A PRESSURE-SUITED AERONAUT COULD NOT ONLY SURVIVE IN THE VACUUM OF THE UPPER ATMOSPHERE BUT COULD FALL SAFELY BACK TO FRIENDLY AIR. WITHIN WEEKS OF *EXCELSIOR III*, THE AIR FORCE PROPOSED FLYING KITTINGER 100 MILES FROM EARTH IN THE NOSE CONE OF A REDSTONE ROCKET TO THE LIMITS OF KNOWN SPACE TRAVEL AT THAT TIME (VON BRAUN'S V-2 ROCKETS HAD BEEN THAT HIGH), THEN EJECT HIM INTO THE EXOSPHERE. KITTINGER WOULD THEN CONSERVE HIS TRAJECTORY TO RISE AS HIGH AS POSSIBLE AGAINST GRAVITY, MANY MILES HIGHER, FALLING BACK THROUGH THE ATMOSPHERE AS BEFORE. SINCE IT WAS ALL A VACUUM ABOVE 63,000 FEET, WHAT WOULD BE THE DIFFERENCE IF YOU WERE EIGHT MILES HIGH OR 100 MILES ABOVE IT?

"IT WASN'T NECESSARY [TO GO HIGHER], AND FOR THIS REASON," SAYS KITTINGER'S FORMER PROJECT SUPERVISOR, DR. STAPP, FROM HIS HOME IN ALMOGORDO, NEW MEXICO. "SEVEN HUNDRED SIXTY MILLIMETERS OF MERCURY IS THE ATMOSPHERIC PRESSURE AT SEA LEVEL. AT 104,000 FEET, IT'S SIX MILLIMETERS OF MERCURY. NOW, HOW MUCH WORSE DOES IT GET AT ZERO MILLIMETERS? [CHUCKLES] FROM A FEW OUNCES OF ATMOSPHERIC PRESSURE PER SQUARE INCH TO NOTHING?"

AS FAR AS THEY COULD TELL, GOING HIGHER WAS JUST A MATTER OF HAVING A GOOD SUIT AND ENOUGH AIR. KITTINGER WANTED TO DO IT.

IMAGINE THE IMPLICATIONS: PEOPLE ALWAYS PICTURE THEMSELVES, IN SCIENCE FICTION AND ELSEWHERE, AS BLASTING THROUGH SPACE IN ROCKETSHIPS. WHAT IF THE SPACE SHUTTLE COULD JUST DIP INTO THE ATMOSPHERE, DUMP OUT A FEW TIRED ASTRONAUTS, AND LET THEM PLUMMET BACK TO EARTH WITH A PARACHUTE ON THEIR BACKS, WHILE THE SHIP STAYED IN ORBIT? THIS IS ESSENTIALLY WHAT KITTINGER DID. IT'D SAVE A LOT OF HOLES IN THE OZONE BY REDUCING ROCKET BLASTOFFS AT CANAVERAL. THE EXPOSURE TO THE NAKED SKY FEELS WRONG, BUT MAYBE THAT'S ONLY BECAUSE WE'RE THINKING WRONG. FOR INSTANCE, MILITARY RESEARCH DIVERS WORKING AT SUPER-DEEP DEPTHS HAVE EXPERIMENTED WITH A SCUBA SYSTEM SO COMPLETELY COUNTER-INTUITIVE IT BRINGS ON A FEELING OF REVULSION: AT DEPTHS WHERE THE DIVER CAN NO LONGER MATCH THE PRESSURE NECESSARY TO MAINTAIN AIR INSIDE THE LUNGS, THEY BREATHE THICK, SUPER-OXYGENATED *LIQ-*

UID. JUST LIKE YOU DID IN THE WOMB. IN A SENSE, THEY ARE GIVING IN TO THE DEMANDS OF THE MEDIUM: DOWN THERE, YOU BREATHE WATER. SURPRISE, SURPRISE, GROWN PEOPLE CAN DO THAT JUST FINE AND NOT DROWN. IT JUST MAKES YOU GAG THINKING ABOUT IT.

THE FLEDGLING SPACE-RACERS AT NASA, CREATED BY EISENHOWER IN JULY 1958 AND THUS A NEWBORN AGENCY DURING EXCELSIOR, WERE SO DISINCLINED TO EXPLORE THE POSSIBILITIES OF THE ASTRONAUT STRIPPED BARE THAT THEY QUICKLY CHOKED OFF THIS AREA OF RESEARCH. IN MAY 1961, HOT ON THE HEELS OF GAGARIN, JOHN GLENN WAS LIFTED INTO SPACE IN A REDSTONE ROCKET FOR A 15-MINUTE SUB-ORBITAL CRUISE. ALTHOUGH KITTINGER WAS THE IDEAL CANDIDATE FOR NASA'S ASTRONAUT TRAINING PROGRAM, HE AND STAPP DECIDED HIS TESTING EXPERTISE WAS TOO VALUABLE TO REPLACE AND HE WAS NOT CLEARED FOR REASSIGNMENT. NO ONE EVER SURPASSED OR DUPLICATED HIS RESEARCH JUMPS. STAPP CANCELED THE EXCELSIOR PROGRAM AND MOVED ALL HIS PEOPLE INTO OTHER AREAS OF RESEARCH. IT SEEMS THAT THE FUNDERS AND RATIONALIZERS OF SPACE TRAVEL IN GOVERNMENT AND THE MILITARY-INDUSTRIAL COMPLEX CANNOT CARE ABOUT ASTRONAUTS, THEIR BODIES, OR THEIR PERCEPTIONS. THEY MUST CARE ABOUT PAYLOADS.

SO MUCH SO, IN FACT, THAT MUCH OF EXCELSIOR'S RESEARCH WAS IGNORED. ALAN SHEPARD EVIDENTLY TRIED TO CONVINCE NASA TO INCLUDE A PERSONAL PARACHUTE SYSTEM IN THE EARLIEST MERCURY SPACECRAFT, BUT THE IDEA WAS FINALLY REJECTED. ACCORDING TO STAPP, THE MERCURY, GEMINI AND APOLLO CRAFT WERE DESIGNED TO GET THE WHOLE CAPSULE DOWN SAFELY IN AN EMERGENCY, AND BAILING OUT OF THE CAPSULE ITSELF WAS RULED OUT. HOWEVER, NONCAPSULE CRAFT SUCH AS THE SPACE SHUTTLE COULD USE IT AND DON'T.

"THE DROGUE CHUTE FORMULA THAT THEY USE TODAY ON THE SR-71 AND THE U-2 [HIGH-ALTITUDE SPY PLANES] WAS DERIVED FROM THE WORK THAT WE DID," SAYS KITTINGER, REFLECTING ON THE INTERDEPARTMENTAL POLITICAL INFIGHTING AND EGO STRUGGLES THAT SHELVED THE WORK FOR WHICH HE'D RISKED HIS LIFE.

"NASA OPTED NOT TO USE IT. THE SPACE SHUTTLE IS REALLY THE FIRST EXPERIMENTAL VEHICLE THAT DID NOT HAVE A MEANS OF ESCAPE. THE *CHALLENGER* FLIGHT [WHICH EXPLODED MIDFLIGHT IN JANUARY 1986, AT LESS THAN HALF THE ALTITUDE OF *EXCELSIOR III*, KILLING ALL CREW MEMBERS], IF THEY'D HAD THE SYSTEM THAT WE DEVELOPED, ALL OF THEM COULD HAVE MADE IT OUT OF THERE. THEY WERE ALL ALIVE WHEN THEY HIT THE WATER."

STAPP ALSO BRINGS UP THE *CHALLENGER*, BUT WHEN ASKED WHY NO ONE EVER WENT FURTHER, HE SAYS, "EXCELSIOR HAD ACHIEVED THE MISSION OBJECTIVE."

EXCELSIOR, ALONG WITH THE MANHIGH AND STRATOLAB BALLOON PROJECTS BEFORE IT, HAD PROVED THAT ASTRONAUTS COULD SURVIVE IN SPACE, NOT BE BURNED UP BY "COSMIC RADIATION," AS WAS FEARED IN THE EARLY 1950S. NOR DEVELOP "BREAKAWAY PHENOMENON," A MAJOR TOM-LIKE PSYCHOLOGICAL STATE WHERE THE PILOT FEELS ENTICED TO SIMPLY DRIFT OFF INTO SPACE INSTEAD OF RETURNING TO EARTH. KITTINGER OUTMODED HIS OWN WORK BY PROVING THAT PEOPLE COULD SAFELY LOOK THROUGH EARTH'S ATMOSPHERE TO MOONSHOTS, SPACE STATIONS, AND BEYOND.

SO HIS TERRITORY WAITS THERE STILL IN THE UPPER ATMOSPHERE, UNEXPLORED.

INSTEAD OF GOING TO THE MOON, KITTINGER FLEW THREE TOURS OF COMBAT IN VIETNAM AND BECAME COMMANDER OF A FIGHTER SQUADRON THAT SHOT DOWN MORE NORTH VIETNAMESE MIGS THAN ANY OTHER. HE FLEW P-26 AIRCRAFT IN 1963-64, A-26S IN '66-67, AND F-4'S IN '71-72. HE FLEW 483 COMBAT SORTIES IN OVER 1,000 HOURS OF COMBAT. KITTINGER WAS SHOT DOWN ON MAY 11, 1972 ("BY THE WORLD'S GREATEST FIGHTER PILOT," HE JOKES), AND SPENT A YEAR AS A POW, ENDURING EXTENSIVE TORTURE IN HANOI UNTIL HE AND APPROXIMATELY 550 OTHERS WERE FREED UNDER THE 1973 PARIS PEACE ACCORDS. IN 1985, KITTINGER MADE THE FIRST SOLO BALLOON CROSSING OF THE ATLANTIC.

IN LIGHT OF HIS DRAMATIC AND ONGOING CAREER, PERHAPS IT'S NATURAL THAT KITTINGER HIMSELF NEVER EQUATED HIS JUMP WITH ANY BREAKTHROUGH, AND NEVER EVEN LOOKED BACK ON IT AS THE HIGHLIGHT OF HIS CAREER.

"OUR PROJECT MADE JUST A SMALL CONTRIBUTION TO WHERE WE WERE GOING," HE SAYS, EXHIBITING THE SANGUINE, TIGHT-LIPPED ATTITUDE CHARACTERISTIC OF MILITARY SCIENCE. "IN MY HUMBLE OPINION, THERE'S NO SUCH THING AS LARGE LEAPS IN OUR SOCIETY, AND IN OUR DEVELOPMENT. THERE'S JUST VERY SMALL INCREMENTAL STEPS, AND IF WE'RE FORTUNATE ENOUGH TO MAKE OUR LITTLE CONTRIBUTION, THEN WE'RE VERY FORTUNATE INDEED."

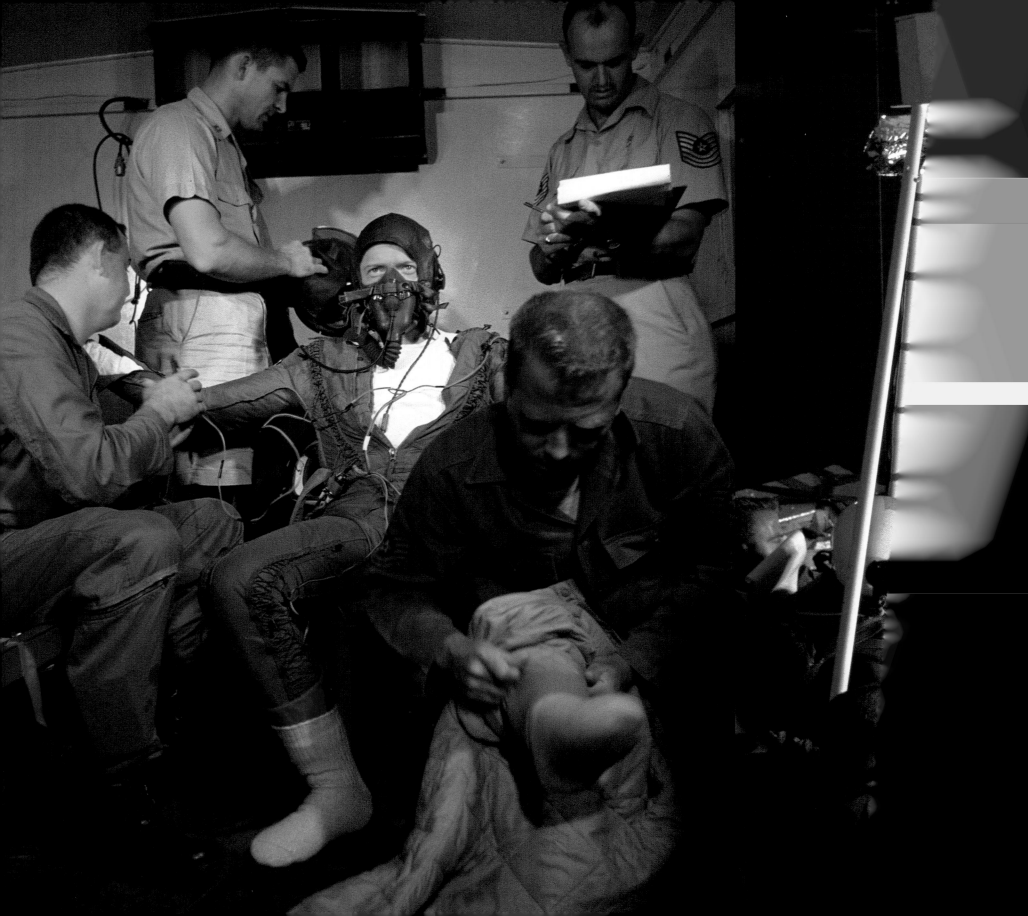

015
history

desire

017
history

2 SPEED

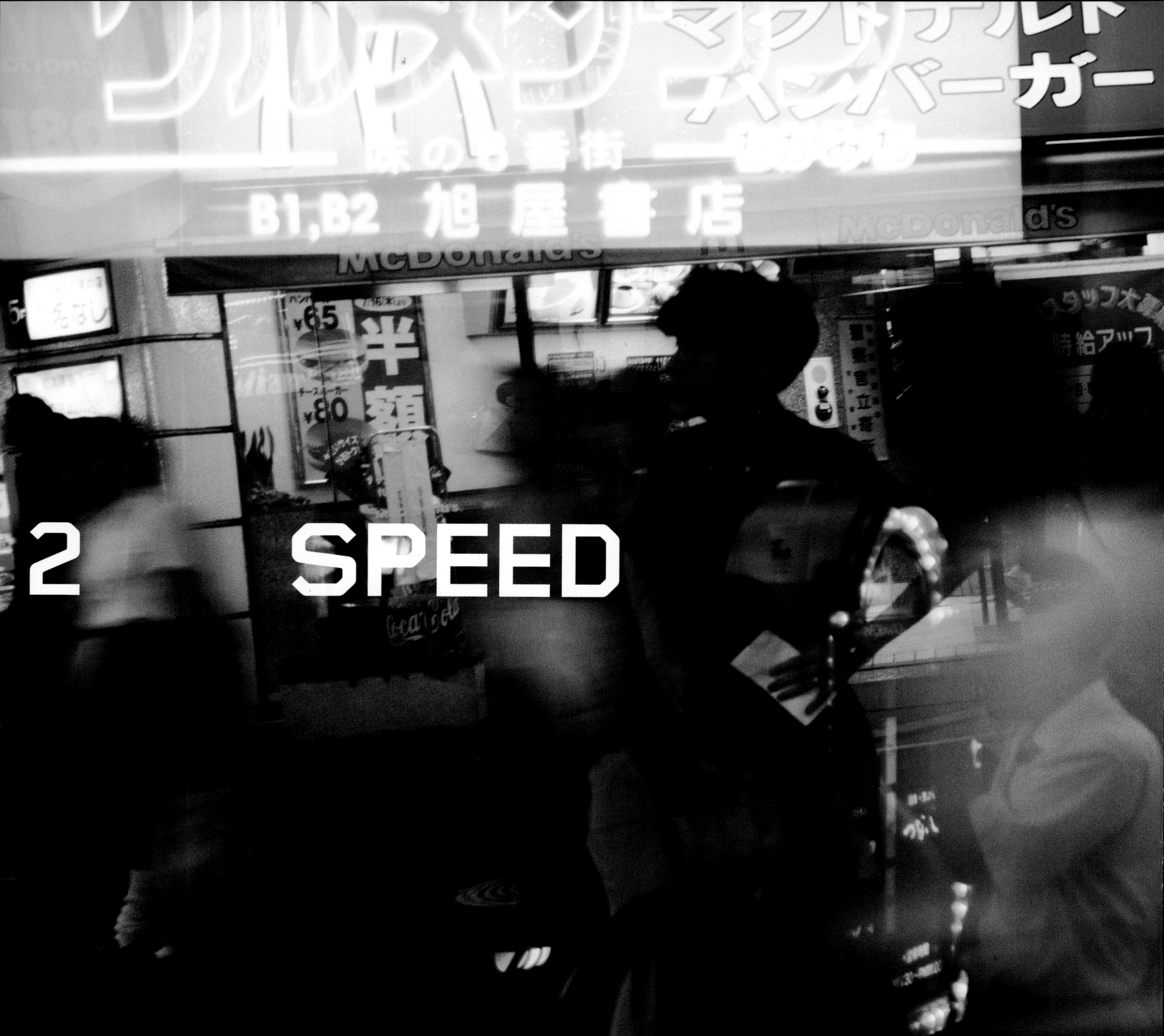

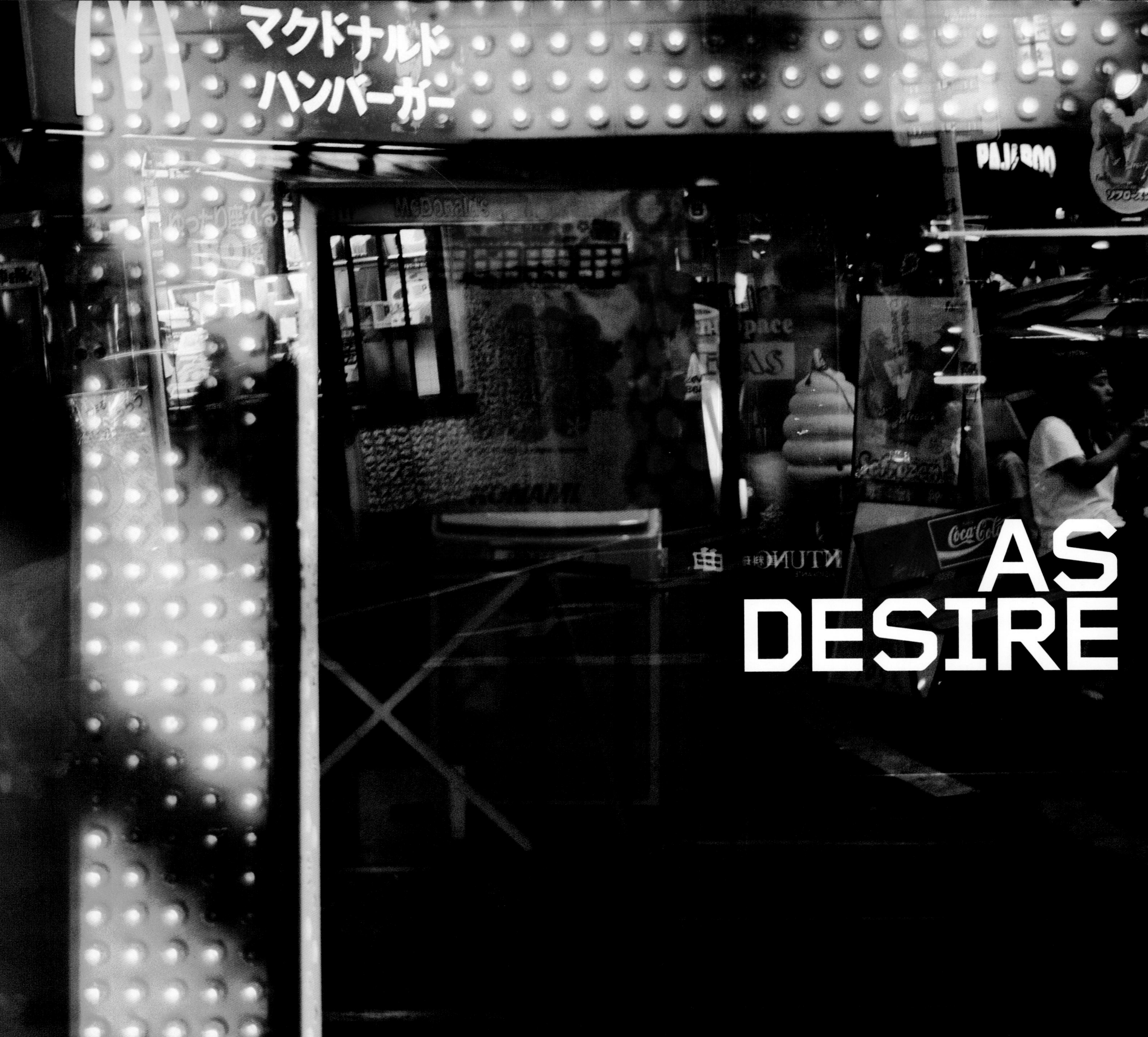

AS DESIRE

1プレイ
¥50 渋谷会館
新しい
マシン
2ゲーム
100円
GAME
3F MONACO
1 PLAY 50 YEN
3F GAME
2F MONACO
PLAY 50 YE
2012

TOKYO YOUTH
ENDING THE FUTURE

"ELLE N'EST JAMAIS FATIGUEÉ. QU'EST-CE QU'ELLE FAIT?" ↳ JAPANESE CLOTHING ADVERTISEMENT SHOWING A FASHIONABLE GIRL CROUCHING IN TOKYO'S BUSY SHIBUYA SHOPPING DISTRICT. THE ENGLISH HEADER READS "BAD GIRL BUT GOOD GIRL." THE FRENCH READS: "SHE'S NEVER TIRED. WHAT DOES SHE DO?"

ve the friends that I made at school. But I wanted to learn something, not what they give me at school. It's not that I
...nd, but I wanted to learn something else in life."

...ed out of high school at 15 and moved into her own apartment in the Miguro section of Tokyo. Five years ago this would
...Now she's the knife. The middle class has shattered. She is the first generation to be born knowing it. A revolution is
...f Tokyo and she is it.

...ecognizes itself in her, but only up to the point where she rejects their institutions. She's educated and well-spoken. She's
...'s eroticized by dirty old men — not in the hiked-up school uniform and glued-on "loose socks" that are popular this
...ché *kogals* her age. She spends her nights in the neon brillance of the street, but not in the also-popular sleazy Hawaiian
...ater dye in their hair and the Roxy surfwear. She sidesteps the vicious parade of trends. She's culturally ambitious. She's
...z dance, voice and culinary arts. She studies language by attending "manner parties" at the French Embassy. She wants to
...herself, from books and friends, skeptical of art instruction.

...used to be rare in Japan: an individualistic critique. This critique is where acceleration is now most evident in the infamously-
...ture.

...move and pays her rent. They respectfully disagree on many things, but they agree on one: the slow, turgid grind that has
...cial climbing since the 1950s — as well as the raft of social taboos one drags up that ladder — are finished. Ayuchi and
...g risk, but a calculated one. They are responding to a cultural shift which has given young people, and teenage girls in
...ng of power at this moment in contemporary Japan. The fact that that power could be conditional or false is exactly what
...about this extraordinary moment in her city.

...e are considered strange within Japan," says Ayuchi, sipping a juice after midnight in a Shibuya street cafe. "In Japan,
...e same most of the time. So me and my friends respect each person's own individuality. For me, it comes naturally,
...ficult to live in Japan because of that."

That speed, that ability to accelerate, is pouring down into Japanese youth culture like fuel into a runaway reactor core. The smell of blown minds hangs in Tokyo's sooty air. The national goals represented by the commodity fetishes and the general commitment to post-WWII "modernization" are finished. When stopped on the street, an astounding number of young people will mention WWII as being the beginning of a national drive to become like the United States, adding that this had been largely accomplished by the late 1970s. Their Big Bang was the moment the Bubble Economy burst in the mid-80s and they realized that just being a US-style Western economy was not an identity in itself, nor even a guarantee of prosperity. As a result, Japanese youth are in a somewhat manic search for meaning. Rapid changes in global technology and information that used to be viewed through the lens of consensus are now open to individual interpretation. Personalization of culture requires a violent reversal of perception.

"Speed of harmonization can be good or bad, depending on the way that it's directed," says Murakami. "When it's happening in a very closed space, in a top-down fashion, certainly that's a very unhealthy form. But when it's based on each and every individual's motivation, I think the way in which that speed can then work, based on these personal motivations, is highly effective, a quite welcome thing."

Down on the street it's a war. Children rush back and forth across a battlefield lit by roaring electronic video screens and screaming neon 24 hours a day, displaying a meaningful array of missions and uniforms. The war is between sovereignty and belonging. Between media images and self-image. Between the future and the right now. The only weapon (right now) is style and the only tactic is speed.

Hitomi Kamata and her friend Chiori Nakajima shout over the zillion rattling balls careening inside a small, seedy pachinko parlor on the Shibuya pedestrian zone. They are pushed up against the wall by a crush of tens of thousands of bodies as they acknowledge the complex interplay between fitting in and standing out.

in a week, sell in the millions of units, and be gone in the space of two months. But Hitomi wants a look all her own. It's too easy to ape the looks that dominate the smoldering wet summer nights. As though illustrating her point, she steps back to let pass a trio of schoolgirls, with their tartan skirts and Sailor Moon blouses, so classic as to almost go unnoticed. Then comes a pair of the surfer-girls, with their oddly unsettling chemical tans and flip-flops. Only the weak do that, she says, only the victims.

"When I was a high school student, merchandise people would come and make a propaganda by saying it is 'frequently used by high school girls,'" says Chiori. By "propaganda," she means an implied desire in the form of an advertisement or a magazine feature. She and Hitomi are both at university, studying English, but we talk through a translator. "And then they make bullshit photos. They create it like it's happening already, and then that instigates the market. A lot of times, we could be invited to a party, and then there'd be like some merchandise, and then they'll take photos as if these high school girls have done this party. Whereas it's prefabricated."

High school girls are not only the market. They are the validation. Their foul mouths and snap judgments are considered the only honest indicator of emerging desires. Advertising, TV, news broadcasts, magazines, and marketing of all kinds are dominated by the roaring voices of young girls shrieking "BUY! BUY! BUY!" Young men are changing, too, of course, but are kept out of the limelight, mostly because the girls' sexuality is so salable. Consider, for instance, the Lovegety, a gadget by the makers of the super-successful Tamagotchi pendants: a matchmaking toy, the Lovegety has three mood settings — "talk," "karaoke," and "get2." When someone of the opposite sex with the same mood is within five meters of the wearer, a little alarm goes off and the two check each other out. Girls buy the pink Lovegety in modest numbers. Boys' blue models, however, are always sold out, possibly indicating that boys are desperate for a way to speak out in a society where girls have now been allowed a very loud public voice.

"With that lack of the common goal of modernization, communication became something that was no longer so easy," says Murakami. "This was something that was felt most sharply among young girls. **Actually, that's where the majority of power is located in Japan: in these young kids.**

"Certainly they do have the power to consume, but the power I'm talking about is not actually them putting something into play, it's rather this lack of language."

In his seminal work *Speed & Politics*, historian and social critic Paul Virilio contends that the modern city (and its extension, the modern state) maintains only an illusion of the movement that was once their revolutionary power. He argues that circulation (movement around and around, going nowhere) is the true opiate of the masses, and that one of the functions of modern society is to steer dromomaniacs — a word which once meant "deserters" (under France's ancien régime) or "compulsive walkers," but which now might mean "movement junkies."

Is *dromomania* not the American dream? A cherished — though largely false — perception of freedom to move, to escape into a wilderness that was always the American heritage? (As evidence, I might offer our compulsion to surf the Net or the cable TV channels. Or our insane preoccupation with traffic, which really amounts to going to work and then getting home again where we started, day after day.) "The time has come," Virilio wrote in 1976, "to face the facts: revolution is movement, but movement is not a revolution. Politics is only a gear-shift, and revolution only its overdrive...." If so, Japan has adopted the American Dream only too well. Virilio warns, in part, that there is a totalitarian control scheme behind dromocratic society: the freedom to move becomes a requirement to move. Perhaps Japanese youth, not too far removed from a history of benevolent totalitarianism, are better equipped to recognize this than the Americans or Western Europeans who dominate world media.

This generation of Japanese youth has grown up rejecting the old mantras heard at work and home. Parents and teachers are still parrotting tired, discredited lines: go to a good school, get good grades, get into a gargantuan Japanese firm, marry safely. But even progressive Japanese businesses are copping to the new reality, announcing that they won't hire kids no matter how good their grades are if they don't have specialized skills and creative (i.e., individual) ideas.

These new girls are loud. As they openly scrap in the street to define the new talk, they also define the future dialogue. Thus, Murakami is right: the power to imagine the new individual lies with them, for better or worse. They will generate and regenerate a new language of desire. The fetishization of commodity has now been appropriated into personal strategies for constructing identity. Often with the same manic energy.

Their bids to power take on all forms, most of them pretty raw by default. The entrepreneurial kids start boutique clothing lines, small-time computer services, closet-sized record shops, or 'zines they hope will attract advertisers and grow legit. Crime among teens is on the rise. Chatting with Chiori and Hitomi, three *lon ge*, surfer-looking guys with long dyed-brown hair (the Japanese pronunciation of the English word "long"), slouch against the wall with cellphones in hand, methodically picking girls out of the crowd and sweet-talking them into taking work as bar hostesses ("liquor business"), escorts, telephone club girls or full-time whores.

Methamphetamine is the new drug of choice in the streets of Tokyo. The band SPEED's song "Go Go Heaven" is an instant anthem among high school girls, reportedly a slang title meaning "55 heaven," which is a 55-year-old salaryman sugar daddy who can give a young girl the clothes, bar tab, and arcade-game chump change she needs without the old-timey strings attached. Experimental noise music like Masonna, Aube, or the "fetishcore" performances of Merzbow's Akita Masami — who processes sounds into raw, extreme textures, often like a chainsaw run against sheet metal, and performs this live as a soundtrack to pornographic films — has established a niche right next to the unending stream of *idoru* or idol-singers and Euro-style J-Pop. Structure no longer has the same meaning it once had: a Friday night performance by Osaka's wildly experimental free music gurus the Boredoms is jammed by fans inside the 120-degree furnace of Tokyo's Liquid Room as though it were a pagan ritual, the most spiritually important concert event of the summer.

In this new, less-structured environment, girls are largely setting the youth culture agenda. Of course this happens partly because they are sexy, and they have been enculturated to believe that their sexuality is their most valuable commodity. Openly acknowledged for decades as an irresistible fetish, schoolgirl sexuality is a national obsession. Older men slavishly worship them. Housewives and office girls watch near-constant TV news reports about schoolgirls. All advertisements for sex papering the walls of Roppongi and Shinjuku phone booths show pictures of little girls. It's part of the girls' self-image, reflected in every product they voraciously consume and every dollar they thus deposit in the pockets of the dominant culture. The *Popteen* magazine available at any train station, clearly aimed at 12 to 16-year-olds, has advice columns on anal sex and many graphic depictions of sex acts. On a 1996 trip I bought one of the top girls' magazines in the conservative Hilton bookshop. In among the cosmetics ads and advice columns was a photo-novella section called "Rape Fantasy," which depicted a young girl being violated by an older man.

Though controlled by a culture of male violence, the girls are rising to the bait of their implied power. They are trying to wrestle some real control from their mediated self-image. Their true power may lie in the new languages Murakami mentioned, their styles and behaviors that take Japanese ambition to the extremes of speed. For instance, the *kogals*.

In the densely packed shopping zones of Shibuya, Harajuku, Shinjuku and even Ikebukuro, you can't miss 'em: packs of loud, bratty 14-to-16-year-old girls stashing their schoolgirl uniforms into train station coin lockers and donning long fur coats, super-short minis, high-heeled boots and Louis Vuitton handbags. The name probably comes from the words *kou*, for "high" as in "high school," and *gyaru*, for "gal." Because they can't pronounce the "l" in *kogal*, they say "kogyaru." They're *cho-mabu* (slang for mad sexy) and every salaryman's wet dream. They mob the clubs, shamelessly pricktease, and keep the luxury shops in business. They're bad girls, splashing their amorality around with an almost desperate savagery, hiking their skirts on escalators, baring their breasts in the photo booths that print instant stickers called "print club," getting drunk on someone else's tab if they can.

A hilariously accurate essay by Eric Planet de Jesus in *Giant Robot* magazine describes them as "a lot like Iris in *Taxi Driver*. They wanna look like elegant hookers in blaxploitation flicks, but end up looking like pimps. They look like an Eleganza catalogue, circa 1973. They look like the bitches in *The Killing of a Chinese Bookie*." Tremendously successful as a predatory class, the *kogals* rose with the speed of a Japanese trend, in the space of one season, and would probably laugh if you still used that term by the time you read

But they're more than just a trendy style. The *kogals* are pure acceleration. Their commodity is their schoolgirl sexuality, and it's fleeting, so they're selling *right now*. They piss on the old morality. They'll take it up the ass for a Prada handbag or boots, then give the old guy's phone number to one of their friends who needs a new D&G overcoat. The polite term for this transaction, which swept the media over the last four or five years, is *enjo kosai*, which translates literally as "compensated companionship."

Enjo kosai is not called prostitution because it has little to do with survival. Sometimes it only means meeting an older salaryman for drinks and a few pictures at print club, but the serious money is in sex. They sometimes take their dates into the "Love Hotel" districts, where nice rooms can be had by the hour. *Enjo kosai* is most common among middle-class girls who still live with their parents and attend good schools. Their parents don't know. And if they did, they wouldn't say anything because they're afraid that their girl will lose status among her friends if she doesn't have the designer gear. Literally enslaved to the off-the-rack couture identity they have claimed for themselves, the girls dismiss *enjo kosai* as just an occasional lay to get the brand names — Prada, Louis Vitton, Dolce & Gabbana — that are out of reach for the average middle-class family. The general reluctance to voice social criticisms in the Japanese press has, predictably, done more to glorify the girls than to chastise or lament their loss of innocence. Eager to capitalize on a good sex story, news crews roam the shopping districts trying to grab impromptu interviews. Incredibly, the girls talk bluntly to the cameras. The general subtext to newspaper and TV stories about *enjo kosai* is that no one can criticize

these girls for being super-efficient consumers. They are only as ruthless as the marketing machines they emulate. And, of course, their out-of-control spending habits help drive the economy.

Hitomi motions across Shibuya: "There's a big department store, One-Oh-Nine, which is across from Big Camera. Usually these young girls hang out on the second floor, and older guys hang out looking for these girls, and they all meet up." Chiori and Hitomi make it clear they have never done this, but that they've had plenty of opportunity. Every girl says the same thing, and they know exactly how it works. "The recent trend has been that old men look for girls that are more subtle...chic ones rather than the crazy, provocative kind." By provocative, she means the surfer girls or *kogals*. "These girls are so experienced, they only go if there's a lot of money involved...and they have almost scary attitude, so these older men now wants to go for maybe novice."

"It's sort of like everyday life," says Ayuchi gaily. "Two years ago [when she was 14] friends from the same school go to karaoke bars. A friend of mine would go up for an hour, and come back with 70,000 yen [$500 in 1998]. I would be waiting in a karaoke bar. So that was my reality. Friends would introduce older men to each other, so they switch and swap. They use telephone clubs, too [phone sex services where girls arrange in-person dates with the callers]. Telephone clubs are such a regular thing in Japan. It's sort of like playing a video game at game centers."

By all accounts, *enjo kosai* was at its peak in 1996, but continues today. In Japan, even this re-named prostitution is more or less trendy. It's what the popular girls are doing this year. Estimates of the numbers of girls actually engaged in some form of *enjo kosai* range from 10–20 percent, and in some sensationalized magazine reports to 70 percent.

Hitomi and Chiori come to Shibuya three or four times a week. Two surfer girls in front of an arcade say they spend most of every day on this battlefield. One is 20, the other 16. They shock our translator by blurting out, "We're against *enjo kosai*!" Why? "We don't like old man!" They laugh maniacally, explaining that the economic crisis has sunk *enjo kosai* prices too low, and move off.

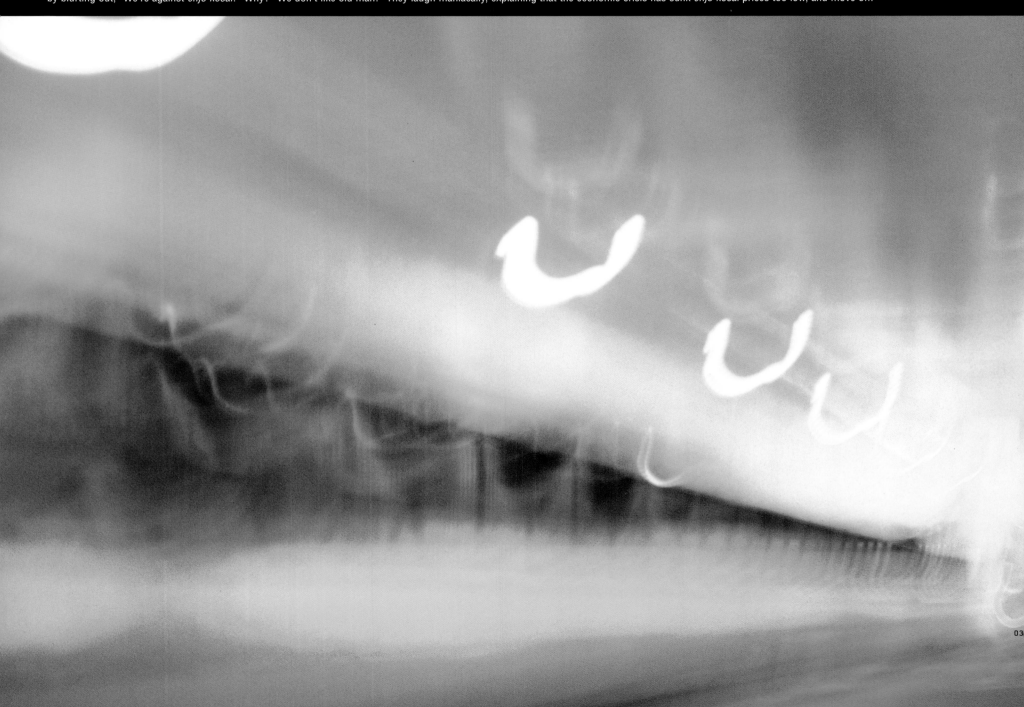

渋谷
霞が関
竹橋
入谷
浜崎橋
銀座
箱崎
有明
大井
辰巳
葛西
船堀橋
浦安
大黒
要地点までの所要時間
詳細な経路はMEX
警察官
首都高速 インフォメーション
ブのために……
路交通情報をお知らせします。
高速道路公団
神奈川県警察
不審物を発見した
ただちに110番で
または非常電話で
お知らせ下さい。

KENT
CABIN
North Carolina

CABIN

合流注意

所沢33
ら 37-14

Kogals accelerate to meet the opportunity that exists for them in the current chaos of Japan. Their strategy is to fuck, fight, and flee. They might be weirdly reifying the 1950s crazes by selling themselves for recognized name-brands, but they are a symptom, grasping desperately for a power that still eludes them, an identity validated by anything other than their availability for sex. Young Tokyo has simultaneously given rise to a new, floating class of outsiders like Ayuchi Watanabe who are trying to internalize global acceleration in some less conspicuous and less trendy way. Or at least some way that doesn't make them feel so overtly exploited.

Japanese people seemingly no longer agree that it's important to agree. **The new agreement is only that it's important to want things**. As Andy Warhol once said, "Pop is about liking things." Japanese youth are pure pop. Wanting things is one source of identity. **The emperor *is* his new clothes.**

The idea of rarity, of one-of-a-kind objects, has spawned urban legend at the Harajuku boutique retail outlet called A Bathing Ape. The company designer and founder, known simply as Nigo, has since changed his approach, but his original strategy reveals much about the appetite for individualized hip. Every morning, he'd fill the store with one line of carefully chosen merchandise — mostly T-shirts, sweatshirts, jeans and inexpensive sportswear bearing logos and phrases based on the film series *Planet of the Apes*. This is not haute couture but shockwear, validated by Nigo's friendship with pop icons like the Beastie Boys. Shoppers, mostly girls, would line up outside in the wee hours. The doors would then fly open at the appointed hour and the shop would instantly sell out. Every day.

Nigo's commodity was rarity. To be seen in a "Bape" T-shirt was something unusual, each piece a lightly recontextualized slice of Americana. He says that the urge to possess them is more complex than simple kitsch. It's a chance to own pre-validated identity at a time when identity itself is in question. Content has been flushed out of the culture, and these surface forms substitute as speed strategies.

Nobu Kitamoura, founder of the well-established Hysteric Glamour boutique clothing line, agrees with Nigo's analysis if not with his approach. Working more as an artist, he believes in a complete aesthetic. However, he too has struggled with the question of identity in his clothing, which borrows from '70s American pop culture.

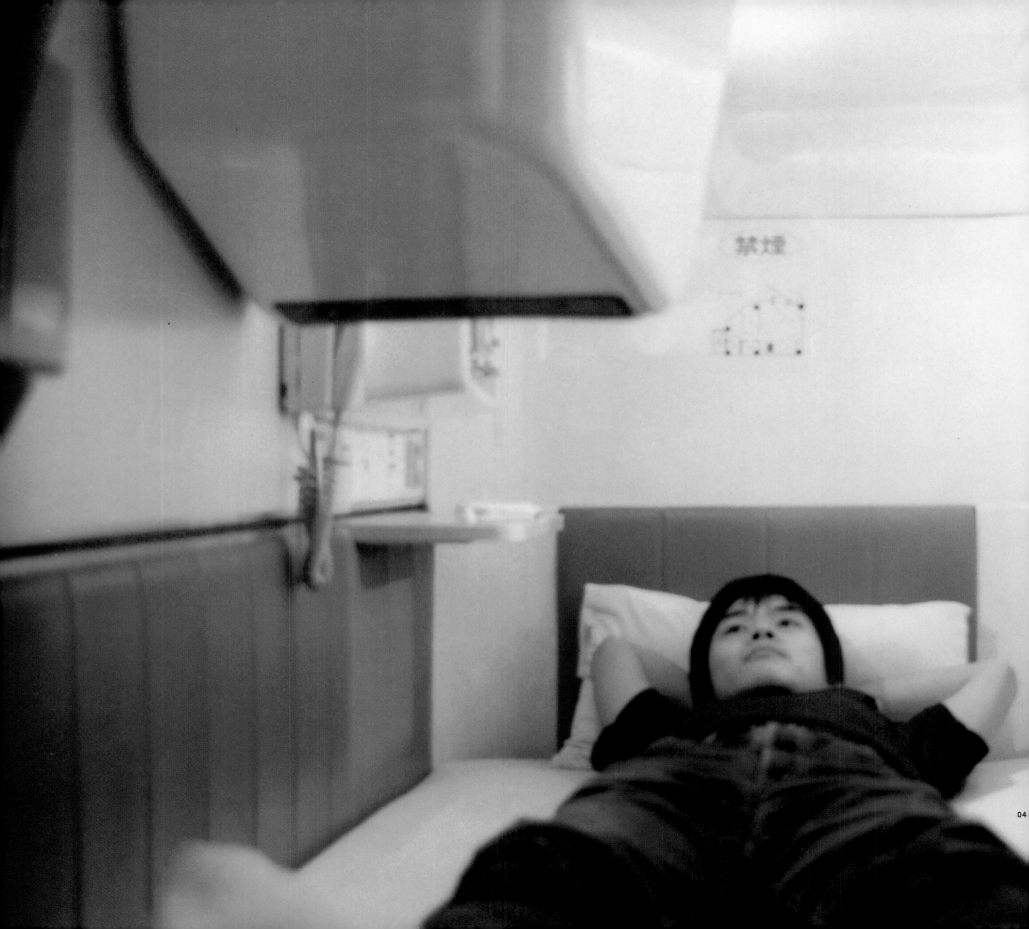

"When I was young, I had a kind of complex about why I'm Japanese," he says, sitting in a bean bag chair in front of a huge red Mobil gas station logo. "Up until like 27 or something, I am listening to American music and English music. But then some people from England told me about how they love Japanese writing, how some characters have power and others elegance. I never saw this. We don't look at the beauty of our own culture. Now I am okay about it."

"Everybody wants security," says Ayuchi, who also says she'd like to open a restaurant or a salon for intellectuals. "I feel insecure, like I don't have balance. Although [enjo kosai] is against the law, I don't think that it's the wrong thing to do. When you are at the center of this spinning circle, you can't understand what you are doing. Those are the enjo kosai girls. They have to understand themselves by experiencing it. But if you are not in the center of this movement, you would observe it and see what is going on, and that's where I am."

Murakami is writing a new novel now whose protagonist is one of a growing number of young people dropping out of junior high. In his book, they end up saving Japanese society. When I tell him about Ayuchi, he nods, "There are a lot of them now."

Speed has been internalized. As Doug take a few photos of Ayuchi, he hear her singing a Madonna song softly to herself: "Oh we are living in a material world, and I am a material girl..."

3   SPEED

04

↳ 1 Marilyn Ivy, "Formations of Mass Culture," in Postwar Japan as History, ed. Andrew Gordon (Berkeley: University of California Press, 1993), 239.

2 Carol Gluck, "The Past In The Present," in Postwar Japan as History, ed. Andrew Gordon (Berkeley: University of California Press, 1993), 75.

3 Ivy, "Formations of Mass Culture," 241.

4 Gluck, "The Past in the Present," 72.

045
desire

3   SPEED

AS
MEDIA

URBAN STR
INVADE RUR
AMERICA

"THEY KILLED MY BROTHER," SAYS ONE YOUNG LAKOTA SIOUX GANG MEMBER, KICKING AROUND A DRIVEWAY IN THE RESERVATION VILLAGE OF WANBLEE, SOUTH DAKOTA. "SO I HAD TO KILL ONE OF THEM. MY HOMEBOYS MADE ME DO IT. THEY SAID THEY WAS GONNA KILL ME IF I DIDN'T DO IT. BUT I WANTED TO DO IT ANYWAYS."

→THAT IS THE GANGLAND CODE. IT'S OLD, NEVER CHANGING, AND WHEREVER THERE ARE GANGS IT'S THE SAME. ON ANOTHER DAY ON THE RESERVATION WE TALK WITH A 21-YEAR-OLD BANGER NAMED A-DOG. HIS IRON-HARD EYES FLASH BRIEFLY IN A FLAT-TOOTHED SMILE. HE KNOWS ABOUT KILLINGS, TOO. HE PULLS A T-SHIRT OVER HIS WIRY BROWN FRAME WHICH READS "IN LOVING MEMORY OF MICHAEL."

A-DOG AND HIS COUSIN BOOM-BOOM ARE GANGSTER DISCIPLES, A NATIVE SPLINTER GROUP OF THE INFAMOUS CHICAGO CRIMINAL GANG. THEY STARE DOWN THE STREET AT SOME KIDS WHO CLAIM A GANG CALLED DOS MOB. THE REMOTE VILLAGE OF WANBLEE IS AN ISLAND OF TENSE GANG WARFARE. RAW AGGRESSION IS THE ONLY RESPECTED CURRENCY HERE. AT LEAST ONE CHILD FROM EVERY HOUSEHOLD CLAIMS A GANG.

WIND-TOUSLED PRAIRIE SQUEEZES IN ON THIS CIRCA-1970 U.S. DEPT. OF HOUSING AND URBAN DEVELOPMENT PROJECT LIKE PARADISE SEEN THROUGH THE BARS OF A PRISON, SHRINKING THE 25 FEET SEPARATING EACH IDENTICAL HOME FROM ITS NEIGHBOR. TUCKED IN THE NORTHEAST CORNER OF THE PINE RIDGE RESERVATION, WANBLEE'S APPROXIMATELY 1,500 RESIDENTS (300-400 IN THE CLUSTER HOUSING) ARE ISOLATED BY THE VAST EMPTINESS OF PRAIRIE AND THE CHALKY CLIFFS OF THE BADLANDS, TWO HOURS BY CAR FROM THE BRIGHT LIGHTS OF RAPID CITY, HUNDREDS OF MILES FROM THE URBAN CENTERS OF SALT LAKE CITY, MINNEAPOLIS OR DENVER.

LIKE THE MAROONED CHILDREN IN GOLDING'S *LORD OF THE FLIES*, THE ONLY PRIZE FOR WANBLEE GANGS IS POWER. THESE KIDS, HOWEVER, ARE SHIPWRECKED RIGHT WHERE THEY WERE BORN. IT IS GANG IDENTITY ITSELF WHICH TRAVELED, A DEEPLY URBAN IDEA CARRIED HERE AT THE SPEED OF CABLE TV AND RENTAL VIDEOS AND THE DESPERATE PEREGRINATIONS OF WANBLEE YOUTH. GANG STYLE AND THEIR STYLE OF VIOLENCE WAS ONLY TOO EASY TO TRANSPLANT. GANG SETS FROM CHICAGO, SALT LAKE CITY, OMAHA, DENVER AND LOS ANGELES SHOT THROUGH THE SIOUX COMMUNITIES FROM PINE RIDGE TO ROSEBUD TO EAGLE BUTTE IN THE SPACE OF ONE SUMMER BACK IN 1990, QUICKLY OVERWHELMING FRAGILE NATIVE PRIDE WITH MEDIA-VALIDATED BLACK AND LATINO CULTURES.

INDIAN COUNTRY GREEDILY SUCKED UP THAT VALIDATION. ACCORDING TO ONE POLICE OFFICER'S MILD HYPERBOLE, A HOMEGROWN GANG CALLED THE NOMADS CLAIMED HALF OF THE MALE TEENS ON THE PINE RIDGE RES BY NOVEMBER 1997. WANBLEE ITSELF HAS AT LEAST SIX GANG SETS AT WAR WITH ONE ANOTHER, MOST OF THEM COUSINS OR AT LEAST RELATED BY TRIBE SINCE TIME IMMEMORIAL. THE SPEED OF THE INVASION INCREASED ITS SHOCK POWER. LIKE A TSUNAMI TRAVELLING SMOOTHLY AT MINIMUM HEIGHT THROUGH DEEP URBAN WATER, GANGS SLAMMED INTO SOUTH DAKOTA'S PURELY RURAL AND ISOLATED SIOUX RESERVATIONS WITH A STATURE THAT OVERSHADOWED ALL ELSE. NOW THE VIOLENCE, THOUGH LARGELY LIMITED TO HOUSEHOLD-ON-HOUSEHOLD STREET FIGHTS AND INDIVID-UAL KIDS GETTING "GANGED," IS PANDEMIC.

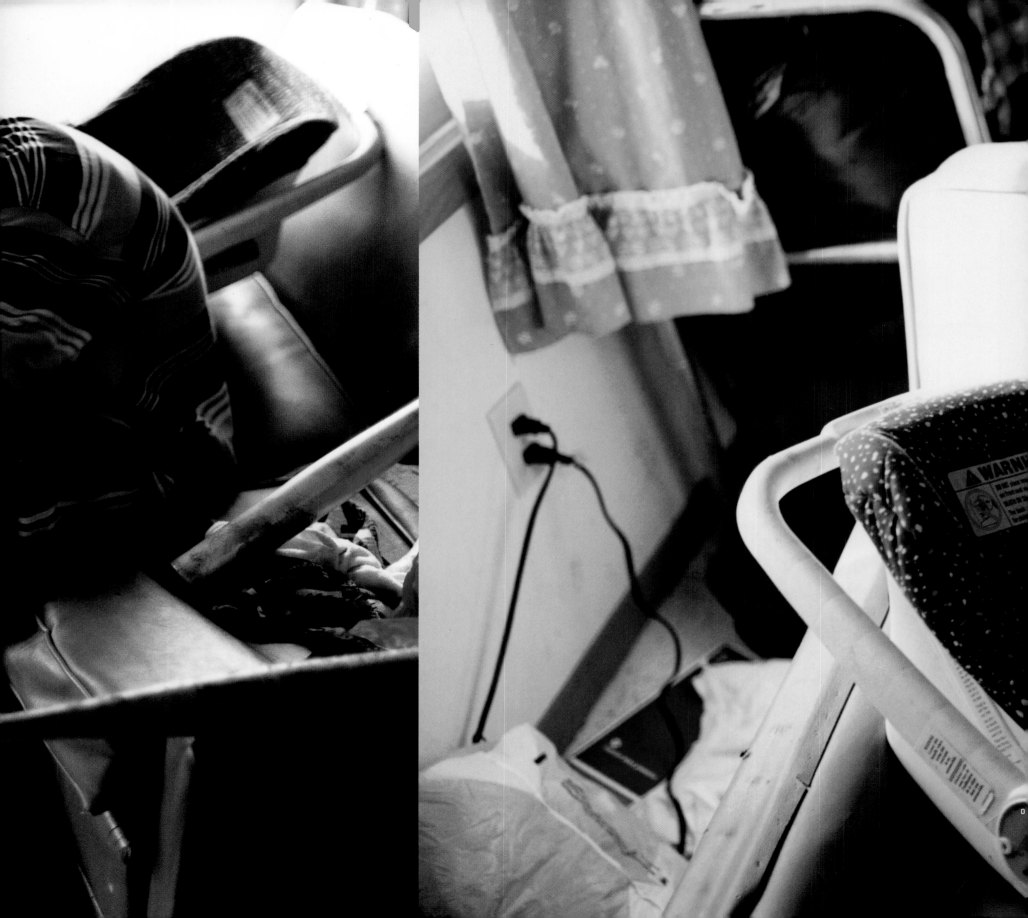

THE FORCE WITH WHICH GANGS HIT INDIAN COUNTRY IS AN INDICATOR OF JUST HOW ISOLATED AND POWERLESS NATIVE YOUTH REALLY ARE. THE SPACES BETWEEN THEM AND "MAINSTREAM" SOCIETY ARE ACCELERATION ZONES, WHERE THE STRENGTH OF IDEAS – ESPECIALLY ENTIRE PACKAGE LIFESTYLES LIKE GANG CULTURE – IS AMPLIFIED AND WARPED BEYOND RECOGNITION. THESE ZONES OR GAPS, WHERE THEY CAN BE PERCEIVED, ARE CRITICAL TO UNDERSTANDING THE GLOBALIZATION OF CULTURE AT FIXED POINTS LIKE WANBLEE (AND, BY EXTENSION, EVEN MORE REMOTE POPULATIONS). EXPLOSIVE CHANGE AND FUTURE SHOCK THERE BRING ON HYBRIDIZATION OF IDENTITY, EXTREME CULTURAL FORMS, AND EVEN ECONOMIC MUTATIONS.

IN THIS CASE, HOWEVER, THE ACCELERANT AND ACCELERATED ARE BOTH VIOLENCE.

THE DUCE (SIC) CRIPS ACROSS THE STREET SOMETIMES POP A CAP AT A GANGSTER DISCIPLE, AND THE GDS SHOOT BACK. THOUGH KIDS ON BOTH SIDES WILL TELL YOU THAT GUNS INDICATE "REAL" – BIG CITY – GANGS AND THAT UP HERE THEY JUST BATTLE HAND TO HAND, A FALL BREEZE BLOWS A COLD-WAR BOREDOM THROUGH THE BULLET HOLES IN BOTH HOUSES. THE NAMES ARE URBAN FAMILIARS. THE GDS SOMETIMES CLAIM AS SOUTHSIDE GANGSTER DISCIPLES OR THE INSANE GANGSTER DISCIPLE NATION. THE DOS MOB IN THE BLUE HOUSE 80 YARDS ACROSS THE GRASS HAVE RECENTLY MUTATED INTO THE HAPPY HONKY HUNTERS OR TRIPLE-H, A DENVER SET, AND CLAIM DOMINANCE. AN L.A. SET CALLED THE NORTH SIDE BLOODS ARE MENTIONED, BUT ONLY AS NEWCOMERS. SPRAYPAINT TAGS HAILING THE BOYZ, OR TBZ, FADE FROM ALL 40 OR SO IDENTICAL BRICK HOMES. TBZ ARE ORIGINAL GANGSTERS OUT HERE, A NATIVE SET FROM RAPID CITY.

"THE BIGGEST INFLUENCES ON THE YOUTH ON THE RESERVATION NOW ARE HISPANIC CULTURE AND THE BLACK CULTURE," SAYS PINE RIDGE POLICE OFFICER JOE CROSS. "YOU CAN TELL BY THE STYLES OF DRESS, THE LINGO. A LOT OF THEM TRY TO SPEAK SPANISH. AND FROM THE GANG NAMES LIKE DOS MOB. YOU'LL FIND HISPANIC NAMES HERE ON THE RESERVATION, LIKE ROMEROS, MARTINEZES, RODRIGUEZES. BUT MOST OF THESE YOUTH HERE ARE LAKOTA, AND THEY HAVE TRADITIONAL LAST NAMES LIKE CHIPPS, QUIVERS, SWIFT HAWKS, BALD EAGLES."

CROSS AND HIS PARTNER TIM MCGRADY LIVE IN WANBLEE AND WORK THE GANGS. BOTH GREW UP HERE, AND RECRUIT THE YOUNGEST BANGERS INTO THE BOXING CLUB THEY RUN OUT OF THE POLICE SUBSTATION GARAGE. SATURDAY SMOKERS ARE AN IMPORTANT DIVERSION FROM HOUSE-BURYING SNOWDRIFTS THAT CAN STUN THIS AREA IN WINTERTIME.

"PERSONALLY, I SEE THEM AS WANNABES," SAY MCGRADY OF THE GANGSTERS.

"BUT THEY HAVE POTENTIAL FOR VIOLENCE," ADDS CROSS. "THEY MIGHT SHOOT AT YOU, BUT IT'LL BE MORE A SCARE TACTIC. MY BIG WORRY IS THAT ONE DAY THEY'LL BE FORCED INTO A BIG GUN SHOWDOWN AND THEY WON'T MISS. THEN ONE OF MY BOYS'LL BE DEAD HERE, MY NEIGHBORS."

"WE'VE SEEN THE EMERGENCE OF OVER 50 SEPARATE GANGS JUST IN THIS COMMUNITY SINCE 1990," SAY RAPID CITY POLICE CAPTAIN CHRIS GRANT, WHO'S WRITING A MASTER'S THESIS ON NATIVE GANGS AND HAS DELIVERED OVER 200 LECTURES ON THE SUBJECT. THE DIFFERENT SETS COME AND GO, BUT THEIR VIOLENT CLASHES HAVE DOMINATED HIS POLICE WORK. GRANT SEES THESE GANGS AS TRANSPLANTS, AN OPPORTUNISTIC CULTURE GRAFTING PERFECTLY ONTO NATIVE ECONOMIC AND SPIRITUAL HARDSHIP.

"THERE IS NOTHING WITHIN THE NATIVE AMERICAN CULTURE THAT IS ABOUT GANG ACTIVITY," HE SAYS. "THERE'S NO UNIQUE GANG STYLE. SO NATIVE AMERICAN ADOLES-CENTS, YOUNG ADULTS, WILL ACT AND TALK AND USE THE SAME SYMBOLISM AS BLACK AND HISPANIC GANG MEMBERS – CALL EACH OTHER NIGGER AND HO AND BITCH. THEY'LL USE HISPANIC TERMS LIKE POR VIDA, MEANING 'FOR LIFE,' AND MI VIDA LOCA, MEANING 'MY CRAZY LIFE.' VERY RARELY DO WE SEE ANY KIND OF DISTINCT AND UNIQUE NATIVE AMERICAN GANG STYLE LIKE BROWN PRIDE, FOR EXAMPLE, OR NATIVE MOB. ASK THE GUYS IN ROSEBUD TO TALK TO YOU ABOUT EAST SIDE SUREÑO 13. SUREÑO 13 IS A SOUTHERN CALIFORNIA, HISPANIC, PRISON-BASED GANG. SUREÑO 13 IS ON THE ROSEBUD RESERVATION. IT'S EMULATED BEHAVIOR. WE DON'T HAVE THAT KIND OF BLACK AND HISPANIC POPULATION IN THIS PART OF THE COUNTRY. WE GET NAMES LIKE KILLER PARK CRIPS, OR THE HIGHLAND BOYS, AND WE DON'T HAVE A 'HIGHLAND' AREA. OFTEN TIMES THESE GANG STRUCTURES MOVE IN WHEN PEOPLE MOVE HERE AND BRING GANG-INVOLVED KIDS WITH THEM."

GRANT CALLS THIS "CULTURAL TRANSPLANTING." BANGERS CALL IT RECRUITING, OR, AS ELLIOTT BLUE COAT SO ELOQUENTLY RENDERS IT, "BRINGING THE PAIN."

"'CAUSE IF YOU AIN'T MAKIN' SOMEONE FEEL PAIN, THEN YOU FEEL PAIN YOURSELF, FOR WHAT YOU DID AND SHIT," SAYS ELLIOTT, SITTING IN CUSTODY IN THE TRIBAL LAW ENFORCEMENT BUILDING IN TINY EAGLE BUTTE, SOUTH DAKOTA. "IT'S CALLED 'BRING THE PAIN.' IT'S TO GROW BIGGER. IT'S LIKE A RECRUITER IN AN ARMY. GANGS ARE BUILT ON CORRUPTION, RIGHT? LOYALTY."

ELLIOTT IS ONE OF THE LOCAL LEADERS OF AN L.A.-VIA-SALT LAKE CITY GANG CALLED THE TONGAN CRIP GANGSTERS, OR TCG. THIS GANG ISN'T HISPANIC OR BLACK, BUT BUILT AROUND THE VIOLENT STRUGGLE FOR SECURITY BY TONGAN ISLANDER COMMUNITIES IN SOUTHERN CALIFORNIA. BACK THERE, THE TONGAN'S MORTAL ENEMIES ARE THE SONS OF SAMOANS, OR SOS. OUT IN EAGLE BUTTE, A COMMUNITY OF ONLY A COUPLE THOUSAND, THEY BATTLE A NEWLY FORMED BLOOD SET CALLED THE ODD SQUAD. WHEN I ASK HIM HOW GANGS GOT TO EAGLE BUTTE, HE QUIPS, "I BROUGHT 'EM HERE."

BUT THE RISE OF NATIVE GANGS IS MORE COMPLEX THAN THAT. AS NOTED IN MALCOLM KLEIN'S EXCELLENT HISTORICAL STUDY, THE AMERICAN STREET GANG, IT'S ONLY THE STYLE THAT MIGRATES. THE ROOT CAUSES ARE LOCAL.

"THE IDEA OF A GANG [WAS] HERE, BUT THEY NEEDED A LEADER TO CONTROL IT," SAYS ELLIOTT. "WE WOULD LIKE SEE GANGS ON TV OR WHATEVER, SO WE HAD A LITTLE GANG BEFORE I LEFT, IT WAS CALLED DARK SIDE BOYS. SO WHEN I CAME BACK, WE JUST ALL GOT TOGETHER AND STARTED IT UP."

ELLIOTT IS 22 AND SITS IN EAGLE BUTTE JAIL ON A STATUTORY RAPE CHARGE. HE SAYS HE HAS "ABOUT TEN" GIRLFRIENDS, BUT HE ALSO JUST HAD A SON. HE'S SCARRED AND A LITTLE HANG-DOG. ELLIOTT AND A FRIEND LEFT EAGLE BUTTE YEARS AGO TO ESCAPE RES LIFE IN SALT LAKE. A GREAT NUMBER OF LAKOTA YOUTH END UP IN SALT LAKE BECAUSE THE MORMONS ALSO RECRUIT – FOR THEIR BOARDING SCHOOLS. ONE DAY THE BUS SHOWS UP IN YOUR VILLAGE AND MOM KNOWS IT'S EITHER STAY HERE AND MAKE TROUBLE OR GO THERE AND BE SOMEONE ELSE'S TROUBLE, SO SHE PUTS YOU ON THE BUS. WE HEARD THIS STORY OVER AND OVER IN SOUTH DAKOTA. BUT ONCE IN SALT LAKE, YOU'RE EITHER DOWN OR SQUARE. SO ELLIOTT AND HIS BUDDY WERE BEATEN INTO TCG ONE NIGHT WHILE DRUNK AT A PARTY. HE SHOWS ME THE SCARS. THERE ARE SEVERAL WAYS IN, BUT MOST FREQUENTLY IT'S A CHOICE BETWEEN A SEVERE GANG BEATING OR "DOING DIRT" – ROBBING, DRIVE-BY SHOOTING OR EVEN KILLING SOME-ONE FOR THE GANG. GIRLS ARE MOST OFTEN "SEXED" IN, THOUGH THEY CAN JOIN BY DOING DIRT, TOO.

ELLIOTT AND FOUR OTHERS WERE EVENTUALLY DIRECTED TO BRING THE PAIN BACK TO EAGLE BUTTE. NOW THERE ARE FIVE SQUABBING SETS OF CRIPS – ELLIOTT ESTI-MATES 210 KIDS TOTAL, AND 90 IN HIS CLIQUE – IN LITTLE EAGLE BUTTE, A MAP DOT SMACK DAB IN THE MIDDLE OF SOUTH DAKOTA THAT CONSISTS OF A THREE-BLOCK MAIN STREET, A MODERN GROCERY, A BIG SCHOOL, A GAS STATION/DAIRY QUEEN AND A COUPLE MOTELS. THE ODD SQUAD WAS A FORMER BASKETBALL TEAM, A RAGTAG UNIT MADE UP OF THE BOYS WHO NEVER GOT PICKED FOR GAMES. ODD MAN OUT. WHICH JUST ABOUT SUMS IT UP. THE ODD SQUAD NOW NUMBERS ABOUT 120. "IT'S THE WHOLE TOWN NOW," ELLIOTT SAYS.

THEY'RE NOT DISCONNECTED FROM THE MAIN BODY OF THE TCG GANG, EITHER. ELLIOTT GETS REPRIMANDED FROM HIS HIGHER-UPS DOWN SOUTH IF A SNITCH SAYS HE'S GOING SOFT. ONCE WHILE HE WAS IN PRISON, ELLIOTT'S CLIQUE WAS DEFENDED BY DOZENS OF SLC TONGANS WHO DROVE UP IN TWO SCHOOL BUSES IN BROAD DAY-LIGHT WITH "TCG" SPRAYPAINTED ON THE SIDE.

EVERY NIGHT THEY GO TO WAR, SOMETIMES COLD, SOMETIMES HOT, MOSTLY IN A DARK LITTLE INTERSECTION CALLED CHINATOWN (THERE AREN'T ANY CHINESE IN EAGLE BUTTE, EITHER) ACROSS FROM THE GROCERY. THEY USE BATS AND GOLF CLUBS, BUT GUNS ARE BECOMING A STATUS SYMBOL. JUST LIKE WANBLEE.

"TOO MUCH PEOPLE WITH GUNS, NOW," ELLIOTT ADDS. "WE'RE GETTING PARANOID LIKE THE CITY, MAN. ALWAYS LOOKING, WATCHING MY BACK. IT'S GETTING TO A POINT

WHERE A LOT OF MAMAS AND DADS AND FAMILY MEMBERS ARE GOING TO START CRYING." HE MENTIONS A LITTLE HOMEBOY, 14 YEARS OLD, BADLY PISTOL-WHIPPED BY SOME SQUAD. HE KNOWS HE CREATED THIS, AND KNOWS IT'S OUT OF CONTROL. HOW COULD ONE KID CHANGE THE WHOLE TOWN?

TOO EASY. EVERY KID AND EVERY COP AGREE: *THERE'S NOTHING ELSE TO DO.*

THAT NOTHINGNESS IS NOT BENIGN. NATURE MIGHT ABHOR THEM, BUT IDEAS ACCELERATE IN A VACUUM AND INCREASE IN POTENCY. THE KIDS YANKED THIS LIFESTYLE TOWARD THE RES WITH A TENACITY THAT WOULD NOT BE DENIED, NO MATTER HOW MUCH THE OLD FOLKS TRY TO PASS IT OFF AS A FAD. MAYBE THEY DON'T WANT TO SEE THESE GAPS, EITHER.

L.A. GANG LEGEND SANYIKA SHAKUR, AKA "MONSTER" KODY SCOTT, DESCRIBES THIS GAP IN ANOTHER WAY IN HIS BOOK, *MONSTER*: "IT'S EASY TO PERSUADE THE GENERAL PUBLIC OF YOUR 'RIGHTEOUSNESS' WHEN YOU CONTROL MAJOR MEDIA. BUT THOSE OF US WHO CONTROL NOTHING ARE IN THE PRECARIOUS POSITION OF HAVING SOMEONE GUESS WHAT OUR POSITION IS. THIS LEAVES QUITE A LARGE GAP FOR MISINFORMATION."

TWO KINDS OF VOIDS STAND BETWEEN A YOUNG PERSON ON THE RES AND THE UNITED STATES OF AMERICA: ECONOMIC AND CULTURAL.

THERE ARE NO JOBS. OR, IF THERE ARE, INDIANS DON'T GET 'EM. U.S. BUREAU OF LABOR STATISTICS FOR 1997 SHOW THAT JACKSON COUNTY, WHICH CONTAINS WANBLEE AND WHICH ALONG WITH SHANNON COUNTY MAKES UP THE PINE RIDGE RES, HAS AN AVERAGE UNEMPLOYMENT RATE OF 5.5%. SHANNON'S IS 12%. DEWEY COUNTY, WHICH SHARES HALF OF EAGLE BUTTE, IS AT 12.1%. THE STATE AVERAGES 3.1% FOR 1997, WHICH IS A LITTLE BETTER THAN THE NATIONAL AVERAGE OF 4.9%.

THEN WHY DOES IT *LOOK* LIKE NO ONE'S WORKING? THE 1996 BUREAU OF INDIAN AFFAIRS (BIA) *INDIAN SERVICE POPULATION & LABOR FORCE REPORT FOR PINE RIDGE* TELLS THE REAL STORY: OF THE 38,426 RESIDENT INDIAN POPULATION, 18,986 ARE "POTENTIAL LABOR FORCE" BETWEEN THE AGES OF 16 AND 64 (MINUS STUDENTS AND OTHERS INELIGIBLE FOR WORK). OF THESE, 14,021 ARE "NOT EMPLOYED," THOUGH 4,165 OF THOSE ARE "ACTIVELY SEEKING WORK." IN RAW NUMBERS, THAT'S 74% UNEMPLOYMENT. EVEN IF WE ASSUME THAT THE EMPLOYED AND THOSE ACTIVELY SEEKING EMPLOYMENT ARE THE ONLY TRUE POTENTIAL LABOR FORCE, UNEMPLOYMENT IS STILL RUNNING 46%.

EAGLE BUTTE FARES NO BETTER. A 1995 CHEYENNE RIVER INDIAN RESERVATION (WHICH CONTAINS EAGLE BUTTE) BIA REPORT SHOWS 6,516 PERSONS IN THE POTENTIAL LABOR FORCE AND 5,069 UNEMPLOYED, EVEN THOUGH 4,827 OF THOSE ARE ACTIVELY SEEKING WORK. AN UNOFFICIAL TALLY FOR THE MONTH OF MAY 1998, SHOWS 90% OF THE MEN AND 85% OF THE WOMEN UNEMPLOYED, AS A PERCENTAGE OF THE LABOR FORCE.

SHANNON COUNTY, SOUTH DAKOTA, IS THE POOREST COUNTY IN THE NATION. ACCORDING TO THE 1990 U.S. CENSUS BUREAU POVERTY STATISTICS, THE MOST RECENT AVAILABLE FOR ALL COUNTIES, 63.1% OF SHANNON'S RESIDENTS LIVE BELOW THE POVERTY LINE, WHICH FOR ONE SINGLE PERSON IN 1989 WAS A YEARLY INCOME OF $6,311. FOR A HOUSEHOLD OF NINE PERSONS OR MORE (LIKE MOST RESERVATION HOUSEHOLDS), THE CUT-OFF IS $25,480. THESE FIGURES INCLUDE ALL RESIDENTS OF THE COUNTY – INDIAN, WHITE, AND EVERYONE ELSE – SO INDIAN-ONLY PERCENTAGES ARE OBVIOUSLY HIGHER. THE COUNTY MAKES UP TWO-THIRDS OF THE RESERVATION. JACKSON COUNTY, HALF OF WHICH LIES IN THE RES, IS TIED FOR 63RD POOREST. ZIEBACH AND DEWEY COUNTIES, WHICH MAKE UP THE CHEYENNE RIVER RES AND SPLIT THE TOWN OF EAGLE BUTTE, ARE 7TH AND 29TH, RESPECTIVELY. NINE OF SOUTH DAKOTA'S RESERVATION COUNTIES ARE AMONG THE NATION'S 50 POOREST.

BUT THERE ARE GOOD DAYS ON THE RES: SOCIAL SECURITY INSURANCE AND DISABILITY CHECKS COME ON THE FIRST OF THE MONTH. STATE WELFARE CHECKS COME AROUND THE FOURTH OR FIFTH. LOTS OF FIGHTING OCCURS AROUND THOSE DAYS.

THIS KIND OF ECONOMIC SEPARATION FROM THE REST OF THE U.S. IS BOUND TO PRODUCE SOME HYBRID ADAPTATIONS. ONE MIGHT BE THE UNBELIEVABLE CHARACTER OF ALCOHOLISM ON THE RES. SINCE THE SIOUX RESERVATIONS ARE BOTH POOR AND TECHNICALLY "DRY" – SALE OF BEER OR LIQUOR IS ILLEGAL – DRUNKS THERE EXPERI-MENT WITH CHEAP, ALTERNATIVE SOURCES OF ALCOHOL. OFFICER EDWIN YOUNG OF THE ROSEBUD TRIBAL POLICE SHOWED ME A LITTLE HILLSIDE OF SUMACS OUTSIDE THE VIL-LAGE OF ST. FRANCIS, AFFECTIONATELY KNOWN AS "LYSOL PARK." THOUSANDS OF LYSOL CANS LAY STREWN IN THE GRASS, EACH ONE WITH A TINY PUNCTURE HOLE.

"THE DRUNKS ALL CARRY A NAIL," YOUNG TOLD ME, "THEY POUR IT INTO A SODA OR DILUTE IT WITH WATER." LYSOL IS 79% ETHYL ALCOHOL. HAIRSPRAY IS IN SUCH HIGH DEMAND THAT THERE ARE BOOTLEGGERS ILLEGALLY SELLING NAME BRANDS LIKE FINAL NET. COLOGNE IS POPULAR AND CAN BE CHOKED DOWN WHEN MIXED WITH SWEETENERS LIKE SUGAR, THOUGH IT CAN'T BE QUITE AS *BON MARCHÉ* AS AQUA NET. THIS SEASON, ONE GANGSTER TOLD US, MOUTHWASH IS ALL THE RAGE. ONE GOOD THING ABOUT PEOPLE WHO DRINK MOUTHWASH, HE SAID: AT LEAST THEIR BREATH SMELLS GOOD.

THE LESS OBVIOUS ACCELERATION ZONE, BUT MAYBE MORE IMPORTANT TO YOUNG PEOPLE, IS CULTURAL. MAGNIFIED BY THE ALIENATION THEY FEEL, POP CULTURE SEEMS MORE IMPORTANT ON THE RES, WHERE IT IS EXOTIC, THAN IT WOULD BE ON URBAN STREETS, WHERE ITS STARS OR LANDMARKS ARE MORE FAMILIAR. THAT'S NOT TO IMPLY AN EMPTINESS *WITHIN* INDIGENOUS SIOUX CULTURE. FAR FROM IT. LAKOTA SIOUX HISTORY AND CULTURE IS RICH AND ALIVE, EVOLVING INTO A MODERN IDENTITY THAT REMAINS ENVIABLY CLOSE TO LANGUAGE, SONGS, RITUAL AND RELIGION, FOOD, MEDICINE AND WAYS OF GOVERNING THAT ARE THOUSANDS OF YEARS OLD. RATHER, GANGSTERS HAVE EXPOSED A GAP IN THE OWNERSHIP OF POP CULTURE. WHICH, FOR THE YOUNG, IS THE *DOMINANT* CULTURE.

AND NOWHERE IS THAT MORE EVIDENT THAN IN WANBLEE OR EAGLE BUTTE OR ROSEBUD. IT'S NO MYSTERY WHY THEY TAKE TO GANGSTA FORMS. RAP VIDEOS ON MTV MIGHT NOT REFLECT NATIVE CULTURE, BUT IS THERE ANY SHOW ON THE TUBE THAT DOES? AT LEAST HIP HOP AND GANGSTA RAP ARE ABOUT RAGE AND DRUGS AND OPPRES-SION AND THE NEED FOR POWER – REAL STUFF ON THE RES – AND NOT SOME NO-STYLE OFFICE CHUMPS MAKING WHINY SITCOM JOKES ABOUT THE MINUTIAE OF THEIR YUP-PIE DREAMS.

"I'M NOT AT ALL LAYING THIS AT THE FEET OF THE ENTERTAINMENT INDUSTRY, BUT TO A CERTAIN EXTENT MOTION PICTURES, TELEVISION – AND TO A HUGE EXTENT, AS FAR AS I'M CONCERNED, THE MUSIC INDUSTRY – HAS GLORIFIED GANG BEHAVIOR," SAYS CAPTAIN GRANT. "GANGSTA RAP MUSIC IS A POWERFUL, POWERFUL MEDIUM FOR THAT 12 TO 19-YEAR-OLD AGE BRACKET WHO ARE INFLUENCED BY THOSE MESSAGES. NONE OF THE MEDIUMS CAUSE PEOPLE TO BECOME GANG MEMBERS, BUT ALL OF THEM HAVE THE POWER TO CONTRIBUTE TO THAT MENTALITY. SEVERAL YEARS AGO, AFTER A PARTICULAR MOVIE CAME OUT, A GANG STRUCTURE STARTED HERE THAT WAS THE SAME AS THE GANG STRUCTURE IN THE MOVIE."

LARRY ROMERO KNOWS ALL ABOUT IT: WHEN *AMERICAN ME* CAME OUT IN MARCH 1992, ALL THE KIDS IN WANBLEE COPPED A MEXICAN ACCENT. LARRY HELPED ORGANIZE DOS MOB DURING A WAVE OF LATINOPHILIA. THOUGH HE HAS SOME MEXICAN BLOOD, MOST OF HIS HOMIES DO NOT. REALIZING THIS, HE AND THE ORIGINAL MEMBERS CHANGED HORSES MIDSTREAM AND STARTED CLAIMING HAPPY HONKY HUNTERS, OR TRIPLE H. THIS DENVER SET VALUES NATIVE PRIDE AND, OSTENSIBLY AT LEAST, FIGHTS THE WHITE MAN. THIS SEEMED TO MAKE MORE SENSE. BUT THERE ARE NO MOVIES ABOUT INDIAN GANGS, NO COOL SLANG, NO STYLISH LOOKS OTHER THAN THE ALSO-BOR-ROWED COWBOY GETUP, NO CAR CULTURE, SO TRIPLE-H HASN'T REALLY CAUGHT ON UP HERE. NOW LARRY HANGS OUT AT THE SUBSTATION HOPING TO BECOME A COP.

COLORS CAME OUT IN APRIL 1988. THAT YEAR, THERE WERE ONLY A COUPLE GANGS ON ANY OF THE SIOUX RESERVATIONS, MOST OF THEM NATIVE-INFLECTED 1950s-STYLE NEIGHBORHOOD GANGS LIKE THE KNIGHTS (FORMERLY THE DRAGONS), WHO USED TO CONTROL SOLDIER CREEK ON THE ROSEBUD RES. KNIGHTS FOUNDER ERIC BLACK LANCE (ROUBIDEAUX) SAYS HE WAS INSPIRED BY THE ARTHURIAN KNIGHTS OF THE ROUND TABLE. BY THE TIME JOHN SINGLETON'S *BOYZ N THE HOOD* CAME OUT IN JULY 1991, A NEW STYLE WAS COMING STRAIGHT OUTTA COMPTON AND NO OTHER PLACE MATTERED. BLACK WAS BEAUTIFUL FOR ABOUT A YEAR, BEFORE *AMERICAN ME* GOT EVERYONE THINKING MEXICAN. WANBLEE BANGERS THEN STARTED DIGGING OTHER GANGSTER MODELS, WORKING BACKWARDS THROUGH THE TRENDS. THEY WATCHED JOHN CARPENTER'S *THE WARRIORS* TO GOOF ON THE KOOKY COSTUMES. OF THE ITALIAN MOBSTER MOVIES, SCORSESE'S *MEAN STREETS* IS SYMPATHETIC, *GOODFELLAS* IS RIGHTEOUS, AND COPPOLA'S *THE GODFATHER* IS HEAVY, BUT *SCARFACE* IS #1. THEY WATCHED IT SO MUCH THE TAPE IS WORN OUT. DON'T HOLD YOUR BREATH FOR *THE WILD ONE*, OR THE RE-EMERGENCE OF THE SUPER-STYLIZED JETS SINGING *WEST SIDE STORY*. NATIVE GANGS WANT THEIR ROMANCE BLOODY.

INDAN BANGERS WANT TO LIVE OUT THE SAME KIND OF MAD-DOG BRAVADO THAT KILLED GANGSTA RAPPERS BIGGIE SMALLS – NOTORIOUS B.I.G. – AND OF COURSE TUPAC SHAKUR, THE TRAGEDIAN SON OF BLACK PANTHER AFENI SHAKUR, WHO'S RECORD COMPANY PROJECT *THUG LIFE* BECAME NOT ONLY A POPULAR TATTOO BUT A GANGLAND MANTRA.

POOR, CROWDED, UNEMPLOYED AND HABITUATED TO SUBSTANCE ABUSE AND DAILY INCIDENTS OF VIOLENCE, GANGS HAVE A LOT TO OFFER TO RES YOUTH. CONTROL, FOR ONE. A REVISED AND REPURPOSED FAMILY. A POP MYTHOLOGY. GANGS FILL A VOID IN THE PERCEPTION OF POWER. IT DOESN'T MATTER THAT THERE'S LITTLE MONEY TO BE MADE HERE SELLING DRUGS OR ANY OF THE OTHER BUSINESSES IN WHICH GANGS ENGAGE. THE KIDS IN WANBLEE TOWN ARE DESPERATE TO BELONG TO SOMETHING MADE REAL BY TELEVISION, PART OF A NATIONAL DIALOGUE.

ONE EVENING AT DUSK, WHILE DRIVING OUT OF THE WANBLEE CLUSTER HOUSING, A HALF DOZEN 8 TO 10-YEAR-OLD KIDS RAN INTO THE STREET BEHIND OUR CAR, YELLING, "YO! YO! WHAT'S UP! TALK TO ME! I'M IN A GANG!"

OF COURSE, GANGS WERE ALWAYS WITH US. CHAUCER USED THE TERM IN 1390. IN MORE MODERN TIMES, THE INFAMOUS FORTY THIEVES GANG RULED LOWER MANHATTAN IN 1925. MALCOLM KLEIN, AS PUBLISHED IN 1992 AFTER OVER 30 YEARS OF EXHAUSTIVE RESEARCH, LOCATED GANG STRUCTURES IN 54 URBAN CITIES PRIOR TO 1961 – MOST IN THE SOUTHWEST, WHERE MEXICAN-AMERICAN GANGS SET THE STYLE. THESE WERE THE CLASSIC "YOUTH" OR "JUVENILE DELINQUENT" GANG STRUCTURES MYTHOLO-GIZED BY *WEST SIDE STORY*, INCLUDING WELL-KNOWN SUPERGANGS LIKE CHICAGO'S BLACKSTONE RANGERS, VICE LORDS, AND DISCIPLES, SOME OF WHICH ARE STILL AROUND TODAY.

INDIANS HAD 'EM, TOO. THEY SAW THE MOVIES. ROSEBUD SHERIFF WOODROW STAR FONDLY REMEMBERS DRESSING UP LIKE LATINO *PACHUCOS* IN THE 1960, WHICH THEY TRADED IN FOR RODEO STYLE IN THE 1970, AND BEATING UP ON THE LONGHAIRS DURING BOTH DECADES.

BUT EVERYTHING CHANGED FROM THE MID-'70 TO 1980. KLEIN'S WORK SHOWS THAT THE NUMBER OF CITIES REPORTING GANG ACTIVITY ROSE TO 94 BY 1970 AND TO 172 BY 1980. AFTER THAT, HOWEVER, IT EXPLODED: BY 1992 THERE WERE SIMILAR GANG STRUCTURES IN OVER 800 CITIES, INCLUDING 91 ALL-AMERICAN PICKET-FENCE TOWNS WITH LESS THAN 10,000 RESIDENTS. BY NOW THEY'VE SPREAD INTO FARM TOWNS, WHITE SUBURBS, HAWAIIAN ISLANDS AND RURAL OUTPOSTS. KLEIN NOTES THAT GANGS, ONCE ESTABLISHED, ALMOST NEVER FADE OUT, ADDING: "THE PROBLEM RARELY GOES AWAY."

FOR *MONSTER* AUTHOR SHAKUR, THE NEW HIGHLY POLITICIZED AND QUASI-PERMANENT STRUCTURE OF GANGS (FEATURING ALLIANCES, LITERATURE, INTERNAL GOVERN-MENTS, ETC.), MILITARY-STYLE AUTOMATIC WEAPONRY, DRUG DISTRIBUTION ECONOMIES, AND SUBSEQUENT VIOLENCE CAME STRAIGHT OUTTA SOUTH CENTRAL L.A. BY HIS AND OTHER'S ACCOUNTS, HOWEVER, IT DID NOT START WITH CRACK COCAINE, AS IS WIDELY BELIEVED. TURF WARFARE BEGAN A STEADY ESCALATION IN SOUTHERN CALIFORNIA AROUND 1975 AS GANGS PROLIFERATED. BY 1980, "MONSTER" AND HIS EIGHT TRAY CRIPS WERE AT FULL-SCALE WAR WITH THE ROLLIN' SIXTIES CRIPS. THE SCORES OF CRIP-ON-CRIP MURDERS AND THE HAIL OF BULLETS THAT FLEW THAT SUMMER GRABBED THE MEDIA BY THE CROTCH AND NEVER LET GO. GANGLAND GOT IN THE MEDIA LIKE A VIRUS AND INFECTED THE REST OF THE NATION. WHEN CRACK FIRST APPEARED IN THE U.S., IN 1982 IN LOS ANGELES, THOSE STREET ARMIES WERE SIMPLY THE PERFECT TOOL TO MOVE IT.

SO THE PRESENCE OF GANGS ON THE RES IS PART OF A GENERAL RURALIZATION. BUT THE RES ISN'T LIKE THE REST OF THE U.S. GANGS HERE ARE PARTICULARLY PERNICIOUS. ELSEWHERE IN AMERICA, MEDIUM-SIZE TOWNS OF BETWEEN 10,000 AND 100,000 RESIDENTS WILL REPORT HAVING TWO OR MAYBE FIVE GANGS (NEVER JUST ONE: THEY NEED RIVALS). IN WANBLEE OR ROSEBUD, BY COMPARISON, DOZENS OF SETS HAVE SPRUNG FROM A FEW THOUSAND RESIDENTS.

THIS REVEALS THE NATURE OF THE CULTURAL VOID: IT IS LIKE A LAND RUSH FOR A NEW IDENTITY. THE IMAGE OF CRAZY HORSE THAT NOW GLARES OVER THE BLACK HILLS NEAR MOUNT RUSHMORE IS NOT ENOUGH TO SUSTAIN THEM. THESE KIDS WANT THEIR OWN PIECE OF VALIDATED IDENTITY.

AS THEY GROW OLDER, THE NEW MYTHOLOGIES ADOPTED BY NATIVE GANGSTERS SLOWLY BREAK DOWN. BECAUSE THEY'RE NOT MEXICAN, BLACK, OR ARTHURIAN ENGLISH, SOON THEY MUST FACE THEIR GANG'S WORST ENEMY: THEIR OWN SKIN. "THE OTHER DAY I SEEN BEN CHIPPS WALKING DOWN THE STREET, STRUTTING, BARE-CHESTED, WITH FRESH BLOODY PIERCINGS ON HIS CHEST FROM SUNDANCING," SAYS CROSS. CHIPPS IS THE 19-YEAR-OLD LEADER OF THE DUCE CRIPS SET (BEN MEANS TO IMPLY "DEUCE," AS IN L.A.'S 2ND STREET, BUT SPELLS IT "DUCE"). "HE HAD THE BLUE RAG IN HIS BACK POCKET. I PULLED OVER AND SAID, 'WHICH ONE IS IT GONNA BE, BEN? NATIVE SPIRITUALITY OR THE GANG-BANGIN'? 'COS YOU CAN'T CHOOSE BOTH.'"

CHIPPS IS AN OLD LAKOTA NAME. HIS GRANDFATHER CHIPPS IS A POWERFUL ANCESTRAL HEALER. BEN LIVES WITH HIS MOTHER, SISTERS AND BROTHERS IN THE HOUSE ACROSS THE STREET FROM THE BALD EAGLES IN WANBLEE'S OLD HOUSING. HIS GANG NAME IS LI'L TRIGGER. BEN'S UNCLE CHARLES LIVES NEXT DOOR AND WORKS AS A SPIRITUAL LEADER. BEN'S FATHER, TOO, NOW CARRIES THE MEDICINE. BEN IS CAUGHT BETWEEN TWO IDENTITIES: HE GOT INTO THE CRIPS IN AUSTIN, TEXAS, BY EMPTYING A PISTOL THROUGH THE FRONT WINDOW OF A GANGSTER'S HOME WHEN HE WAS ONLY 15, AND NOW HE'S FEELING THE PRESSURE TO KEEP UP THE GANG FRONT – ESPECIALLY WITH GANGSTER DISCIPLE–IDENTIFIED BALD EAGLES READY FOR WAR ACROSS THE STREET – WHILE FEELING MORE AND MORE DRAWN INTO THE WAYS OF HIS FAMILY.

"MY UNCLE, HE'S A BIG PART OF IT," SAYS BEN, SITTING ON THE EDGE OF A HIGH OVERLOOK IN BADLANDS NATIONAL PARK. HE TOSSES HANDFULS OF SUNFLOWER SEEDS TO A BRASSY MAGPIE. "WHEN HE GETS US OUT OF JAIL, WE HAVE TO WORK FOR HIM AT 3 DOLLARS AN HOUR TO PAY OFF THE FINES. HE TAKES US TO SWEAT LODGES ALL THE TIME, PURIFICATION LODGES. BOY, IT GETS HOT IN THERE."

HE SHOWS ME THE SCARS ON HIS CHEST FROM THE SUNDANCE CEREMONIES. HE'S BEEN PIERCED ON 8 OR 10 OCCASIONS, AT ALMOST ALL OF THE SUNDANCES THAT HAVE HAPPENED HERE SINCE HE WAS 11 YEARS OLD. "THE ONLY THING WE HAVE TO GIVE TO THE CREATOR IS OUR SOUL," HE SAYS. "MONEY DON'T MEAN NOTHING TO THEM, SO GIVE FLESH. THEY'RE CALLED OFFERINGS. KEEPS US STRONG, EH?"

I ASK HIM IF HE SEES ANY CONTRADICTIONS BETWEEN THE RESPONSIBILITY DEMANDED BY HIS RELIGION AND THE EXQUISITELY CYNICAL EBK – EVERYBODY KILLER – MEN-TALITY OF THE GANGS.

"WHEN I FIRST STARTED TO GANG-BANG I DIDN'T," HE SAYS. NOW HE'S THINKING TWICE. UNABLE TO GIVE UP EITHER ONE, HE JUST KEEPS THEM SEPARATE. "WHEN I'M IN THE SWEAT LODGE, I DON'T THINK ABOUT THAT. OR WHEN I'M OUT ON THE STREETS, I DON'T THINK ABOUT SPIRITUALITY."

BEN'S LAKOTA PRIDE IS PALPABLE TO EVERYONE AROUND. AS WE SIT ON THE OVERLOOK, A STRANGER WALKS UP AND THEY START TALKING. THE MAN RECOGNIZES BEN'S NAME AND SAYS, "CHIPPS IS A POWERFUL NAME. *WASTÉ* (GOOD). MUCH RESPECT." BEN TAKES IT IN STRIDE. AS WE WALK, HE TELLS ME THAT HIS PLAN IS SIMPLE: GO INTO "NEUTRAL" AS A GANGSTER AND JUST SELL MARIJUANA. "I MAKE IT EXCITING AROUND HERE," HE SAYS. HE CONSIDERS IT A SERVICE TO HIS PEOPLE, AND HIS UNCLE'S REP MAKES IT EASY FOR HIM TO MOVE THROUGH DIFFERENT FAMILIES, GANGS AND NEIGHBORHOODS SAFELY. HIS RELIABLE SOURCE FOR WEED IS A 68-YEAR-OLD WOMAN IN A NEARBY TOWN.

"IT'S OKAY IF YOU SAY I SELL WEED, BECAUSE PEOPLE GOT TO KNOW THAT THEY DON'T GIVE US NO JOBS UP HERE. I GOT A LITTLE DAUGHTER AND SHE GOT NEEDS."

BEN IS ALSO PROUD TO ACKNOWLEDGE THAT HE HAS A COUPLE SKS AUTOMATIC RIFLES, SAWED-OFF SHOTGUNS, AND HAS HAD ACCESS TO A MAC-90 (A CIVILIAN VERSION OF THE AK-47 ASSAULT RIFLE). HE SAYS THERE'S AN ARMY SURPLUS STORE IN RAPID THAT'S SO LOOSE HE CAN SEND IN HIS HOMIE CRAIG LITTLE THUNDER, 18, WITH A HAND-FUL OF CASH AND WALK OUT WITH ANY HOT GUN YOU WANT.

HE'S GROWN COMFORTABLE WITH THE STRANGE AMALGAM OF IDENTITY THAT HE'S COLLECTED FOR HIMSELF. BUT HE RANKLES WHEN HE SEES IT REFLECTED IN HIS YOUNGER FAMILY MEMBERS. HIS COUSIN MICHELLE,16, SEEMS TO BE EVERYWHERE IN WANBLEE, KICKING IT ON DOORSTEPS WITH HER HOMEGIRLS, ALWAYS FLY IN HER BIG

PANTS, SNEAKERS, MIDRIFF TOPS AND BLACK LIPSTICK. SHE IS NERVOUS AND ANNOYED WHEN I ASK HER QUESTIONS. SHE SPEAKS A RAPID-FIRE LINGO THAT FRANKLY SOUNDS MORE BLACK THAN INDIAN. SHE CLAIMS GD.

"SHE LEARNS THAT LOOK AND THAT TALK OFF THE TV," BEN NODS. "SHE LEARNING HER OWN LITTLE SLANG OFF THE VIDEOS ON THE MTV. THAT'S HER TRIP."

NATIVE IDENTITY IS NOT UNHEARD-OF IN GANGLAND; IT'S JUST NOT EMBRACED. THERE ARE A FEW LAKOTA GANGS WITH NAMES LIKE NATIVE MOB.

"THERE'S ONE NOW, IT'S CALLED 'NCG,' NATIVE CRIP GANGSTERS," SAYS ELLIOTT BLUE COAT. "THERE'S ANOTHER ONE CALLED 'BROTHERHOOD,' THOSE GUYS ARE RED. I THINK BEING IN A GANG GIVES A NATIVE AMERICAN A BAD NAME. 'CAUSE WE ALREADY WENT THROUGH A LOT OF WARS AND NOW WE'RE FIGHTING AMONGST EACH OTHER AND SHIT."

BUT NATIVE TRIBES HAVE ALWAYS FOUGHT INTER- AND INTRATRIBAL WARS, AND PERHAPS THAT'S WHY KIDS WITH PRIDE LIKE BEN SEE LITTLE CONTRADICTION IN BATTLING EACH OTHER AS PART OF "IMPORTED" GANGS. IN THE TIME OF THE GREAT OGLALA SIOUX WAR LEADER RED CLOUD, FOR INSTANCE, THE SIOUX FOUGHT PAWNEE, OMAHA, CROW, SHOSHONE, CHEYENNE, GROS VENTRES, ARIKARA, ARAPAHO, AND OTHER TRIBES (AND ALSO DEFEATED THE U.S. ARMY AND DROVE THEM TO A PEACE CONFERENCE). MORE IMPORTANTLY, TRIBAL MEMBERS DON'T ALWAYS AGREE ON HOW MUCH THEY SHOULD BE IDENTIFIED AS A TRIBE. IN THE EARLY 1970S, WANBLEE WAS A HOT SPOT WHERE SIOUX WARRIORS FROM THE TRADITIONALIST AMERICAN INDIAN MOVEMENT (AIM) FOUGHT THE GOONS, BACKERS OF A THEN-NEW, U.S.-BACKED ELECTED GOVERNMENT SYSTEM LED BY OGLALA SIOUX TRIBAL PRESIDENT DICK WILSON—THUS ESTABLISHING A TRADITION OF "COUSIN ENEMIES."

"THERE USED TO BE CIVIL WAR HERE. REAL BLOOD WARFARE," SAYS BLAINE LITTLE THUNDER, HEAD OF ONE OF THE HOUSEHOLDS IN THE CLUSTER HOUSING. HE DIS-MISSES THESE NEW GANGSTERS AS "WANNABES" COMPARED TO THE ISSUE-ORIENTED BATTLES OF HIS YOUNG ADULTHOOD, WHEN HOUSEHOLDS BATTLED OVER THE TERMS OF THEIR SOVEREIGNTY VIS-À-VIS THE UNITED STATES. "GUYS WERE SHOOTING AT EACH OTHER IN 1973 – AIM AND THE GOONS. THAT'S REAL GANGS. BACK IN THEM DAYS, BULLETS WERE FLYING EVERYDAY."

AFTER SEVERAL DEATHS, THE BATTLE BETWEEN AIM AND THE GOONS CAME TO A HEAD DURING A PROLONGED 1973 FIREFIGHT AT THE PINE RIDGE TOWN OF WOUNDED KNEE. AIMSTER LEONARD PELTIER WAS EVENTUALLY GIVEN LIFE IN PRISON – WRONGLY, MANY STILL SAY – FOR BEING PRESENT AT THE CLOSE-RANGE SHOOTING DEATHS OF TWO GOON-BACKED FBI AGENTS.

WANBLEE WAS AN AIM TOWN. AIM AND THE GOONS WORE COLORS TO DISTINGUISH THEMSELVES. AIM WORE RED BANDANNAS. THE GOONS WORE BLUE. JUST LIKE CRIPS (BLUE) AND BLOODS (RED). BANDANNAS HAVE BEEN GETTING FOLKS KILLED UP HERE GOING ON 30 YEARS.

THERE ARE ALSO LONGER-RUNNING INTERNAL CONFLICTS. GANG CULTURE IN WANBLEE IS UNIQUE IN THAT IT HAS BEEN RECONTEXTUALIZED TO FURTHER A BITTER, TRIANGULAR FAMILY FEUD THAT PRE-EXISTS THE CLUSTER HOUSING ITSELF – A FEUD THAT THE KIDS SAY STARTED AMONG THEIR GRANDPARENTS OR EVEN EARLIER.

OFFICE JOE CROSS SITS IN HIS SUBSTATION AMONG THE HEAVY PUNCHING BAGS AND THE TIRED UNIVERSAL WEIGHT MACHINE AND FLOW-CHARTS IT ALL OUT, FAMILY BY FAMILY. BEN'S FAMILY, THE CHIPPS, ARE ALLIED WITH THE QUIVERS AND THE DOYLES. THEY MOSTLY BECAME THE DUCE CRIPS. THE BALD EAGLES ARE ALLIED WITH THE PROVINCIALS, LOAFERS AND BLACK BEARS; THEY CLAIM GANGSTER DISCIPLES. ANOTHER FAMILY CALLED THE BETTELYOUNS BECAME THE DOS MOB, THE LATIN KINGS, AND THEN TRIPLE H. HISTORICALLY, THE FEUD WAS KNOWN BY THE THREE MAIN FAMILY NAMES – CHIPPS, BALD EAGLES, AND BETTELYOUNS. IF YOU RAN WITH ONE OF THEM, THAT'S THE NAME YOU TOOK NO MATTER WHAT YOUR GIVEN NAME. IT WASN'T SUCH A LONG STRETCH, THEN, TO GANG IDENTITY.

RURAL RES FAMILIES WHO UNITE AND FIGHT ALONGSIDE ONE ANOTHER NOW TAKE THEIR PLACE IN THE 1990 URBAN GANG STRUCTURE. THEIR FAMILY NAMES "REPRESENT" JUST LIKE THE OTHERS. ON A TRIP INTO THE NEIGHBORING TOWN OF KYLE, BEN INTRODUCES US TO HIS HOMIES KEITH AND JAMES BROWN. THEY ARE PART OF A MUCH-FEARED BATTLE CLAN KNOWN IN RAPID CITY SIMPLY AS THE "BROWNS." IT'S ONE OF THE EASIEST GANGS TO JOIN, BUT THE HARDEST TO QUIT; YOU'RE SIMPLY BORN INTO IT.

THE MIX OF GANG STRUCTURES IN ONE SMALL TOWN BECOMES A BAFFLING MATRIX OF ALLEGIANCES. ONE OF THE BROWNS' FRIENDS, A YOUNG MAN NAMED STACY, SHOWS US THE FOUR HORIZONTAL BURNS (DONE WITH A HEATED KNIFE BLADE) THAT MARK HIM AS AN OG MEMBER OF TBZ. TOGETHER, THEY RUN DOWN THE LIST OF GANGS THAT CLAIM PARTS OF KYLE, WHICH IS ONLY SLIGHTLY BIGGER THAN WANBLEE. THEY HAVE PIRU (BLOODS), TRE TRE GANGSTA CRIPS, NOMADS, NIGHTWALKING CRIPS, TBZ, GD, NORTH SIDE GANGSTER DISCIPLES, FOLK NATION (ALL GANGS OF CHICAGO ORIGIN ARE SPLIT INTO EITHER FOLK OR PEOPLE NATIONS, MUCH LIKE BLOODS AND

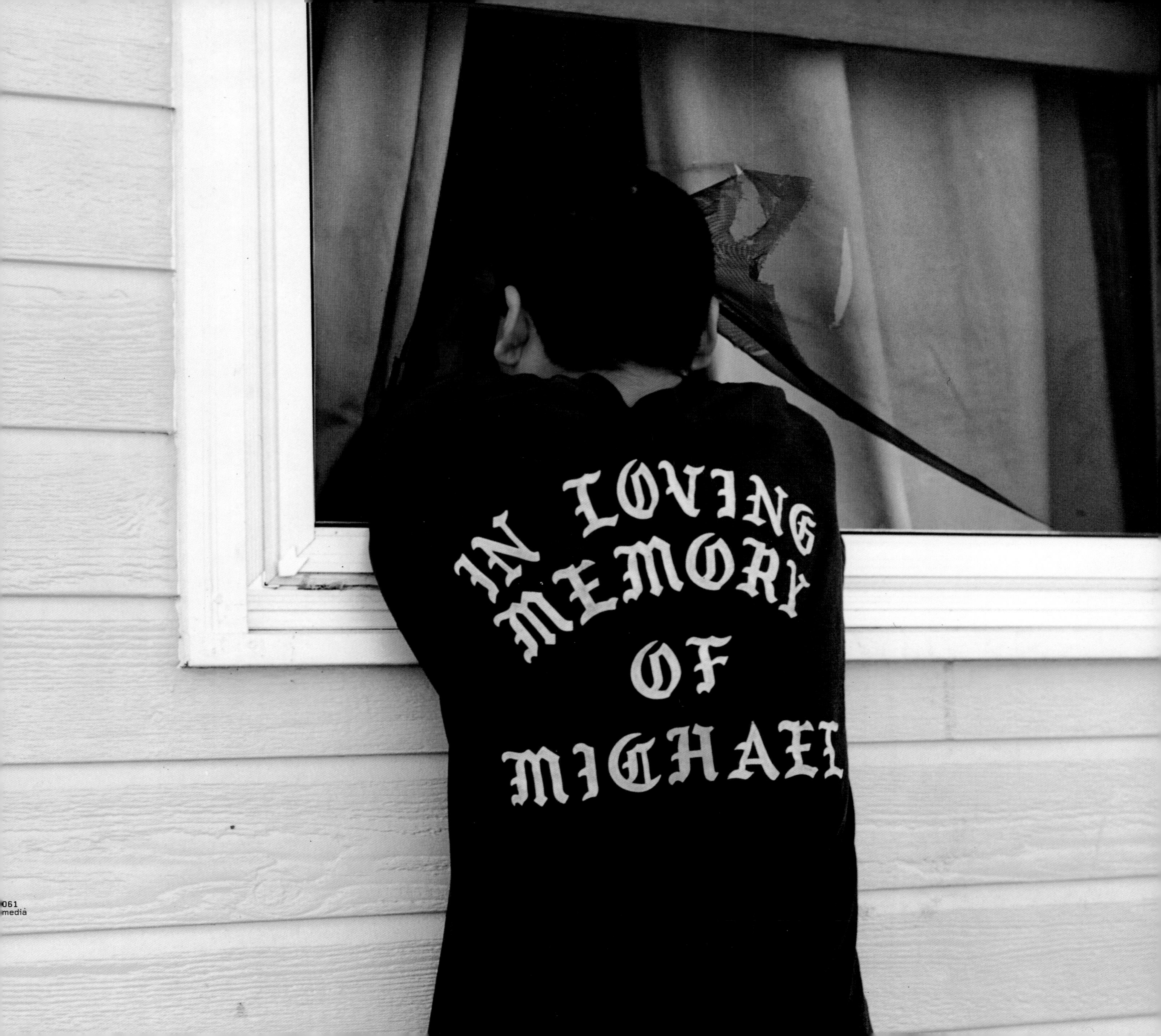
IN LOVING
MEMORY
OF
MICHAEL

CRIPS IN LOS ANGELES; THE GD ARE FOLK), NATIVE OUTLAWS, NORTH SIDE BOYS, AND *SUREÑO* 13. THE NAMES MEAN EVERYTHING. FAMILIES END UP SPLIT. COUSINS MEET IN THE DARK INTERIORS OF THE HOUSING CLUSTERS AND BEAT EACH OTHER IN THE HEAD WITH GOLF CLUBS AND BATS. THE MOST COMMON CAUSE FOR A GUY TO REQUEST GETTING "JUMPED OUT" OF A SET – A PRO- LONGED BEATING DELIVERED BY GANG BROTHERS IS THE ONLY WAY TO QUIT THE GANG, AND MANY GANGSTERS SAY THEY'RE PRETTY SURE THEY WOULDN'T SURVIVE IT – IS HAVING A PREG- NANT GIRLFRIEND FROM ANOTHER SET.

THE TRIBAL GOVERNMENT IN THE TOWN OF PINE RIDGE, THE RESERVATION SEAT THAT GOVERNS WANBLEE, DOESN'T THINK THERE IS A "GANG PROBLEM." EVERETT LITTLE WHITEMAN, DIRECTOR OF PUBLIC SAFETY, ACKNOWLEDGES THE PRESENCE OF GANGS BUT WANTS TO BELIEVE THEY'RE A PASSING FAD. HE MAY BE RIGHT, AND BY THE TIME YOU READ THIS THEY MAY BE GONE, WASHED UP AS QUICKLY AS THEY WASHED OVER THIS RES. SHOCKING PERCENTAGES OF THE ORIGINAL GANGSTERS ON EVERY RES ARE IN PRISON, LEAVING THE RANKS OF HARDCORE WARRIORS DEPLETED. BUT, AS MANY PATROLMEN, CRIME PREVENTION SPECIALISTS, TEACHERS, AND PARENTS POINT OUT, A GANG EITHER IS OR ISN'T. IF A WANNABE PULLS THE TRIGGER, THEN ALL YOU GOT IS SOMEBODY DEAD.

A-DOG AND THE BALD EAGLES KNOW ABOUT DEAD. HIS OLDER BROTHER MICHAEL WAS KILLED BY A GUNMAN AT A PARTY IN MINNEAPOLIS. AS BEN CHIPPS SAYS, "THE GDS FRONTED HIM THREE POUNDS OF WEED TO SELL OUT HERE AND HE SMOKED IT ALL UP, SO WHEN HE WENT BACK THERE THEY SMOKED *HIM*."

WHETHER OR NOT THAT'S THE WHOLE STORY, THE CIRCUMSTANCES WERE AS GHOSTLY AND SURREAL AS A SHAKESPEAREAN TRAGEDY. GANGSTER DISCIPLES THREW A BIG PARTY, EVIDENTLY INTENDING TO USE IT AS A COVER TO BEAT SOME SENSE INTO MICHAEL. WHEN THEY EVENTUALLY REVEALED THEIR TRUE PURPOSE, HE RESPONDED BY PULLING A GUN. LEAVING THE PARTY, ANOTHER GD EVIDENTLY RAN UP ON MICHAEL AND SHOT HIM IN THE BACK. THE KILLER THEN RETURNED TO THE PARTY AND PROCEEDED TO BRAG IT UP TO EVERYONE. AFTER RESISTING EFFORTS BY OTHER GANG MEMBERS TO CLEAR HIM OUT OF TOWN, HE ATE A BUNCH OF ACID, THEN MADE A "LAST VISIT" TO HIS GIRLFRIEND. THEY SMOKED A BLUNT, THEN HE TOOK A WALK, WHICH ENDED AT A POLICE STATION, WHERE THE KILLER WALKED IN, ANNOUNCED THAT THE PISTOL HE'D LAID ON THE COUNTER WAS LOADED AND THAT HE'D JUST USED IT TO KILL MICHAEL BALD EAGLE AND THAT HE WOULD LIKE TO LIE DOWN IN ONE OF THEIR CELLS AND TRIP. HE GOT LIFE.

THE BALD EAGLES HAVE WEAPONS STASHED IN WANBLEE. THEY'VE HAD A COUPLE GUN BATTLES WITH THE CHIPPS, APPARENTLY HALFHEARTED THOUGH THEY INVOLVED HIGH-POWERED AUTOMATIC RIFLES AS WELL AS CRAPPY OLD SAWED-OFF .22s. THE TOWN'S TOO SMALL TO SHOOT ANYONE, THEY SAY. NOWHERE TO RUN AND HIDE, NO CITYSCAPE IN WHICH TO DISAPPEAR. EVERYONE'S A SNITCH. EVERYONE'S RELATED. GUNS GENERALLY COME OUT ONLY WHEN SOMEONE'S DRUNK.

MOSTLY, THEY POSE IN THE YARD. AND WAIT.

"THOSE GUYS ACROSS THE STREET TALK SHIT," SAYS A-DOG'S COUSIN D MONEY, WHO JUST ARRIVED FROM SALT LAKE CITY TO HIDE OUT IN THEIR GRANDMOTHER'S HOUSE. HE STANDS IN THE DRIVEWAY AND POINTS AT EACH HOUSE IN SUCCESSION. "THOSE GUYS IN THAT HOUSE RIGHT THERE TALK SHIT. THAT HOUSE TALKS ALL KINDA SHIT. BUT THEY'RE ALL TALK, NO ACTION. IF A GANGSTER WANTS A PIECE OF YOU, THEY JUST WALK UP AND SHOOT YOUR ASS. THEY AIN'T NO *REAL* GANGS UP HERE."

D MONEY MOVES NERVOUSLY AS HE TALKS, THROWING DOWN THE FAMILIAR SLOPE-SHOULDERED GESTURES, HIKING HIS BAGGY JEANS UNDERNEATH A HUGE FOOTBALL JERSEY AND RETYING HIS LONG BLACK HAIR. LIKE ALMOST EVERY YOUNG MAN IN WANBLEE, HE RELOCATES CONSTANTLY, SPENDING SEASONS OR WEEKS WITH RELATIVES AND THEN MOVING ON, STATE TO STATE. STAYING IN ONE PLACE TOO LONG MEANS AN INEVITABLE BATTLE. DESPITE HIMSELF, HE MAKES IT PLAIN THAT BATTLE – WHETHER IT INVOLVES GUNS OR NOT – IS ALWAYS REAL.

"ONE TIME THEY TRIED TO RUN UP HERE IN OUR GRANDMA'S HOUSE," SAYS D MONEY'S YOUNGER BROTHER BOOM BOOM WITH A MANIC SMILE. "WE SENT THEIR SHIT IN FOR A CAT SCAN."

THIS IS THE BALD EAGLE BOYS' FAVORITE WANBLEE STORY. ON ANOTHER DAY, THEIR COUSIN ROBBY LOAFER STANDS IN THE SAME YARD ONLY MINUTES AFTER BEING RELEASED FROM POLICE CUSTODY, DANCING FROM FOOT TO FOOT TRYING TO SHAKE OFF THE BURNING EFFECTS OF A FACEFUL OF MACE. HE PICKS UP THE STORY: "THEY CAME OUT ALL BLOODY, BEATEN, ROLLED DOWN THE STAIRS, GS WITH TEETH KNOCKED OUT AN' SHIT," ROBBY SAYS. HE AND BOOM BOOM'S BROTHER, CLOWN, CRACK UP, POINTING DOWN THE STREET AT THE QUIVER HOUSE. "HEY, HE'S SITTING ON THE PORCH RIGHT OVER THERE. HE'LL SMILE, HE AIN'T GOT NO FRONT TEETH! WE GOT THIS STICK WITH FUCKIN' TEETH MARKS FROM THAT MOTHERFUCKER."

"YEAH, FOUR TEETH MARKS IN IT," SAYS CLOWN. "TWO ON THE TOP, AND TWO ON THE BOTTOM."

A-DOG: HE SWALLOWED 'EM.

BOOM BOOM: THERE WAS ONLY SIX OF US. AND THERE WAS ABOUT THREE FAMILIES COMIN' DOWN THE ROAD WANTIN' TO FIGHT US.

A-DOG: YOU COULDN'T EVEN SEE THAT ROAD, MAN. YOU COULDN'T EVEN SEE THAT GRASS, THAT'S ALL YOU COULD SEE WAS A BUNCH OF PEOPLE.

BOOM BOOM: ABOUT 15 TO 20 GUYS AND THE REST ARE WOMEN.

A-DOG: THEY FUCKIN' KICKED IN OUR DOOR, JUST – BOOM! MY COUSIN, HE'S A LEFT-HAN-DER AND HE HAD A BROOMSTICK. AND HE WAS ALL, "WHAT, YOU WANT SOME?!" THEN HE JUST CRACKED HIM ON THE HEAD TWICE WITH IT. THEY WENT WRASSLING BY ME, AND I WAS JUST CHECKIN' 'EM OUT.

BOOM BOOM: THEY WAS SOME *BIG* GUYS, TOO!

A-DOG: YEAH, THEY'S BIGGER THAN US. AND OUTWEIGH US AN' SHIT. I SMACKED HIM ON HIS BACK. ALL THAT PAIN MUST'VE HURT IN HIM SO BAD HE KNOCKED MY COUSIN INTO A CHAIR AND SOME BAGS AN' SHIT.

BOOM BOOM: I COME RUNNIN' UPSTAIRS WITH A CAN O' JUICE, ONE OF THOSE GIANT CANS? (HEFTS A 24-OZ. TIN CAN OF BEANS AS AN EXAMPLE.) THE LAST ONE GOIN' OUT THE DOOR, I COME RUNNIN' BY HIM, HIT THAT MOTHERFUCKER – BOOM! – HARDER THAN FUCK IN THE BACK OF THE HEAD! IT DENTED THAT MOTHERFUCKER OPEN! SENT HIM TO RAPID [CITY HOSPITAL].

A-DOG: THE BACK OF HIS HEAD-PRINT IN THE CAN. THEY TRIED TO SAY THAT THEY KNOCKED OUR GRANDMA OVER THIS BANISTER AN' SHIT.

BOOM BOOM: YEP. IF THEY'D'A DID THAT, THEY WOULDN'T'A NEVER LEFT THIS HOUSE.

A-DOG: WE WOULD'A KILLED 'EM IN HERE. WE BEAT THOSE GUYS UP, SO THOSE WOMEN WERE COMIN' WITH BATS AN' SHIT. "FIGHT US, THEN!" SO I WAS ALL LIKE, "COME ON! I'LL BEAT YO ASS, YOU FUCKIN' BITCH!"

BOOM BOOM: AND THEY ALWAYS BREAK OUR WINDOWS, EH? EVERY WINDOW GOT BROKEN A COUPLE TIMES. ALL OUR CARS OUT THERE GOT THEIR WINDSHIELDS BUSTED.

A-DOG: THESE ARE WHAT WE HAVE TO USE DOWN HERE: BATS. I LIKE THIS ONE. LOUISVILLE SLUGGER.

→chance

→chance

4 SPEED

TREASURE IS

AS
CHANCE

"YOU WANT A METAPHOR? WE HAVE ROCKET FUEL PUMPED INTO OUR DRINKING WATER. THERE IS A ROCKET FUEL PLANT THAT HAS LEACHED ROCKET FUEL INTO LAKE MEAD. THAT'S WHAT WE'RE DRINKING RIGHT NOW." ↳ PATRON AT GAMBLER'S BOOK CLUB.

"OH, IT'S GOTTA BE REAL. WE'RE REAL, AREN'T WE? I DON'T SEE ANY ROBOTS WALKING AROUND." ↳ DONALD "SARGE" CUNNINGHAM, AT ST. VINCENT'S RESIDENTIAL PROGRAM FOR PROBLEM GAMBLERS, ON THE "ACTION" IN LAS VEGAS.

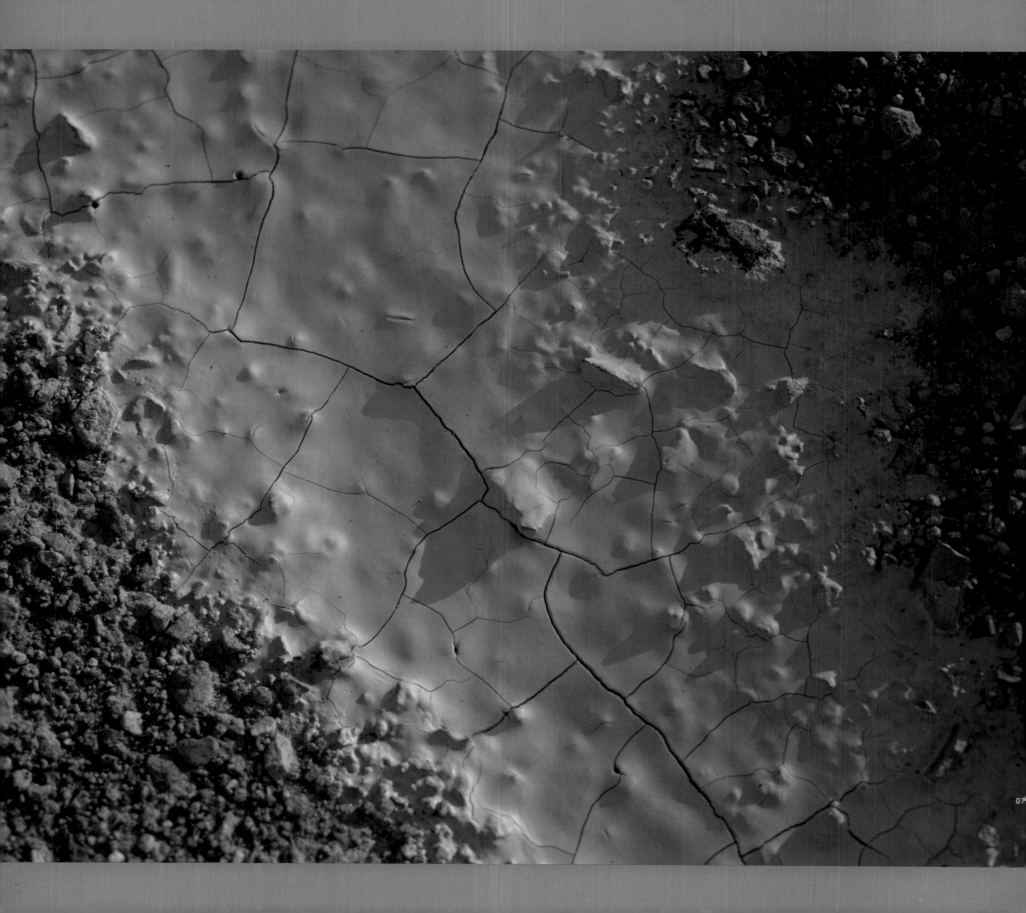

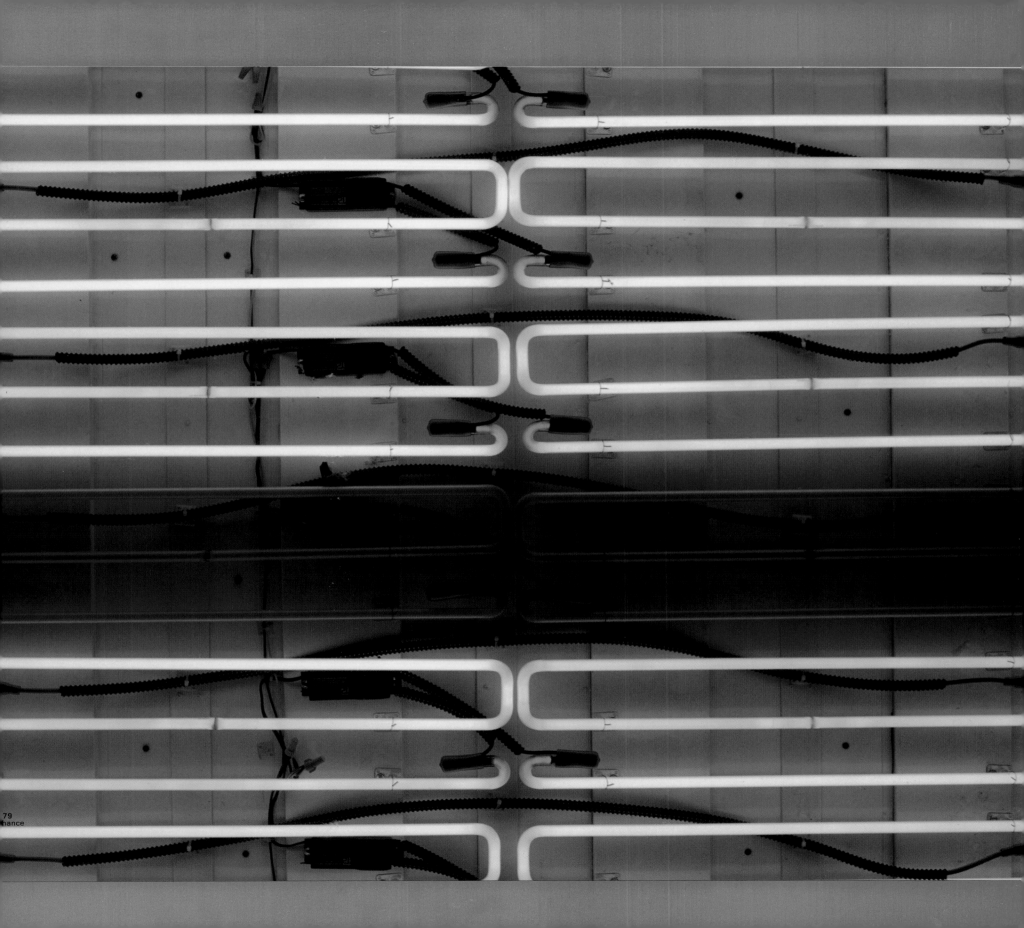

hance

→ Luck is just about the fastest thing there is. Faster than light. Light has a velocity, 186,000 miles per second, but luck, the way we experience it, is instantaneous: one instant your hope is in play, the next you either win or lose.

Las Vegas is less a town than a promise of instant karma. Want to know how you're doing with the gods? There's an actual place you can go to find out. You'll get your answer in dollars.

Of course, the supplicants, like pilgrims everywhere, choose their answers selectively. You can lose your ass all week and then hit one good score and go home thrilled, even if you've actually lost money on the week. Because the gods have answered. You knew your luck was there, hanging behind a veil in that other world, and you just had to play long enough to realize it. To let it manifest itself. That thrill is the same for the nickel-slot tourist or the million-dollar baccarat player. And it's nothing to scoff at. One throw of the dice can get you ahead. A half-hour hot streak can make you truly and instantly rich. In any table game in Las Vegas, a $100 bet let ride 13 times in a row, and won, will make you a millionaire. The odds against it are basically impossible. But it happens several times each year.

This is more than just getting rich quick, which is why a million-dollar baccarat player would care. It's an act of Creation. It's making something out of nothing, just like God. It's an act of God. It's a shamanistic act of influencing the uninfluenceable, rolling the bones like an old witch doctor. It's magic. Magic entertains people, and having luck in Las Vegas is the best show there is. You are a different person afterwards.

"For the guy living from paycheck to paycheck, winning five grand could change his life," says P. Moss, owner of Las Vegas' Double Down Bar. A lifelong sports bettor, Moss sees the average Joe play for a lifetime waiting for that big score. "Housewives, grandmothers, they'll bet $5 on a parlay card; bet ten teams, it pays 1,000 to 1. So they get back $5,000 for their $5. Or 15 teams, it's 100,000 to 1. They know they're not gonna win, but they're throwing out $5 to win $150,000 on stuff they're watching on TV. So they get a little action. They don't want to bet $5 to win $5. What's the point? They care about betting on something with long odds; if they should get lucky, it's gonna change their lives."

No one deserves it. There's no such thing as "due." No work will earn it. Like salvation, it's just plain free. It's truly divine. *Anyone can do it.*

Or, seen another way, no one can do it. It can't be done. It just happens.

Unless, like Moss, you learn to measure luck by the amount of money made over time. There are pros in Las Vegas who are more than lucky. And that's what counts now. The new Las Vegas, where money is now more important than fun, asks an intoxicatingly complex question: Is luck faster than skill? Moss knows the answer. So does any professional, like blackjack player Tom Collins. In fact, Tom Collins is the answer.

Tom Collins pushes furtively through the rear door of the casino like a defrocked priest needing to cop some holy water. He carries in a radiant aura of 4 a.m. desert heat that sloughs off in the indoor chill. Instantly the familiar liquid rush is on him. He floats in on the promise of communion with the unknowable. It's there, in the totalitarian sensation of cheap carpet, cigarette-smoked felt, vinyl worn by the forearms and buttocks of a million farting pilgrims, institutional cleanser, oxygen-fluffed air conditioning, the buffet smoldering medieval somewhere below, all of it washing downstream on that sound. It gives texture to the teflon edifice of Las Vegas, the only assurance of a pulse, the sound of dropping coins, of the flapping tab on the wheel of fortune, of jackpot bells, of the monotone voice on the public address. But above all, the sound of dropping coins. The rush he feels is one of belonging to that flow. Here is the camaraderie of all those citizens in all those casinos acknowledging one another before the one true object of the American religion. The rush of fast money.

Money is speed. To have it is to have mobility. Contemporary global culture preaches that money is accumulable in amounts approaching a terminus of total mobility — to be able to move in and out of locations, in and out of personas, even backward and forward in time. Money can buy reality, change it instantly, which is acceleration. This is why it's equated with luck.

Tom Collins can control that flow. You could say he has an accelerator. He counts cards.

"Blackjack is unique," he says. "It's the only game where the player can gain a positive edge over the casino."

Raised by a gambler, Tom Collins was playing in the casinos at age 13. He's been a professional blackjack player for 30 years, though he manages to play only infrequently and almost never in Las Vegas. "Positive edge" means that, statistically, the game of 21 has predictable patterns. The good counter can have a 1.5 to 2% advantage over the house. His game is exactly what it seems: a sure thing. Mathematically sound. He doesn't cheat. He wins by skill.

Other than a biased roulette wheel, which are discovered by pros who surreptitiously time them for wobble and are coveted as great secrets, it's the only legal sure thing in Vegas.

"There's two kinds of counts," says Tom Collins, moving among the tables. "There's a running count and a true count. With the running count, you're keeping track of the cards that have been in play. The true count are the cards that remain to be played, and there are formulas for figuring these out. Dr. Edward O. Thorp was the first person to propose a counting system, along with Julian Braun, an IBM computer expert in the early '60s who worked with Lawrence Revere. Thorp's book, *Beat the Dealer*, and Revere's book, *Playing Blackjack as a Business*, changed the entire world."

This is no exaggeration. Collins' business depends on bettering the instantaneous speed of luck, which changes the nature of the world considerably. He rattles on as we walk:

"Basically, Thorp proposed a system whereby you assign each card a value. What you do is mathematically add and subtract as the cards come into play. The basic theory is that the more tens and aces that are available, the more favorable position the player is in. The less tens and aces are available, the greater the number of small denomination cards, the greater the advantage the house has. When the count goes positive, it's positive for the player. When

the count goes negative, it's positive for the house. So as the count progressively gets more positive, you're supposed to bet more.

"I use a multilevel count, meaning that I'm keeping track not only of the true count and the running count, I'm keeping track of the side count of a few different cards. Aces and nines, particularly. If there are eight aces in a double-deck game, and I've seen two go by, well, that means there's six more coming."

Improving the speed of luck sounds like a contradiction, because there's still luck in it, which is precisely why so few people do it.

"It involves a massive amount of memorization," he adds. "There is an absolute correct move for every situation, and it has nothing to do with emotion. No hunches. If you lose, you lost because you lost, but you still did the right thing. If you win, that's what's supposed to happen."

A 2% advantage means he wins slowly, over time. Tom Collins is a grinder. He makes money. You always hear about the high rollers making bank, but the high rollers don't play like this. They win and lose like the suckers, just in bigger amounts and wearing louder clothes.

In theory, Tom Collins is engaged in the perfect capitalist enterprise — and a perfect ramp-up in personal acceleration. If speed can be accumulated, and if he could just play his game unimpeded, he would have more speed than anyone. He could clean out the house. Given enough time, he could own Las Vegas. If Las Vegas casino gaming were really *gaming,* he could. But it's not. It's gambling — wagering on games of pure chance, or 50/50. What the tourist doesn't know is that the chance here is not so much pure as it is forced. Las Vegas, and blackjack in particular, is the only game in the world in which pros are penalized for playing better. The casinos will brook no improvement upon dumb luck.

In a place where real speed is outlawed, then, only outlaws will have speed.

Which is why Tom Collins has to wear this beard and this hat. He's humbled himself before the tourists and their god of luck. He doesn't want to offend their desperate superstitions. You would not notice him in his jeans and his worn shirt. Playing by any other odds than blind chance angers the accountants, and he's been banned from every blackjack table in Las Vegas. He is a real person, a middle-aged man living in Las Vegas as you read this. The Griffin Agency, a casino security firm, encourages pit bosses to memorize his picture. Not because he's a crook, but because he's a winner. He's found an edge, a legal speed that threatens the cadre of corporate bean-counters who now run Las Vegas by remote, from headquarters in Beverly Hills (Hilton) or White Plains, New York (Sheraton/ITT/Starwood). He represents the ideal of Old Vegas. Back when it too was about speed. But now we have to refer to him as a drink that no one drinks anymore.

"When they talk about luck in Las Vegas, it's just the way they have there of talking about time," wrote Michael Herr in *The Big Room.* "The whole city's a clock. Luck is the local obsession, while time itself is a sore subject." Las Vegas dealers routinely dispense with their mantra — "good luck" — to remind you that chance is all that stands between you and the passage of *good time.* When you have luck, you make money, and when you make money off pure luck in Vegas it's instantaneous, beyond time. Good time is actually not time at all. It's POOF! PRESTO! Beating the clock once seems to undo losing to the clock for days on end. The lucky don't mind having a clock around, then, because they've conquered it.

Strangely, everyone in Las Vegas feels lucky. Even though, technically, they are not. They fly to Vegas to experience the passage of "good" time. This is how the lack of clocks and sunrises really works.

At first a clockless Las Vegas seems malign, a cheap trick encouraging you to lose yourself in a sort of epileptic fit of timelessness, stuffing your wages into the Megabucks slots until you wake up to the tearing sound that is you fishing the last wrinkled dollar from the secret velcro pocket of your wallet. But that's being charitable. Casino time is actually an extremely slow, plodding, heel-dragging grind designed to make money off the *illusion* of speed. Since luck is timelessness, and there's no apparent time here, you can't believe how lucky you feel. You have to suspend your own disbelief. As though starring in your own movie. Which is entertaining for just about anyone.

The drinks, the half-naked waitresses, the buffet and the roaring sound of dropping coins that is Las Vegas all work this angle: no time is good time, and good time is lucky.

Tom Collins is one of the big reasons why people believe in their own luck. When he plays, more often than not his pile of chips grows very quickly. Tourists believe speed is transferable. They are not discouraged if they

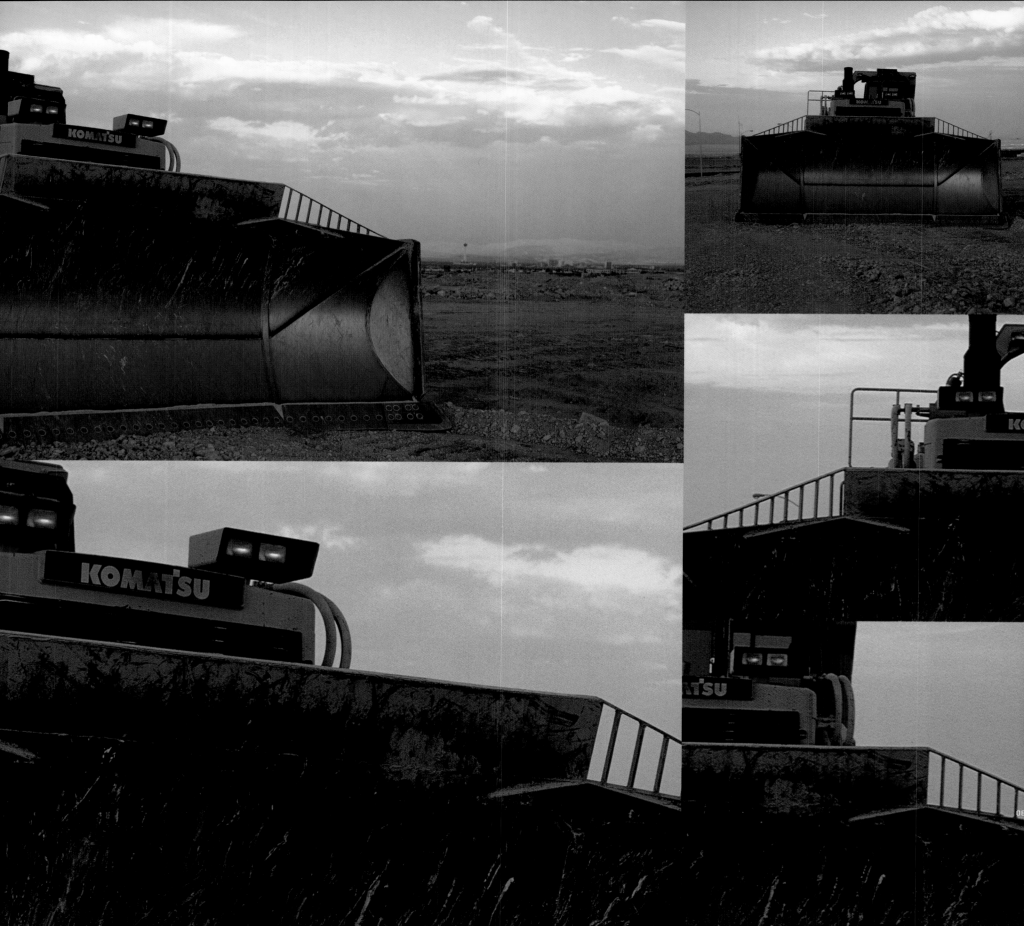

find out he has a system; on the contrary, they're even more intrigued, because of course that really is transferable. *I could learn to be lucky.* Most of them look at it as being a bit underhanded, which is also attractive because everyone in Las Vegas other than Tom Collins and pros like him is slumming.

Moss sees them every day in his bar. Sports betting is huge in the United States, expanding now to massive offshore booking operations and Internet accounts that make money off the dude who thinks he knows a lot about sports.

"Everybody thinks if they read the sports page every day, they know how to gamble and bet the sports. Nothing could be further from the truth," says Moss. "You win a lot of money, you lose a lot of money. One day, I'd have $5,000 in my pocket. The next day, I'd be eating off a free breakfast coupon.

"Professionals get up at six in the morning. It's easier now 'cause of the Internet. They can read twenty out-of-town papers. They look at the sports page and all the statistics, they do the math, so by the time the line comes out at 8 or 9 in the morning, they've done three hours of work and they're ready to jump on it while the line still might be vulnerable. And then they spend the next few hours seeing where the line moves."

Folks have the same fantasies about the stock market, which entertains in almost exactly the same way.

But you know Vegas is a con because, unlike Wall Street, they won't let true talents play.

"There is no percentage in being a professional," says Tom Collins. He's in awe of the tourist, who can play freely but rarely win. "It's the only profession that doesn't reward you for achievement."

But who is really courting luck? The tourist blows into town, takes a big shit, and leaves. But the pro loses slowly, only trying to leave more room for luck to show itself in the long run.

"See, the bookkeepers are running the joint," says Howard Schwartz, marketing director of the Gambler's Book Club, one of Las Vegas' most honored repositories of gambling wisdom. "Years ago, they used to say, 'Let 'em play, they'll lose eventually.' Nowadays, the bookkeeper says, 'Wait a minute. We're supposed to be keeping between 13 and 16% from the blackjack tables. We're down to 8%.' The racetracks have failed to see that, too. But they're taking 18 to 25%. Let them win! What's the difference? They ought to be picking these people up with a limousine. Keep them betting."

Back in the late 1970s, when the casinos believed that card counting worked but didn't believe it would actually hurt them, late blackjack counting genius Kenny Uston would play up to five tables simultaneously at Caesars, with millions on each, and win. But that was when the illusion was a little less mean and outrageous players like him were worth the risk to the casino for their entertainment value alone. When Uston beat the casinos in Atlantic City out of a huge jackpot, they sued him for counting. He took it all the way to the Supreme Court and won — precisely because it's not cheating — but the Atlantic City casino subsequently changed the rules of play and put him out of business. Now they use the words "Kenny Uston" as a negative example, the absolute rarity of players of Tom Collins' skill notwithstanding, and it's impossible to get a decent game in Atlantic City. Big blackjack players shun the place. By keeping the game out of the fairway and off in the rough of dumb luck, the town fathers in gambling towns everywhere play a hugely fat margin, like 99.5 to 1, that you won't win. It's like planned obsolescence. Or a democracy of cripples.

Gambling used to be about a stylized disregard for money. In the New Vegas, money is the only thing that matters. Tom Collins spends his casino time ducking security like an old-timey riverboat gambler, taking people's money until he senses he's about to be run out on a rail.

"I went into the Frontier the other day, just to see what it was like again, and I sat down to play for five minutes." The Frontier was struck by unions for six years and nobody, especially not a resident, would cross the picket line. Now it's reopened as the New Frontier. "A professional blackjack player will do something called 'spreading.' It's where you raise your percentage bet versus the minimum table bet. If you were to go from one five-dollar chip on one spot to playing two spots of table maximum of 500 dollars each, you may be allowed to do that once, then you'll be asked to leave. I decided to push the envelope.

"I went from five dollars to 50 dollars on two hands. The count was like, plus 20. It was ridiculous. I couldn't help it. Tying my hands behind my back. Of course I won. I got a split, dealer showing a three. I get a couple of nines. Split 'em, with 50 dollars up, but now there's 100 dollars on that one spot, 'kay? I make my numbers. I get two face cards. Next thing I know, I pull a blackjack. She turns over the three, there's a four, a ten. Has to stand at 17. I look up and I say, "Lunch is over, I better get going." She's whispering to the boss the whole time. He called upstairs. 'See ya.'"

These days, they simply ask him to leave. In the old days they used to take Tom Collins out back and beat the shit out of him. Not for cheating, he's not. They beat him for destroying the sacred illusion of luck. They beat him for playing in real time. In Las Vegas, real time threatens the entire economy.

Tom Collins: Professional gamblers don't want speed. A professional gambler is interested in accuracy. The house wants speed. They have the house edge. The casino wants speed because they have mathematical formulas, devised by all the little bean counters, as to how many hands of blackjack you can play — it's generally accepted to be about a hundred hands an hour. So they use shuffle machines and all kinds of things to speed up the game. They don't want seven people sitting at a table because that slows the game down. They'd rather see three to four people at a table, the dealer goin' right around. No sloppy drunks.

The tourists, on the other hand, want action. Craps is a perfect metaphor. You get a hot craps table, people are putting more money up and parlaying that. It goes to this feverish pitch.

The public has a misconception that you can win a lot of money in a very short span. The lunatics come here with the beat-up Chevys, the microwave, the little fridge and the beer in the back, their kids and their wives in tow. They move into a motel, and they think they're gonna hit it rich. I can't tell your how many millions of them have come and gone. Very, very, very few of them make it.

Professional gamblers don't look for big scores. You have an acceptable loss in mind, after which you walk away from the table. "Professional" means you don't chase. You play with absolute discipline. Professional gamblers approach it as a business with a moral center.

You don't play drunk. The idea isn't to carry on — "Oh, I'm on a roll, I'm gonna stay on my roll." The bad part of a roll is, you never know where it's going to end. That roll can be negative. I have literally seen people lose 20 to 30 hands. You don't get too high and you don't get too low. If you lose a hand of blackjack and you had some big money up, you don't spill your drink, throw the chips, curse the dealer, pound the table, throw your cards. You lost. Next. And if you win, you don't jump up and down — "I won! I won!" You don't start high-fiving everyone at the table. You take it gracefully. You make your goal and you walk out.

Howard Schwartz: You have to almost turn yourself into a machine. A slow-moving, computerlike mechanism to grind out the profit. The smartest sports bettors in the world are like very sharp housewives shopping in supermarkets or watching the ads. You wait for the right number, you wait for somebody to make a mistake.

"I liked it better when the Mob ran everything," says Ms. Bettye, better known on the seedy end of Fremont Street as "Ladybird." She's been here 31 years, and has worked for everyone in town. Now, she says, sitting on the hood of her car and playing with her three strapping grandsons, it's too corporate. Some of the last privately owned casinos (Mob casinos were considered "independent" compared to the new corporate hotels) were on Fremont, all incorporated now under the mall-like enclosure of the Fremont Street Experience. This was OLD Old Vegas, Glitter Gulch, where the original casinos operated before Bugsy threw up his ecstatic Flamingo and created the Strip in 1946.

The last of Old Vegas died with the Horseshoe's Benny Binion on Christmas Day 1989, Ladybird points out, and most everyone agrees with her. Binion's Horseshoe is still family-owned, run by Benny's daughter Becky, but it's changed with the times. It was once the only casino in town that would cover any bet from any player. Benny believed in no-limit gambling for the common man. The most illustrative Horseshoe story has been repeated many times: in 1980 a nondescript fellow wandered into the casino carrying two suitcases, one empty and one containing $777,000 in hundreds. He changed it to chips and placed the whole pile as one bet at the craps table. Benny said he'd cover it. The fellow tossed, won, filled the two suitcases with $1,554,000, and walked away. He never came back. That's not grinding. That's style.

The Fremont Street Experience is a contrived bit of historical novelty meant to lure a few of the guests from the obscene 1980s Family-Oriented Theme Resorts like Treasure Island and Excalibeur five miles up the Strip. Some prehistoric residents of the El Cid and Ogden House are still propped up at the Horseshoe's legendary poker tables, for years the site of the widely televised World Series of Poker. But Binion's wouldn't cover a three-quarter-million-dollar bet by an unidentified stranger today, because the accountants run the joint.

And since no one else ever would, needing permission from their corporate head offices and seriously impeding play to do so, the era of true gambling has folded. Sure, big-money high rollers — called "whales" in Vegas parlance — are still flown in at casino expense to play the high-stakes rooms at the Hilton and the MGM Grand, but these people are celebrities. They are registered, IRS-tagged, known quantities. Ultra-gamblers like Australian media magnate

Kerry Packer have been known to tip dealers with houses and $25,000 chips. The point is, they also tip the casino heavy and their winnings or losses are on the books. A mysterious millionaire who refuses to give a name and a tax ID number would have a hard time getting a game in Vegas today. The accountants can't stand untidy losses. You gotta pay to play. Leaving the tourists, and a few criminalized professionals, to grind.

This has exposed the raw sickness of the place, a place that used to be about the suspension of disbelief but which now you're asked to really believe in. Like it's shouting at you, wide-eyed: "Well, you believe in *MONEY*, don't you?!" This is its true speed, at last. As Nick Tosches wrote in his intro to *Literary Las Vegas*: "For that — malignant banality, the pestilent have-a-nice-day smile of devouring venality — is the spirit of Vegas, the spirit of the dream itself."

Vegas is dead. Long live Las Vegas! The spectacle still mounts toward the heavens on light beams shot from pyramids in a kind of Morse code to the saints, but its spirit is broken. Like a hyena eating its own entrails, the actual residents and recently turned civic leaders of Las Vegas have internalized the illusion of speed. Now they seek to substantiate it, make it manifest as a New City.

Causing truly quixotic mutations. Life outside the casinos has taken on the moonlit quality of an advertisement; content is no longer as desirable as the simulation of content. The spores of the speed illusion have sprouted into a quasi-real suburbia of unprecedented reach.

Las Vegas is now the fastest-growing city in America, physically and numerically, spreading straight out over the desert from the otherworldly backbone of the Strip. It is as though the janitors and animatronics of Disneyland overthrew the imagineers then normalized the "Happiest Place on Earth," turning the Pirates of the Caribbean and Space Mountain into a laundry and a school.

As of 1998, 20,000 new homes are sold every year in Las Vegas and 10,000 are resold, accommodating 6,000 new residents per month, the highest percentage of in-migration in the U.S. The population has grown from 277,230 in 1970 to over 1,200,000 in 1998. By comparison, Orange County, California, the boomtown of the 1980s, has a population of 7 million and sells 5,000 new homes per month. In 1986, 20,000 people worked construction, remodeling the constantly changing casino face of Las Vegas; ten years later it had tripled to 65,000 on the strength of building its suburban butt.

The whole place is new, so it seems to contain that mobility that everyone wants. Because Las Vegas is ahistorical, with little or no roots beyond a few silver mines and the casinos that get pulled down and rebuilt, an architecture in constant play, each wave of immigrants are seen as new pioneers, remaking the place in their own image. With one grand caveat: the current wave of pioneers is making it just like the place you've dreamed of getting away from.

Las Vegas has become a phantasmagorical hybrid whose lions proudly pooh-pooh its former status as a Xanadu in deference to something infinitely worse: a place programmed to be just like the mall, just like that synthetically rendered idea of a fictitious Middle America. Warping their message of Progress into a lurid, spirit-crushing howl.

The new "community of churches and schools" is championing a speed and mobility it doesn't really have. It's just siphoning speed straight off the casino mythology in a boom of grotesque, uncontrolled Sun Belt development. Meanwhile, every year the casinos make less money off gaming and more and more off entertainment and ancillary sales. The desert is blooming — in a profusion of *les fleurs du mal*.

"When I started working on Summerlin in 1991, there was one road," smiles Jay Moss, the affable former Las Vegas division president of megadeveloper Kaufman & Broad. Summerlin is a 22,000-acre parcel below Red Rocks to the west, owned by Howard Hughes. "Today, there are three off-ramps, multiple traffic lights, we have a hospital, we have medical centers, we have office buildings, we have numerous parks. I have watched, in just six years, a new town actually develop. The whole cycle from raw land to housing to schools to parks to commercial to the McDonald's that's now at our corner, and hospitals and retirement homes.

"It was basically master-planned," he adds, then takes it a step further. "It's not even a master plan, it's a new town, such as Irvine [CA]. It's the revelations of the '70s and '80s that some of these master plans become new towns."

Why would a million new permanent residents move to Las Vegas in the last two decades? Why would a million more be expected in the next? Jay Moss claims the town is in year ten of a reliable, 30-year expansion. The fact that the town of Las Vegas is quite obviously the Worst Place on Earth has been obscured behind the cardboard cutout sundown. But that is exactly what drew Meyer Lansky, Bugsy Siegel, and the Jewish mafia here in the first place. The hellhole that festered just beyond the parking lot was a guarantee that the tourists would never leave the casinos.

092

Families are moving here who don't go in the casinos at all. Many of them, in fact, are quite against the casinos. It's easy to see why they come: making a new life here is supercheap, superfast, and of a choked egalitarian quality. Yes, just like the casinos.

Write a check, roll out the lawn, plug in the Christmas tree, and start bitching about the legal prostitution. New towns rise overnight under dreamy names promising watery leisure — Oasis Canyon, Boca Park. Project housing for the middle class, they're probably destined for the same eventual institutional blight and decay. Brightly colored "ready to move in" flags flap in the dawn wind puffing down over Summerlin and off Railroad Pass above Green Valley and Henderson to the Southeast. Every piece of desert to the horizon is flagged for new towns. But it won't stop there. Since over 70 percent of Nevada is federal land, just sitting there stark raving empty, the expansion is potentially limitless.

Except for one little hitch. There's no water. Since development here is as simple as scraping the iron-flat desert and pouring one kind of concrete for roads, another for foundations, and another for yards, water is really the only setback. So developers ease fears with a veritable gusher of wet, alpine, verdant if not downright sopping names, the single most awe-inspiring display of ecstatic optimism Las Vegas has ever belched forth: Malibu Canyon. Falling Water. Chardonnay Hills. Kew Gardens. Santa Fe Shadows. Buffalo Highlands. The Willows. Heather Glen. Fallbrook. You'd think the place was a boggy tidal estuary overripe with vineyards and infested with big game.

No wonder the grinders are getting squeezed out. They throw a queer light on the city's own reliance upon illusion. Las Vegas is busy making money hand over fist — real money, not magic money — building neoburbia. Trying to put real meat on a skeleton of dreams and blind luck. But even the semblance of permanence is a bummer in the temporal city. In fact, the city is grinding away on a margin just like the one Tom Collins plays, hoping none of the tourists catch on. He's one nagging reminder of an identity crisis they hope they'll never have to face.

Perhaps, then, the town hasn't changed very much at all. It's always been a populist enterprise, giving the people what they want. As Felix Dzerzinski, early Soviet mastermind of strategic disinformation, once said, "Westerners take what they want for reality, so let's give them what they want!" Maybe neoburbia is simply what people want now, this year's dream. The fastest move-in, something-for-nothing deal available anywhere in the country.

"There's no moral center in Las Vegas," says Tom Collins, walking out of the casino to find that a new day has risen unannounced. He is evidence that, curiously, it is the professionals and the grinders who really see the city for what it is, and who probably love it for all the right reasons. The rest are just opportunists, the kind of momentum players who'll move away when the deals dry up.

"It's kind of a personal challenge to maintain integrity and honesty, and have a moral base when there's total anarchy around you," he says. "Professional gamblers find a center of calm in the spinning madness. We're ground zero. Treat it as if you were living in Topeka with access to this other little magical curtain you can part and enter into any time you feel like it."

→economics

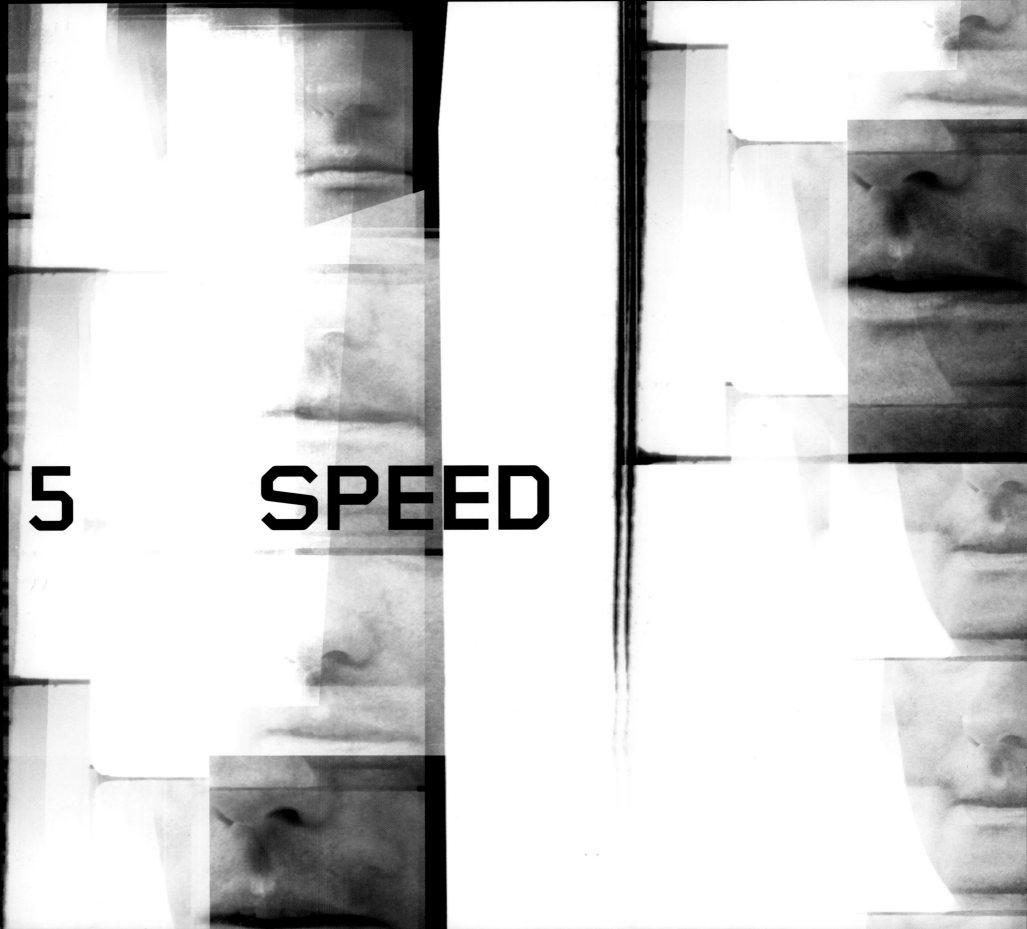

5 SPEED

ECO

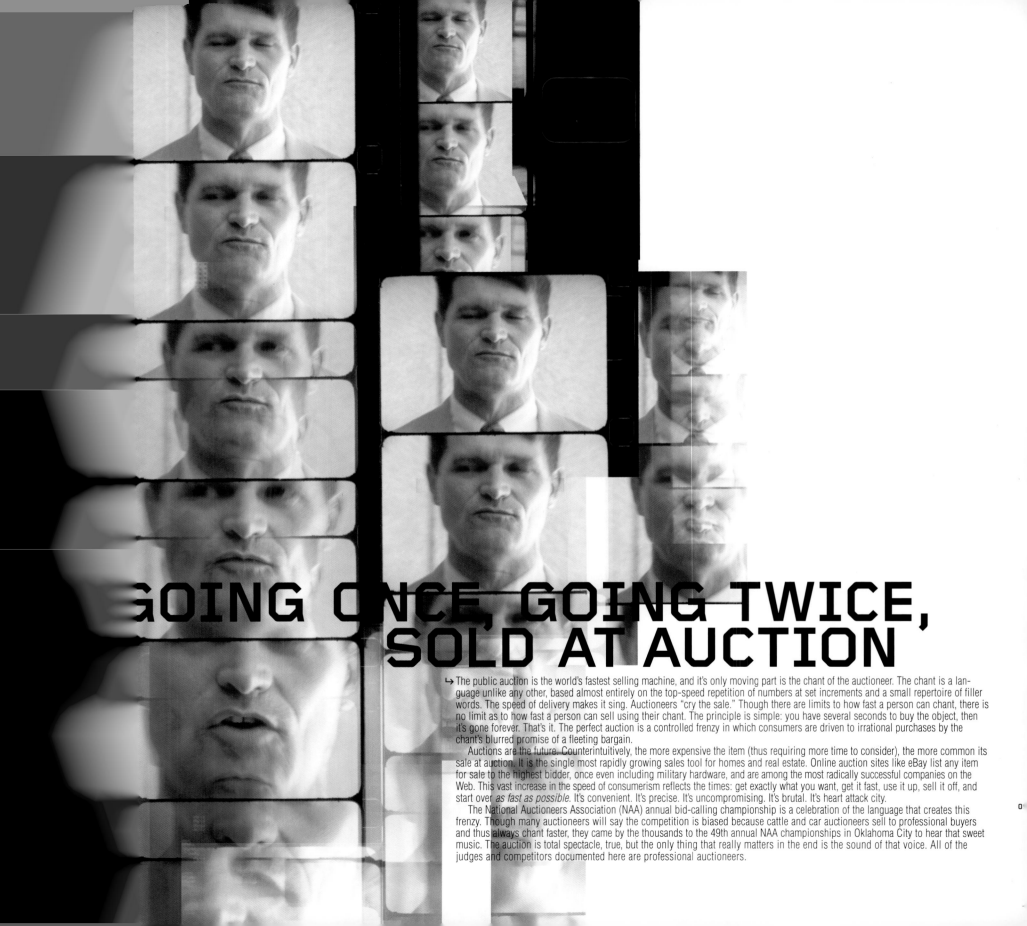

GOING ONCE, GOING TWICE, SOLD AT AUCTION

↳ The public auction is the world's fastest selling machine, and it's only moving part is the chant of the auctioneer. The chant is a language unlike any other, based almost entirely on the top-speed repetition of numbers at set increments and a small repertoire of filler words. The speed of delivery makes it sing. Auctioneers "cry the sale." Though there are limits to how fast a person can chant, there is no limit as to how fast a person can sell using their chant. The principle is simple: you have several seconds to buy the object, then it's gone forever. That's it. The perfect auction is a controlled frenzy in which consumers are driven to irrational purchases by the chant's blurred promise of a fleeting bargain.

Auctions are the future. Counterintuitively, the more expensive the item (thus requiring more time to consider), the more common its sale at auction. It is the single most rapidly growing sales tool for homes and real estate. Online auction sites like eBay list any item for sale to the highest bidder, once even including military hardware, and are among the most radically successful companies on the Web. This vast increase in the speed of consumerism reflects the times: get exactly what you want, get it fast, use it up, sell it off, and start over *as fast as possible*. It's convenient. It's precise. It's uncompromising. It's brutal. It's heart attack city.

The National Auctioneers Association (NAA) annual bid-calling championship is a celebration of the language that creates this frenzy. Though many auctioneers will say the competition is biased because cattle and car auctioneers sell to professional buyers and thus always chant faster, they came by the thousands to the 49th annual NAA championships in Oklahoma City to hear that sweet music. The auction is total spectacle, true, but the only thing that really matters in the end is the sound of that voice. All of the judges and competitors documented here are professional auctioneers.

FAST MONEY

GARY COFFEE. Stonewall, Oklahoma: I had an old-timer tell me one time: "If you catch on fire with enthusiasm, they will come from miles around to watch you burn."

DARLENE DAVIS. Emmett, Idaho: Red's my favorite color, I use it in my auctions. All my auction crew has red shirts. I have a red house, two red Irish setters, a red barn, a red pickup that I take all around. When I go on site I'm usually in all red — whether it's red boots and jeans or a red dress or a red suit. I like red.

LARRY GARNER. Carrollton, Ohio: People are in a hurry to get from the cradle to the grave. When people are through with an automobile or a gun or a house, they need the money and they want it as quickly as they can get it. We are the only viable industry that can convert any asset on the earth today into cash.

PAM ROSE. Toledo, Ohio: Our generation, we're very fast-paced. Our generation is gonna be so receptive to auctions, they're gonna love it.

BRENT EARLYWINE. Kokomo, Indiana: By the year 2010, a good 30 percent of our real estate is going to be sold at auction. In Australia, that's already the predominant way to sell real estate.

TROY LIPPARD. Enid, Oklahoma: When you do an estate sale, it's an accumulation of maybe 50 or 60 years of their life that we are going to sell in about two or three hours time, on the average.

MARTY ROGERS. Union, Iowa: What we try to do is get the most possible money for them on that day.

PAM ROSE: I love to set records at auctions. It's an adrenaline thing.

LARRY GARNER: The faster you can sell the items going down the line, the more money they will bring. There used to be an auctioneer out of Texas who sold heavy equipment. He would put a 'dozer there and a 'dozer there, and he would put a flag there: when he walked by and hit that flag, he sold that 'dozer. And he never stopped walking. Whatever the number was; if you weren't done bidding, you were out. Very distinctive, very clear, but speed. You had to be a bidder *now*. "Pay attention, ladies and gentlemen, we're gonna sell the machines as I walk by them, and you snooze you lose."

GARY COFFEE: You got to move the auction. They don't want a comedian, they want a professional auctioneer.

PAM ROSE: We get right down to business and we truck through that stuff. I say, "Folks, I sell fast, get your cards in the air, there's not a lot of time."

MARTY ROGERS: We separate them into bid callers and auctioneers; you can be a contract bid caller, where you're just the mouth. You cry the sale and go home.

LARRY GARNER: Rome was sold at public auction prior to its demise.

BRENT EARLYWINE: Sometimes I get hyped up and try to get a pace maybe every 30 or 40 seconds saying "sold." But they have to come along with you. Let's say a guy is making his decision just a little slow; if you sell it to the other guy one time, next time he's making his decision a little quicker. They call it "shutting out."

PAM ROSE: The stock exchange is an auction.

GINGER CASTLE. Kimball, Minnesota: The Big Apple Circus felt our fee was a little exorbitant. They were only really expecting $5-$10,000, tops, and they hired us and made $136,000.

C.D. "BUTCH" BOOKER. Colfax, Washington: Registered cattle are sold maybe one every 30 seconds or at the least one every minute. Twenty-five to 30 years ago, they would have been sold much slower, with a lot more talking and a lot more salesmanship. They would grind. This day and age, there's nothing more important at an auction than momentum.

BRENT EARLYWINE: You could be selling a $50,000 tractor and it's on a screen, you don't have to worry about moving it. They're averaging probably about a minute pace in many cases.

GINGER CASTLE: When I'm hired by Paul Newman, their gala raises everything they need to operate that camp [for kids with cancer or blood-related diseases], which is over a million dollars. Just in one day.

THE CHANT

BRENT EARLYWINE: It's getting the mind and the tongue to work in sequence at a very rapid pace.

BUTCH BOOKER: I'm interested in having that number hang out there so that the individual can know the money that's bid and the money I'm askin', and make a decision. The easier it is for them to bid, and the quicker we'll be done for the day.

MARTY ROGERS: Auction was thought to be just performed by artists that have that special gift. Now it's moved into more of the science of the profession.

BUTCH BOOKER: The chant is necessary because people like it. It's similar to a form of entertainment.

GINGER CASTLE: I always wanted to do something musically. Auctioning gives me the wonderful feeling of performing, but I don't have to sing!

LARRY GARNER: Showmanship has an element in there. Within the chant itself is the excitement. When you're bidding on the item, there's at least one or two or maybe a half-dozen other people with it, the anticipation is: "Can I outbid him?" I think the speed and the energy that we put into selling that item is there. It creates this atmosphere that is not in a store.

GINGER CASTLE: I am the evening. When I'm hired for these large nonprofit organizations, I am the entertainment. Once their dinner is over, they don't have a band or anything like that, they have the auction.

BRENT EARLYWINE: Back when [my father] started, he sold everything. He was selling real estate back before it was popular selling real estate at auction. Farm animals to monkeys to horses, he's sold it all. He was 14 [in 1948] and he was selling at Auction City California, two sales a week. One of them was on TV and that was the bill they played, that he was the youngest auctioneer in the world. He's 64 years old and he's still selling very successfully.

GINGER CASTLE: (jumps up on a table and goes into a tap routine) I can tap dance, too!

THE TECHNIQUE

MARTY ROGERS: You have three parts to a basic chant. You have a statement, a suggestion, and a question. The statement is the bid: "One dollar." The suggestion is: "Now two." The question is: "Would you give two?"

GINGER CASTLE: It's the "auction fever." Even though Christie's and Sotheby's are very exciting, and I've worked for Butterfield's, it's not exciting to me to hear them just ask for numbers. It's exciting to hear how fabulously the guy or the woman can chant.

BRENT EARLYWINE: You do have that *hum,* but you don't want to be at the same pitch all day, because they will just fall asleep on you. You have to go, "Forty-five and a bid FIFTY!" You have to throw some strong fluctuation in there which will wake a crowd up.

PAM ROSE: If you ever go to an Amish sale, they're so *enjoyable* to listen to. They can almost put you to sleep, like they're singing a lullaby.

GARY COFFEE: Do not irritate your audience.

TROY LIPPARD: If you got a real good farm, you can keep a crowd about six to eight hours pretty easy. But if it's just household items, you're looking at three hours.

MARTY ROGERS: You have to have those numbers flow in your head like a ribbon, and you can pick a number anywhere you want to.

GINGER CASTLE: If you have to think about what the next increment is, that's when you totally mess up.

MARTY ROGERS: A southern accent lends itself to the auction process because you have to get country. You don't say "one hundred," you say "hunnerd." You have to make that roll. I work with a gentleman out of Wisconsin and they have very short choppy speech. He had a very difficult time with an auction chant.

THE FILLERS

LARRY GARNER: Some auctioneers, if I said, "What's the filler word in between your numbers and you gotta tell me now," they couldn't do it.

TRACY SULLIVAN. Prague, Oklahoma: "Give to me." It becomes, "giddime," with three syllables, or "gimme" with two.

MARTY ROGERS: "Are you able to buy 'em," and that just shortens to, "able to buy 'em," and that gets further shortened to, "abtabom" — "abtabom three, abtabom four, abtabom five." The other one is: "would you give," and that comes out kind of as "woody." "Woody give," instead of "would you give." "Woody give one, woody give two, woody give three."

BUTCH BOOKER: It's not really "would you?" It's "wujya?" After a while, I found that the letter "w" was slow, so I use "now." I use "here" and "there" and "over there" and "over here" and "down there."

GINGER CASTLE: I use "now" a lot, I use "wujyubidda," and then "bidda." And then repeating the number; you can get a pretty good roll on some numbers.

THE TONGUE TWISTERS

TROY LIPPARD: You do a lot of number drills, you do a lot of tongue twisters. There's one: rubber baby buggy bumpers.

MARTY ROGERS: Round the rocks the rough and raggedy rascal rudely ran.

BRENT EARLYWINE: Betty Botter bought some butter but she said this butter's bitter if I put it in my batter it'll make my batter bitter so she bought a bit of better butter put it in her bitter batter made her bitter batter better so it's Betty Botter bought a bit of bitter butter — and so on.

GINGER CASTLE: The handle goes up and the hammer goes down.

TROY LIPPARD: Tommy Atatumus took to T's, tied them atop of two tall trees...you can go on and on.

READING THE CROWD

GINGER CASTLE: You know that you have the crowd when they're actually bidding *crazy.* You ask for a number and five or seven cards go up right away.

PAM ROSE: I'm very controlling. (laughs) It's a problem. I just can't help it. I can make decisions very quickly. I expect my buyers to, and I expect everyone else to.

LARRY GARNER: There are three reasons that people go to auctions: first of all, an auction is a family gathering. When you're collecting items such as firearms that are theft-oriented and you can't afford the insurance on them, you're very comfortable coming to my auction center every month to talk about your latest acquisition.

Secondly, there's an entertainment element. It's exciting, it's fast-paced. If you go to a gun show, there's no impetus to buy that gun. But in my auction, the high bidder goes home with it.

And lastly, everybody, including auctioneers, goes to an auction with an item in mind that we're gonna get this rare bargain.

BUTCH BOOKER: Everybody talks about the bargain. You never hear anybody say, "Boy, I'm so proud, I went to Las Vegas and I lost $250 playing craps!" I'd say 80% of the time the items are bringin' as much or more than through the want ads. An auction is really the only place where the seller can get more than they ask.

PAM ROSE: Have you ever gone to a dealer or a broker on a property and you wonder if there's really somebody on the other end? Well, you know it at an auction. You're starin' at 'em.

GINGER CASTLE: I mean, you hafta survey the crowd and figure out if there's anybody big.

TRACY SULLIVAN: A good ringman is worth his weight in gold. He's out in the crowd talkin' to people. Lots of times he knows 'em. If I'm selling tractors and I'm at $11,500 and we know it's worth 13, he'll stand next to the guy in the crowd and go, "Now Bob, you know that's worth 13 so go 12-5," and the guy'll usually do it. Sometimes he'll even bid *for* the guy if he knows him real well. Like, "He's in!" What's the guy gonna do? He's not gonna shame out after he's been bid.

BRENT EARLYWINE: People kind of swell up. They don't want to be the back-up bidder. Not that you want to take advantage of anyone, but you want to take full advantage of the situation.

PAM ROSE: If I'm selling 50 homes, I'll do a ballroom sale, where they're all on one site. Someone always ends up buying something that they never planned on. I sold a guy 18 homes, he never saw one of 'em! He regretted it.

TRACY SULLIVAN: I'm gonna give you the secret to auctioneering right here: the wink and nod. Let's say I'm working out a bid between the two of you, going back and forth. If we're close, you'll just be nodding real easy. I notice you're trying to fade, then I lay the killer on ya: I turn my palm up like this and look you in the eye and nod. Nine times out of ten you'll nod back and the auction's on again. Now, can you imagine how much more effective that is if you got a ringman with his hand on the guy's arm? It's no contest, man; he's gonna bid.

TROY LIPPARD: In this business, you watch the crowd. You'll see looks, you catch little hints here and there that maybe they didn't think that was right.

MARTY ROGERS: There's a lot of psychology in this process. It's not a lot of trickery, it's just knowing human nature.

PAM ROSE: Let's say you're going along, "Give 25, would you give 30, would you give 35," and people are talking? Then you just lower your voice, and they all pay attention. Or you just sell something. Let's say I know it's worth 30 dollars: "Five, five to give ten? Sold it, five dollars." And everybody goes, "Awww! My gosh! I could'a had that!" Believe me, the next item'll go a lot better.

MULTIPLE CONVERSATIONS

TROY LIPPARD: Somebody can be talking to me about a situation going on in the field office, and I can still hear selling numbers at the same time.

LARRY GARNER: A good auctioneer can hold a conversation with you while he's doing the chant going down the line, and the public doesn't even know what's going on, and you're still selling the item.

PAM ROSE: I can listen to someone's conversation sitting right in front of me. I can auction and still pay attention to all the bidders, and I can still hear every word they're saying. I'll say, "I heard that."

BRENT EARLYWINE: My bid call is a lot of numbers with "wujyubidm," and then also communication with the audience and my crew, like "you're out," "this is a nice piece," "give me a cup of coffee," "get this next item," "I want a sofa next."

LARRY GARNER: We're selling along and the buyer may quit me, and I may tell him, "You can't buy that way, sir, it's this way. It's like Alka-Seltzer: why don't you try it one time, you'll like it. One time might buy it." And consistently run the numbers. That conversation has become my filler words. Now we've got a one-on-one.

THE TRADITION

GINGER CASTLE: I first started with my mom and dad. When I was 10 years old they sent me to auction school in Mason City, Iowa, the Worldwide College of Auctioneering. I used to get two dollars an auction to work the food booth. My dad said, "You know, Ging, even if you sell one item, I'll double your pay; I'll give you four dollars." Hey, I was a businesswoman at that point.

BRENT EARLYWINE: My father had a consignment auction every Saturday night. I kind of picked it up subliminally. When I was in high school, the last thing I wanted to be was an auctioneer. Every Saturday night, here I am at the auction, and all of my buddies were out running around.

PAM ROSE: My father had a large real estate brokerage company. He went to an auction and he really caught on to this concept, because it was a way to get things done much quicker. He was always kind of a visionary. So he immediately went to auction school, and I remember us thinking, "He's nuts."

GINGER CASTLE: I went to the schoolboard meeting, and they only give you 15 minutes to talk. Well, let me tell ya, I got done and they were like, "Wow."

▌→destruction

6 SPEED

AS
DESTRUCTION

DEMOLI TION D
ERBY

"HERE, ONCE AGAIN, WE MUST LOOK AT THE SPEEDOMETER OF THE RACING ENGINE. THE COMBAT RACECAR: AN EXISTENTIAL MEASURE OF THE WARRIOR'S BEING, THE DIZZYING FLOW OF TIME, A RAPIDITY-TAX ON THE COVERED METER THAT RUINS THE EARTHLY INHABITANT, BUT SIMULTANEOUSLY DESTROYS THE SUBSTANCE OF ITS CONQUEROR AND MEASURES THE SURVIVOR'S REMAINING HOURS."

↳ PAUL VIRILIO, *SPEED AND POLITICS*

→ A great blazing Pacific sunset ignites the husks of some 30-odd American cars rusting into the dirt at Valley Flowers in Carpinteria, California. Owner Walter VanWingerden peeks through his fingers at the spray of hot metal his torch draws from a hole in a 1966 Chrysler 300. It's the night before the demolition derby at the Ventura County Fair and the heat is on. For Walter, derbies are always prefaced by this same last-minute, grease-smeared ritual: transforming the icon of American mobility into a customized sacrifice. It's got to have the right destructive potential, the right semblance of durability, the right look of ritual preparedness, or that sacrifice is meaningless. This aesthetic is just as important as the self-image reflected in the car he drives to church.

"First enduro I ever drove in I won Second Place. I got a trophy for bein' the most banged-up car still running," says Walter, smoking a cigarette and holding a 10-gallon gas can. "It's that car sitting over there behind the El Camino. It was unbelievable, how destroyed it was. I guess it's that destruction derby blood in me. **Every car I get into ends up banged up.**" He looks down, then motions toward the parking lot. "Want me to move your car?"

Walter's wife, Allison, looks at the cars piled up beneath the farm's towering palm trees. "Yeah, it's quite a collection of automobiles," she says. **"I'm as into it as he is, though, so there's not a lot I can say. Got oil for blood, I guess.** I saw this one [the Chrysler] and I said, 'Aw, I used to drive one like this. Do we have to drive this one in the destruction derby?' We found a couple clear steering wheels. I love those. I said, 'Save these. I'll mount these on the wall!'"

Walter won last summer's derbies at the now defunct Santa Maria Raceway and the Ventura County Fair. So he returns as reigning champion. He's picked the right car. The Chrysler 300 sedan — similar to a Chrysler Imperial or New Yorker — is arguably the best derby car allowed. Its boxy construction, good bumpers, and heavy steel full frame protect the big-displacement engine, making it fast and durable. The rear leaf-spring suspension is far superior to shocks, as they tend to let the rear sag and make charging in reverse impossible. For these reasons, mid-'60s Chryslers are some-times banned from derbies. They last too long and the idea is to get it over quick.

Station wagons are now generally forbidden for the same reason, despite the fact that the 1976 Chevy station wagon is regarded by many as the ultimate derby car — heavy, leaf-sprung, a 350-cubic inch engine, and widely available parts. Impalas and Caprices are also good. Lots of drivers swear by the Cadillac, but a well-driven Chrysler will take it out. Mechanics regard Ford and Mercury as weak, hard to keep running and tending to rust out where the body connects to the frame.

Walter chains the doors shut as he talks, wrapping thick chain through holes in both front and rear and securing them tight with a padlock. His young friend Matt fires up an air-powered paint gun by the lights of the farm's carport-like machine shop. As the radio blasts Lynyrd Skynyrd, Led Zeppelin, and the Black Crowes, Matt paints it black.

Walter found this car in the *Recycler* newspaper and trucked it home from Sylmar. He has an Imperial that he bought only five miles away from this one. Like the others it sits, a totaled but revered donor, stripped for parts, rusting, numbered, capable of running with a few hours' work.

"I got it for 150 bucks," says Walter. "The guy wanted more, but I talked him down, used the ol' bullshit. He thought I was restoring it, and then he started to feel bad, so he dropped his price."

"And you bought it to wreck it?"

"Yeah," he smiles.

For Walter, this is poor man's racing. Derby cars are the cheapest racers to put on the dirt at tracks like Ventura. The modifications needed are extensive, but they don't require custom parts (except maybe a roll cage — Walter ignores them — and a racing seat harness) and can be done very quickly with ordinary farm tools. Overnight, in this case. The VanWingerden family, including Walter and his brothers John and Kees (say "Case"), their brothers-in-law Hans and Marco, and their wives and children, are first- and second-generation immigrant Dutch flower farmers who love to race. Hans' enduro racer sits on the gravel apron of the shop, still caked with mud from the last race at Santa Maria. For them, this is not about combat. It's about the love of speed.

But it's the speed of destruction. Demolition derby (or destruction derby or smash-up derby, as they're sometimes known) is the quintessential American racing event. Although the combustion-engine automobile was invented by Karl Benz in Germany in 1885 (granted, Swiss engineer/inventor Isaac de Rivaz built a "car" in 1813 and some even say he set the world's first land speed record) and aggressive driving is celebrated by almost all cultures, smash-up derby is most popular in the U.S. They are also known in Canada, Australia and New Zealand — possibly indicating that the English left a legacy of vehicular anger in their former colonies. It is raw catharsis, the realization of powerful vio-lence latent in the rolling automobile and a death wish mythologized by (perhaps even essential to) American culture. Like the American cult film, *Vanishing Point*, derby is about the car as death sled.

Whereas most racing mirrors the day-to-day driving experience — surviving accident and obstacles to arrive quickest at the destination — demolition derby rewards the predatory vehicle that can prevent the others from arriving at all, destroying itself in the process. It is a tacit recognition of the great temptation dangling at the end of the road, the true promise of the American dream of mobility: disappearance. Just like Clint Eastwood in *High Plains Drifter*. It's in the national character for Americans to long for a frontier. Beyond the edge of civility and calculation, one disappears. Speed is the key to reaching it. The faster the car, the closer to obliteration.

And closeness to obliteration is really living. Or so the myth.

The winner of a demolition derby is thus also necessarily the loser. That vehicle survives, not achieving obliteration, and so their relief is frustrated, incomplete. They have slowed their own destruction, and hastened that of their victims. The losers, on the other hand, celebrate the receipt of all that satisfying speed and disappearance.

Few Americans, other than those who live in New York City, can survive without a car. They are bound to it from birth. The thrill of demolition derby is in symbolic liberation. No more car payments, no more insurance, no more paranoia about accidents or dings or birdshit, no more car wash, no more repairs and tires and sticker-price comparison and one-upsmanship. Just total it and let the junkman have the spoils. The ultimate act of acting out in a childlike society.

Or, as the VanWingerdens do, total it, drag it home like a taxidermied trophy after a big-game hunt, and build a new car out of it for next year's race.

In demolition derby, more is more. Customizing the demolition derby car is as important as the will to destroy it. It was strictly run what ya brung back when Lawrence Mendelsohn put on the first official demolition derby in 1961 at Islip Raceway out on New York's Long Island. Or at least that's what Tom Wolfe wrote in *The Kandy-Kolored Tangerine-Flake Streamline Baby*. (Other histories, namely that of the National Demolition Derby Association — NDDA — suggest that derbies were already known in the mid-'50s as a season-finale "destruction race" event for mostly homemade stock car racers.) But modifications were immediately apparent. According to the NDDA, derbies are now the "financial mainstay of 786 known County Fairs in the United States, as well as hundreds more private Race Tracks and Community Festivals or Non-Profit Organization Fund Raisers." With 50,000 men and women now crashing their cars in derbies every year, having destroyed about a million American freedom machines in the last 30 years in front of untold millions of spectators, the derby was bound to become a regulated science. And a fetish.

Make the car indestructible. Make it pretty. Paint the virgin before throwing her to the volcano. The idea is to glorify the scapegoat's instant retirement. It's more satisfying to destroy a cherry Buick Electra with a custom paint job than some rusted-out Celica that took a wrong turn on its way to the junkyard. More investment means more *Americanization*, thus more symbolic value, thus more pleasure, and thus more catharsis.

Walter begins the Chrysler's transformation with a baptism by fire. Fire is one of the few real uncontrollable dangers to the derby, and all the unnecessary items that can burn, should. He pops out all the windows and dash instruments and removes all the unnecessary chrome, trim, hitches, muffler and the gas tank. That stuff can be sold (recoup the investment). Then a match to the upholstery to gut the interior. He then installs a solo racing seat with a safety harness.

He doesn't have much time, so eschews much of the tweaking that could give an edge in competition. Regulations require the gas to be mounted on the floor where the back seats used to be, minimizing the risk of explosion by impact. He bolts a wooden box containing the battery into the passenger-side front footwell, as the battery left in its original position will often get knocked loose and its box will puncture the radiator. He puts on some bigger tires and overinflates them to get the bumpers up high, then gives the tire sidewalls a coating of grease to repel attack. Higher bumpers tend to bend the car upward on impact, as will pre-kinking the hood and the trunk, and that's an advantage. If the car bends downward, the bumpers could dig into the ground and stop motion. He turns the air cleaner around, away from a potentially exploding radiator, and jams a few extra breathing holes in it. The choke plate is removed from the carburetor and the idle is cranked up to 1,200 rpms. A cable is added so Walter can operate the throttle by hand when and if the accelerator linkage is whacked apart.

After cutting and bending the metal away from the wheelwells to prevent tire puncture, he's about done. He explains that these are only a few of the scores of other possible customizations, but it's already about two o'clock in the morning. **According to Mark Humphrey's self-produced amateur guide** *Demolition Derby*, **about 45 other derby modifications are common, from simple adjustments like delaying the engine timing four to eight degrees to machine-shop endeavors like building custom, puncture-resistant radiators, converting transmissions from automatic to standard by running a shift kit through the floor, making funky double-sidewall tires and installing an oversized heater core from a semi tractor to prevent overheating. Walter points out that you can, in fact, spend thousands building the absolutely ideal demolition-ready car. But it probably won't make any difference. The tiniest impact could take you out, and some car straight off the street with no modifications at all could survive the worst beating to win the prize money.**

Walter cuts holes in the hood and wraps a chain around the front bumper, the front clip, and back through the hood, transforming the front into a chain battering ram. Same for the trunk. Then he sets to kinking the hoods and molding the chained areas smooth with a sledge hammer, much to the chagrin of his sleeping neighbors and family whose house lights burn high up in the foggy Carpinteria hills.

On Saturday, a whole reserve team of VanWingerdens appear, putting the finishing touches on Walter's car and also slapping together a second car.

Marco and Kees and John are there, with a friend of the family named Christina and Kees' wife, Marilyn. The men are in a complete panic, covered in grease and dirt from head to toe. Walter directs them to scavenge key parts off other cars to bring along for pit repairs between the 2 p.m. qualifying derby and the 8 p.m. main event.

His daughters Erika, seven, and Porsche, five, get caught up in the racing fever, zipping quietly over the dusty farm lanes in an electric flower cart. Erika drives expertly, happy to show off. I tell her that she's a good driver and she says matter-of-factly, "I know. I drive all the time, so I'm used to it." She wheels me around the farm, under 20 acres of empty shadehouses and plastic-tented greenhouses and through 40 acres of open fields, where the VanWingerdens grow primarily snapdragons and chrysanthemums.

Allison paints the number 69 on the side of the black Chrysler. Matt and Christina stencil "Flying Dutchman" on the hood in white spray paint.

Kees is the family jester. "Hey, Allison, why is 69 Walt's favorite number? There's a story behind that, right?" They both laugh.

He tells me there's an enduro race and two tanker races coming up at Ventura. In a tanker race, one person runs the throttle and another steers. Marco is going to run in it and tries to recruit a partner.

Marco and John work feverishly on a car they ran in the derby last year. This car had a broken front axle earlier this morning, but now it's fixed. It needs a lot of work. John turns it over and it throbs to life, the whole engine shaking violently in its mounts.

11

"You're going to run this car today as well?"

"Yah," moans Marco. "A few problems with the girlfriend at the moment." They laugh weakly. They look terribly hungover. The others indicate that they're ...ng to enter Marco in the derby as a kind of ad hoc aggression therapy.

Marco looks familiar. We saw him in the Carrows Restaurant the night before in ...pinteria, sitting with three other Dutchmen. The manager suddenly went off on ... long-haired one among them, shouting that he had a lot of nerve showing his ...e after being thrown out a couple nights before. The manager said he didn't ...nt any of the guy's "bullshit."

"Yah," says Marco. "I got out of there real fast. Because of those guys I was ...h. They are always causing some trouble. Giving a bad name to the Dutch people ...his area."

"It's afternoon," says John, straightening his back and looking at his watch. ...me for a beer."

...ntura County Raceway is a 1/6-mile clay oval surrounded by a 10-foot wooden ...ce painted with sponsor's ads. They race 4-cylinder Pony Stock here, plus ...Modifieds, Sprints, and 8-cylinder Street Stocks. I ask a kid racing Pony ...ck if they can bump.

"Oh, everybody bumps," he drawls. "You can't race any class here and ...bump."

The clay's been wet to reduce traction and collision speed for the derby. Bleachers ...nd along the oceanfront side of the track, sheltering the crowds from the ocean ...ds, with the other side open to the midway. The Ventura County Fair is on and ...machines crank and clunk gaily in the flat afternoon light. Like at all county ...s, AC/DC's "You Shook Me" plays somewhere in the background.

...Walter climbs into the Flying Dutchman wearing a regulation firesuit and helmet. ...e 2 p.m. derby begins with three-quarters of a crowd. There are ten cars ...ered — the second VanWingerden crew is nowhere in sight. The cars drive out ...the track and line up in two lines of five facing one another. The National ...hem blaps out and everyone stands up, then they join in the traditional count-

down to ecstasy: five, four, three, two, ONE! The flagman drops the green flag and the cars fly at each other flat-out in reverse in a creaking, metallic, mufflerless roar.

The announcer shouts out in a wash of tinny reverb: "This is America's favorite pastime, ladies and gentlemen: destroying automobiles!"

All demolition derbies start this way, with the big bang. Sometimes they form a circle, sometimes a square, but the initial rush is inward. Walter's 300 leaps into the pile-up like a wolf with its lips curled back.

A bulbous, black 1959 Chrysler Imperial is quickly dominant. It has a big skull & crossbones painted on the hood and the number M1-A1 in white. Proving once again the indestructibility of the '50s-'60s Chrysler, the M1-A1 hunts the others down like a sniper. Picking them off one by one with its extraordinarily high rear bumper, which slides over the top of its victims to crush hoods, radiators, and vital engine parts.

The winning strategy is glancing blows off the front engine compartment, not square hits that might get you hung up in a dance of death that lets others get in a good shot. The target is essentially the radiator and carburetor. If the car overheats or can't get gas, it's done for. The front wheels are also prime. When the front wheels are blown, the car lowers perfectly for a follow-up kill shot. Shattering the steering linkage is crippling. Intentionally ramming the driver's side door is illegal.

Walter has trouble with the Flying Dutchman. He's inadvertently taped over the vent to his gas tank. He quickly stalls out. Then he sits for five minutes and the car restarts. The judges, however, invoke the two-minute rule: if you sit dead for more than two minutes, you're out. They black-flag him. He drives to the flag tower and stalls again, arguing with the flagman out his window.

A car painted "Square Root of -1" gets hung up on another car, spinning muddy tires all over the car behind it. Both cars disappear in a steaming white cloud of erupting radiator leak as Square Root guns it. The tires spin so hard they both blow. Mindy Welch and Karen Hanchett drive their orange "00" car tag-team: one in the 2 p.m. derby and the other in the 8 p.m. They aren't very aggressive, but

they survive for quite a long time. One Grand Fury still has the badge on its side from Wilshire Protection security company. They painted a "54" on it. A guy says to me, "You know that movie, *Car 54 Where Are You?* Heh."

The M1-A1 continues to kill. It's not popular with the crowd. They cheer the underdogs, the cars knocked out which then restart and creep away to survive another moment. Pleasure is attributed not to the predators, but the prey. Let us savor the ecstasy of obliteration for as long as possible.

A light green compact wagon marked "007" becomes the crowd favorite. Little economy wagons aren't illegal like the full-size dinosaurs that preceded them. 007's particular drama is delectable. Someone has driven right through its hood, literally shaving the top engine components right off, including the carburetor, the air filter, all that stuff, right down to the manifolds. Plus both front wheels are smashed off the steering rods, right front gone flat and chewed off by the metal wheel wells to just flapping rubber bits on the rim, and still it's lurching around out there in an unsteerable circle like a dying elephant. It gets hit. Dies. But it turns over, the sound of the starter whining away under the grinding noise of combat. Just as the two-minute rule closes in, it restarts in a cloud of black smoke and the crowd exults! It moves! The announcer is bawling out like a preacher, "Oh-Oh-Seven back in!" Around in halting circles it limps, as brave in death as it was in life, inviting and getting more brutal punishment, a smack from M1-A1, dies again — restarts! The crowd is beside itself, cheering. Why? **More is more! More life means one more chance for death!**

Demolition derby is about delivering punishment, yes, but it's mostly about *taking* punishment. Surviving and dying both as an aggressive act. You win by showing that the other's maximum effort wasn't good enough to put the car down. It's very much like boxing in this way. The best slugger in the world will lose if the man won't go down. This happened to Foreman when Ali did the rope-a-dope in the 1974 Rumble in the Jungle in Zaire. The cars here seem to exude a certain pride in being able to survive the harshest aggression to still go on the attack themselves. Meanwhile, maximum aggressors may be knocked out by the desperation of their delivery.

"No Whining" is a mantra here. One Street Stock competitor has written on his rear spoiler: "I brought some cheese for your *whine.*" No complaining, no niggling about the rules, no dilettantes or perfectionists or rule freaks.

The M1-A1 goes on to win the heat. Walter angrily drives the Flying Dutchman back to the pits.

First-time derby competitors Jeff and Jason are back there working on their car. They wear buzz cuts and Jeff spits pistachio shells as we talk. Their car has written on the side: "You want some? Come on."

"What do you do with the car?"

"Junk it," spits Jeff.

"Is there satisfaction in wrecking the car, or do you try to keep it in once piece?"

"The idea is to win. Do whatever you need to do to survive and win it. Look at that wagon [#007]. That car was *fucked up* and now it's back. That car over there just went right fuckin' over the hood and through it and kept right on going. Took the carburetor and everything else right off the top of the engine. Now look at it. It runs. It's back. That's what it's about right there.

"Everybody helps everybody else. My car didn't start first time out. We jumped it off your friend's truck and it didn't go. We had a bad bushing on the back of the

starter. This guy gave me a starter plate off his car up there, and I slapped it in and it fired right up. We're back."

"The VanWingerden posse reappear for the 8 p.m. main with both cars, Flying Dutchman I and II. John and Walter are driving.

"It was gonna be my brother-in-law [Marco]," says John, "but he had a few problems with his girlfriend."

A fight erupts in the pits after the 2nd heat of the Pony Stock races. The father of the driver of the purple car, #8, strides over to confront the driver of car #75. We watch this from the top of the track announcer's booth. A cameraman up there says that these two teams have real bad blood and fight every time they get together. The dad steps in front of the #75 car as it comes into the pits and gets hit, knocking him down right in the pit gate. Both teams jump in and there's a thin but aggressive melee before fairground security, sheriff's deputies and state troopers move in to separate them. The dad, it seems, is on the ground for a long time with paramedics working on him. The mother of the other driver is a known hothead and she prowls the pits looking to start trouble. This is Saturday night at the races.

Both teams are thrown out of the race, but it's too crowded for them to pull their trailers out, so they have to sit in the pits and stew.

Crew fights aside, injuries are rare in demolition derby. The VanWingerdens, however, are the exception. In their thick Dutch accents, they explain that Kees managed to be the only casualty in the history of the Ventura derby, when he rolled his car a couple years ago.

WALTER: HE ROLLED OVER AND PUT HIS ARM OUT THE WINDOW.
MARILYN (KEES' WIFE): HE PUT HIS ARM OUT. IT MAKES SENSE, DON'T IT? THAT'S WHAT YOU DO WHEN YOU'RE FALLING. HE JUST FORGOT THAT HE HAD A WHOLE CAR COMING DOWN ON TOP OF THAT ARM.
WALTER: HE THOUGHT HE COULD STOP THE WHOLE CAR BY PUTTING HIS ARM OUT.
HANS: HE TRIED TO SAVE IT.
JOHN: "I CAN SAVE IT! I CAN STILL SAVE IT!"
KEES: I THOUGHT I COULD SAVE IT.
MARILYN: THIS WAS BEFORE THEY HAD THAT RULE THAT YOU HAD TO HAVE MESH OR A CAGE OVER THE WINDOW.
WALTER: THEY STILL DON'T HAVE THAT RULE. YOU DIDN'T SEE ANY ON MY CAR TONIGHT, DID YOU?
MARILYN: NO. YOU MEAN, YOU DON'T USE IT?
WALTER: (SMILING) NAW.

Crews work feverishly during the five-hour break between derby heats. The M1-A1 driver points out the vent problem on Walter's tank and they fix it. Walter has also installed a new radiator, beat the hood down, and put on more front chains. The Tulare County Association of Destruction Derby Drivers is sponsoring the orange #43 car driven by Jack Jones, a well-known local derby terror. His crew went to Pick-A-Part, got a new drive line, cut it and welded it in with time to spare between derbies. And your mechanic says your car won't be ready for two weeks! The Association hosts a huge annual derby at the Fresno County Fair in Tulare. They have a pickup truck derby and a main event that draws nationwide: a four-heat, 100-car derby. Jack is the reigning champ. There is talk in their pit about the National Demolition Derby happening later in Reno, Nevada.

A full moon rises over the low green coastal mountains to the southeast. The Pacific wind has picked up onshore and turned cool. The flag is suddenly snapping straight out at attention, and people are huddled in coats and car blankets. The neon of the midway looks hot and bright like campfires in a massive darkness. Mists move in at twilight, making this stuck-in-the-1970s beach town look like Hawaii. A rising western swell breaks at a surf spot nicknamed Pipes right out front.

Oil platforms winkle off the coast between us and the Channel Islands like marching alien colonies closing in, whispering the strange language of extraction, quiet commentary on the smell of oil that hangs in the air over the track and all the gearheads here.

The track manager gives instructions to the derby drivers, the VanWingerden brothers creating a nice "Flying Dutchman I and II" effect in their matching firesuits, as the track announcer thanks the many sponsors — Mr. Rooter Plumbing, Quinn's Caterpillar Equipment, Saturn of Oxnard, etc., etc. The winners of the Pony Stock, I-4 Mods and Street Stock "main event" pose in front of the grandstands and accept their cash and trophy awards. They thank their fabricators, as in: "They build all our heads down there...they do real good for us."

Then the crowd is counting down and the derby is on again.

The 007 wagon is back. The orange #45 car driven by Jack Jones works the field like a surgeon, taking everyone out one by one. The track is fast. It's been six hours since it was watered down, and now it's tacky clay. John's Flying Dutchman I has some serious mechanical problems and gets knocked out almost immediately, as does the M1-A1 that was so effective in the first round. Walter roars around the place in Flying Dutchman II like a huge dog that hasn't been let off his leash in days, stopping only to nip at the others, creaming cars here and there, constantly moving. His passenger-side door gets progressively more and more worked.

At one point, a car goes airborne over the hood of its victim and Walter almost sends it into a roll as he rear-ends the car under it. The crowd leaps to its feet as though watching a breakaway skater charge the goal in a hockey game. The car teeters, lands on its wheels, and clanks away.

Eventually, Walter's Flying Dutchman II is trapped against Jeff and Jason's car while #45 whangs away at him. Walter is gesturing at Jones, calling for him to bring it on. On the next hit, however, Walter's carburetor explodes into flame and the derby is over, with a fire truck screaming onto the field. Jason dives out the driver's side window like a missile, headfirst onto the clay. The announcer croons, "Just a little engine fire, ladies and gentlemen. Nothing to worry about. We got plenty of fire trucks and we love to use 'em." Jack Jones wins it, Square Root of -1 takes second, and Walter takes third. **CLOUDS OF RADIATOR STEAM AND CARBURETOR SMOKE SWIRL IN THE WIND, SNATCHING UPWARD THE SMELL OF BURNT RUBBER, ANTIFREEZE, OILED DIRT TRACK AND COTTON CANDY. AME**
Fireworks start thumping into the ocean air, exploding over the chaos of crushed and tangled metal and marking the end of the county fair.

Later that night, the VanWingerden clan parties in Walter and Allison's backyard swimming pool. Tiki torches blaze. We lounge in the hot tub with cans of Miller Genuine Draft. Greenhouses glow beyond the

PLAY SMELLS LIKE A NOSTALGIC VERSION OF AMERICA AT WORK.

15
estruction

trees that surround the yard, a mix of palms and yuccas and fruit trees hung with citrus and avocados. I know there are avocados, because earlier that day Walter had hassled a Mexican kid in the front yard who held an avocado in his hand. All I heard as we rolled by was, "Oh, so this just *fell* on the ground?"

Walter looks like the kind of nice guy who goes aggro when crossed. He was, in fact, the most openly aggro driver in the derby.

"Did you see my throttle get stuck?!," he shouts excitedly. "My wheels were just spinning and I had the brake on. I didn't want to run into the two guys just sitting there like I did, but I had to run into something to stop and I didn't want to just hit the wall like a dummy. I thought that if I hit something it would snap back out again, and it did."

"When you were locked up with that car, that other guy was freaking out because you were waving the orange #43 car to hit you!" says Matt.

"I thought if he hit me, he might knock the transmission back in gear and I'd go again! I thought, 'Well, I'm stuck here unless something happens, so come on with it.'"

Kees' wife, Marilyn, points out again that Walter never installed his roll cage.

"I can't believe nobody got hurt tonight," he says, ignoring his own unsafe behavior. "That one guy got his bell rung in the first race. He took a shot in the side and he whacked his head against the roof strut. He saw stars. His car was fine, but he just sat there, trying to remember where he was. Shit, I was flying around all over inside my car. My damn seat is knocked loose. I'm amazed I didn't end up rolled over on my back in the back where the back seats used to be. I hit my head on the roof strut and on the ceiling a bunch of times."

All the men say they're running next time. All the wives say no they're not. Except Allison. Walter lies back in the hot tub.

"Well, if I didn't do it, we wouldn't be eating pizza right now. I won a couple hundred bucks for Third Place. So see? It's worth it."

IT IS RAW CATHARSIS, THE REALIZATION OF POWERFUL

VIOLENCE LATENT IN THE ROLLING AUTOMOBILE

AND A DEATH WISH MYTHOLOGIZED BY

19
estruction

(PERHAPS EVEN ESSENTIAL TO) AMERICAN CULTURE.

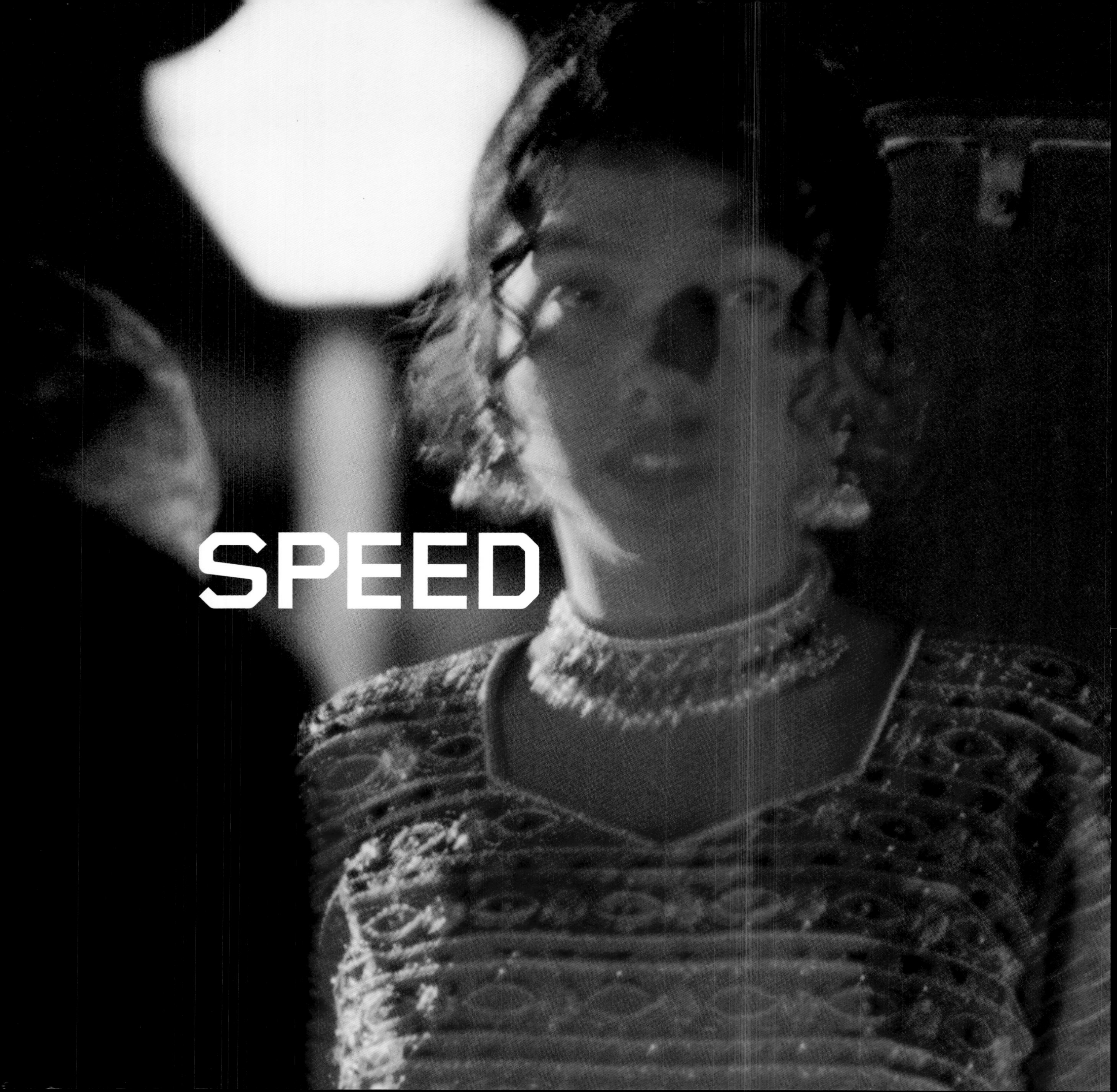
SPEED

AS
FANTASY

BOLLYWOOD DREAMS
900 FILMS A YEAR

"IT IS NOT SIMPLY THE INDIAN CINEMA ITSELF WHICH
IS DREAMING; IT IS ALL OF INDIA. THIS IS A CULTURE
IN LOVE WITH DREAMING. WE WANT TO LIVE IN OUR
FANTASIES. 'I AM A BIG MAN!' (EYES CLOSED) 'OH,
THE THINGS I WILL DO, I AM SUCH A BIG MAN.'"

↳ HYDER ALI, ACTOR IN THE INDIAN TV CRIME SERIAL *RAJA AND RANCHO.*

→THE CROWD BEGINS TO JOSTLE AND WORRY AS IT DEEPENS IN A CRESCENT AROUND MUMBAI'S (BOMBAY'S) LAND-MARK GATEWAY OF INDIA. IN THE SPACE OF 20 MINUTES THE EMPTY PLAZA HAS OVERFILLED TO BLOCK THE STREETS. PEOPLE ARE STREAMING OUT OF THE COLABA DISTRICT AT A DEAD RUN TOWARD THE HUGE ARCHWAY AT THE EDGE OF OILY BOMBAY HARBOR, THEIR DETACHED CURIOSITY QUICKLY GIVING WAY TO A KIND OF DESPERATION.

TWO DOZEN YOUNG MALE DANCERS IN THE TRADITIONAL, LOOSE-FITTING MAHARASHTRA WHITE COTTON ENSEMBLES SOMETIMES CALLED BABA SUITS, COIFS TWISTED UP IN ORANGE *BAGDIS*, PRACTICE THEIR STEPS AS HIT DIRECTOR INDRA KUMAR AND HIS CHOREOGRAPHER QUICKLY BLOCK OUT A DANCE ROUTINE, PART OF A SONG SEQUENCE TO THE FILM *MANN (SOUL)*. BASED ON *AN AFFAIR TO REMEMBER*, IN WHICH LOVERS CARY GRANT AND DEBORAH KERR AGREE TO MEET AT NEW YORK'S EMPIRE STATE BUILDING, THE STAR OF THIS HINDI VERSION IS DANCING HERE IN CELEBRATION OF HIS COMING REUNION WITH HIS LOVE AT THE FAMOUS GATEWAY.

IT'S HIGH NOON ON A SUNDAY. ORDINARILY, BOMBAY LOCATIONS ARE SHOT IN THE MIDDLE OF THE NIGHT. AS 33-YEAR-OLD MEGASTAR AAMIR KHAN BURSTS FROM HIS RUN-DOWN RV AND PUSHES THE 20 FEET THROUGH THE CRANING CROWD, IT BECOMES VERY APPARENT WHY.

THE CRY GOES UP: "AAMIR KHAN!! AAMIR KHAN!!" THE UNIFORMED GUARDS, ARMED ONLY WITH LONG STICKS LIKE MOST INDIAN COPS, IMMEDIATELY BEGIN LOSING CONTROL OF THE CROWD, WHICH HAS SWOLLEN TO A THOUSAND STRONG. TWO OLD GRANNIES BEHIND ME BEGIN SLAPPING THE TOP OF MY HEAD WHILE THEIR NEIGHBORS SHOVE OUR CAMERA GEAR ASIDE. WHEN WE EXPLAIN THAT WE ARE WORKING, A MAN VERY SINCERELY ELUCIDATES: "WE DON'T CARE THAT YOU ARE WORKING, WE ARE HAVING OUR CHANCE TO BE WITH AAMIR KHAN."

AAMIR WAVES QUICKLY TO THE CROWD, GRABS A RECORDER-LIKE FLUTE AND LEADS A MERRY PRODUCTION NUMBER TO ROARING PLAYBACK. KUMAR'S CREW GETS TWO QUICK TAKES. AS THE PRODUCTION ASSISTANTS START MAKING RUNNING ASSAULTS ON THE SURGING CROWD, KUMAR GIVES THE CROSS-THROAT SIGN FOR "CUT!" AND THEN IT ALL GOES TO HELL.

FANS FROM GRANNIES TO INFANTS SWARM THE SET. CAMERAS, LIGHTS, AND DANCING EXTRAS ARE ALL SWALLOWED UP. KHAN'S ASSISTANT AMOS SURFACES SUDDENLY AMID THE SEA OF FACES AND GRABS ONE OF OUR TRIPODS, YELLING, "COME! COME!" WE ARE HUSTLED THROUGH A BEWILDERED MOB, MANY OF WHOM DON'T SEEM TO YET KNOW WHO OR WHAT IS AT THE CENTER OF THE MELEE, AND SHOVED INTO A CAR WITH TINTED WINDOWS, CLOSING THE DOORS AGAINST GRABBING ARMS AND HANDS. THE CAR IS IMMERSED IN BODIES AND CANNOT MOVE. AFTER A LONG MOMENT, POLICE BEGIN CLEARING A PATH ONE YARD AT A TIME AND WE FOLLOW AAMIR'S RV TO A STAGING AREA SEVERAL BLOCKS AWAY. THE

CROWDS FOLLOW, JOGGING BEHIND IN A MASS FILLING THE STREETS, SIDEWALKS AND HARBORSIDE WALKWAY. WE STOP THERE AND AWAIT MORE POLICE AS WAVES OF PEOPLE BREAK UP AGAINST THE SIDE OF THE RV.

AN HOUR LATER, SAFELY REMOVED TO THE OPPOSITE SIDE OF COLABA, FACING THE OPEN ARABIAN SEA, AAMIR GREETS US IN THE RV. "AH, YOUR FIRST RIOT!" HE LAUGHS, WELCOMING US WITH HIS LOVELY HINDI-ACCENTED ENGLISH. "NOW YOU KNOW WHY I CANNOT BE SEEN OUTSIDE!"

INDIAN FILM STARS ARE THE PROPERTY OF THE PEOPLE. LIKE NO OTHER ENTERTAINERS ON THE PLANET, THE ONSCREEN CHARACTERS THEY PLAY ARE FOLDED INTO THE DREAM LIFE OF THE NATION. ACTORS LIKE AAMIR, WHOSE 1998 FILM *GHULAM* AND ITS TITLE SONG WERE A SMASH HIT, ARE MORE THAN CELEBRITIES: THEY ARE THE PERSONIFICATIONS OF A HIGHLY STYLIZED FANTASY THAT THE INDIAN PEOPLE VALUE ALMOST ABOVE ALL ELSE, THE FICTIONAL PARALLEL TEXT TO NATIONAL ISSUES, A VEHICLE THAT RISES EFFORTLESSLY ABOVE THE OPPRESSIVE REALITY OF POVERTY, STRICT SOCIAL CONSTRUCTS, AND RELIGIOUS TENSION IN THE WORLD'S MOST DENSELY POPULATED COUNTRY.

IN SHORT, INDIAN CINEMA IS INVESTED WITH THE HOPE OF THE PEOPLE.

PURE PASSION HAS MADE MAINSTREAM INDIAN CINEMA

ONE OF THE MOST EFFICIENT FORMS OF
MASS COMMUNICATION IN HUMAN HISTORY —
A RUSHING, OVERBUILT, HAPHAZARD
TRADITION OF PURELY POPULIST PITCH-AND-
CATCH WITH AN UNPARALLELED IMPACT. THE
INDUSTRY CALCULATES ITS EVERY MOVE TO
GIVE THE PEOPLE WHAT THEY WANT.
    SUBSEQUENTLY, THE PEOPLE HAVE GIVEN
FILM A PLACE VERY NEAR TO THEIR CULTURAL
HEART, TUCKED IN JUST NEXT TO FAMILY AND
RELIGION. FILM IS THEIR VEHICLE OF LIGHT-
HEARTEDNESS AND FUN. THIS MIX OF FANTASY
AND UNCYNICAL ENTHUSIASM IS THE
ULTIMATE SOLVENT. IT PENETRATES EVERY
INCOME GROUP, CASTE, RELIGION, LANGUAGE,
AND GEOGRAPHICAL DISTINCTION. FILM
MOVES THROUGH INDIAN SOCIETY WITH A
QUICKNESS AND EASE LIKE NO OTHER MEDIA.

BOLLYWOOD, THE GENERIC TERM FOR INDIAN CINEMA, NAMED AFTER THE TWO-DOZEN SPRAWLING BOMBAY STUDIOS THAT PRO-DUCE THE BEST-KNOWN HINDI FILMS, EXTENDS ITSELF THROUGHOUT INDIAN CULTURE AT THE SPEED OF DREAMING. FLUID, PERVASIVE, BOLLYWOOD'S POP FILMS ARE ONE OF VERY FEW CLASSLESS MEDIA IN THIS SUPER-STRATIFIED SOCIETY. IN THE LAST TWO DECADES, IN PARTICULAR, BOLLYWOOD HAS OVERCOME EVEN THE UPPER-CRUST'S RESISTANCE TO POP CULTURE: THE SAME FILM ENJOYED ON VIDEO BY A SUCCESSFUL BRAHMIN BUSINESSMAN AND HIS FAMILY IN THE PRIVACY OF A CHIC BOMBAY HIGH-RISE WILL ALSO PLAY, ON THE SAME NIGHT, TO SEVERAL HUNDRED ILLITERATE PUNJABI FARMING FAMILIES IN A DUSTY VILLAGE MARKET SQUARE DEEP IN THE COUN-TRY, PROJECTED ONTO A SHEET FROM A TRAVELING MOVIE VAN. LIKE MANY OF BOLLYWOOD'S RABID FANS IN RUSSIA, THE ARABIAN PENINSULA, WEST AFRICA, THE MIDDLE EAST, SOUTHEAST ASIA, AND KOREA, THE PUNJABI FARMER MIGHT NOT UNDERSTAND HINDI VERY WELL. BUT THEY WATCH THE FILM ANYWAY, HAVING GROWN UP WATCHING IT THAT WAY. FILM IS INDIA'S NATIONAL DIALOGUE.

CONSEQUENTLY, THESE FILMS ARE MADE FASTER, CHEAPER, LONGER, MORE MELODRAMATIC, LOUDER, IN LARGER NUMBERS AND FOR A VASTLY LARGER AUDIENCE THAN HOLLYWOOD'S WILDEST DREAMS.

"IN 1997, FIVE *BILLION* CINEMA TICKETS WERE SOLD IN THIS COUNTRY," CHUCKLES PRODUCER SUNIL MANCHANDA, ON THE SET OF A COKE COMMERCIAL AT HIS OWN MAD STUDIOS. HE LETS THE WEIGHT OF THAT NUMBER SINK IN. "EVERYONE'S GOING TO THE MOVIES ALL THE TIME."

IN THE LAST TWO DECADES, BOLLYWOOD HAS MADE 800 TO 900 FILMS A YEAR. THAT MEANS APPROXIMATELY THREE RELEASES PER DAY. HOLLYWOOD PUTS OUT ABOUT 250 A YEAR. INDIA'S CENSOR BOARD TALLIES SHOW THAT INDIGENOUS INDIAN FILMS HAVE COME OUT IN 59 LANGUAGES SINCE 1931, FROM ARABIC TO TEA TRIBE. THE MOST COMMON IS HINDUSTANI OR HINDI, AT AN AVERAGE OF ABOUT 150 EACH YEAR SINCE THE EARLY 1970s. HINDI IS ALSO THE NATIONAL LANGUAGE. HOWEVER, ANOTHER 150 TAMIL-LANGUAGE FILMS COME OUT OF CHENNAI (MADRAS) IN INDIA'S DEEP SOUTH. AND ANOTHER 150 IN TELUGU. OTHER IMPORTANT REGIONAL CINEMAS INCLUDE, IN DESCENDING ORDER OF RELEASES: MALAYALAM, BENGALI, KANNADA, MARATHI, GUJURATI, ORIYA, AND PUNJABI.

BOLLYWOOD ALSO WORKS ON THE CHEAP. THE BEST THREE-AND-A-HALF-HOUR MUSICAL EPICS ARE CURRENTLY MADE FOR ABOUT US$2 MILLION, INCLUDING TOP ACTOR SALARIES. THE TECHNIQUES ARE STRICTLY GUERILLA. EVERY FILM REINVENTS THE WHEEL. EVEN THE MOST EXPENSIVE "FLOORS," AS SOUNDSTAGES ARE CALLED IN INDIA, ARE AS FILTHY AS BARNS. THE FLOORS ARE DIRT. VISITING

AAMIR KHAN ON THE SET OF *MANN* AT A
STUDIO CALLED FILMISTAN, WE SAW
MOVIE MAGIC AT ITS MOST BASIC: ON A
HUGE FACSIMILE OF A LUXURY LINER,
KHAN PLAYED A SCENE OBVIOUSLY TRAD-
ING ON THE RECENT SUCCESS OF *TITANIC*.
A HUNDRED FEET OVERHEAD, DOZENS OF
LIGHTING CREW WRESTLED HEAVY LIGHTS
ACROSS SWINGING PLANKS ROPED TO THE
RAFTERS, SOME OF THEM WEARING
LOINCLOTHS, SIMULATING LIGHTNING
FLASH BY STRIKING HOT WIRES TOGETHER
AS WATER POURED DOWN ALL OVER
CAMERAS, JUNCTION BOXES, AND A
SPAGHETTI TANGLE OF WIRING. NONE OF
THE RIGGERS ARE UNION. NOR ARE THE
ACTORS, FOR THAT MATTER. BUT THEY ALL
WORK AT FRANTIC SPEED, AND SUCH SETS
CAN BE BUILT ALMOST OVERNIGHT.

   THESE FILMS ARE SEEN BY 15 MILLION
CINEMAGOERS EVERY DAY IN INDIA. LESS
IMPRESSIVE THAN THE NUMBER OF DAILY
WORLDWIDE VIEWERS OF *BAYWATCH* OR
XENA — BUT WATCHING A HALF-HOUR
SHOW ON CABLE TELEVISION DOES NOT
INVOKE THE SOCIAL ELEMENTS THAT MAKE
INDIAN FILM SUCH A LIFE-AFFIRMING
RITUAL: GATHERING FRIENDS, DRIVING TO
A THEATER, AND PAYING 75-100 RUPEES IN
MUMBAI FOR A TICKET (US$2, IN A COUN-
TRY WHERE THE AVERAGE YEARLY INCOME
IS ABOUT US$350) A WEEK OR TWO IN
ADVANCE. NOT BUYING IN ADVANCE NECES-
SITATES THE ADDED DRAMA OF BUYING
INTO A SOLD-OUT THEATER AT THE MERCY
OF THE "BLACKIES," BLACK-MARKET
TICKET SCALPERS, AT QUADRUPLE OR
EVEN TEN TIMES THAT PRICE. NOR WOULD
BAYWATCH EVER BECOME THE PINNACLE
OF INDIAN POP CULTURE THE WAY FILMS
DO, WITH THEIR UNIQUE ABILITY TO
SELL LOOKS, LINGO, STYLE AND, MOST
IMPORTANTLY, MUSIC. INDIAN FANS WILL
SEE A NOTED FILM IN ANY OF THE MAJOR
LANGUAGES. THEY'LL MEMORIZE THE
SONGS. OFTEN A POPULAR FILM IN TAMIL

OR OTHER LANGUAGE WILL BE REMADE IN HINDI, WITH HINDI ACTORS AND SOUNDTRACK, AND VICE-VERSA. THE AUDIENCE WILL GO SEE BOTH. AND SOMETIMES BUY BOTH SOUNDTRACKS.

THIS UNFETTERED ENTHUSIAM ALSO COLORS THE WAY THEY WILL ENJOY THE FILM WHILE IT IS PLAYING.

"I GO SEE MY FILMS MAYBE TEN TIMES THE FIRST WEEK THEY COME OUT," SAYS AAMIR, WHO MAKES A PRACTICE OF HIDING IN THE PROJECTION BOOTH. "WHEN THE PEOPLE LOVE IT, IT'S PRICELESS. THEY GO MAD. A SONG THAT I DID IN *GHULAM* WAS THE BIGGEST HIT OF THE YEAR. AND WHEN IT PLAYS IN THE FILM, YOU CAN'T HEAR THE SONG BECAUSE PEOPLE ARE JUST WHISTLING AND SCREAMING AND SHOUTING.

"ONE OF THE FILMS I DID WAS MY FATHER'S PRODUCTION AND I HAD CO-WRITTEN THE FILM, EDITED, AND MIXED IT," HE CONTINUES. "I HAD A LOT AT STAKE. AT THAT POINT, THE FILMS THAT WERE SUCCESSFUL WERE REALLY CORNY, HARSH, VULGAR KINDS OF FILMS. AND THIS WAS A SWEET FILM ABOUT THREE KIDS WHOSE PARENTS DIED IN AN ACCIDENT. I WAS LIKE, 'GOSH, I DON'T THINK THIS IS GONNA WORK.' THERE WAS ONE SONG IN THE FILM WHICH IS ONE OF MY FAVORITE SONGS. IT WAS THE FIRST DAY, BUT THE AMOUNT OF CHEERING AND WHISTLING WHEN THAT SONG BEGAN WAS UNBELIEVABLE. I WAS IN THE STALLS, WHICH IS THE LOWER LEVEL, AND THERE WERE THESE GUYS THAT GOT UP FROM THEIR SEATS, CAME OUT IN THE AISLES AND DANCED THROUGHOUT THE SONG. I HAD TEARS IN MY EYES WHEN I WAS WATCHING THIS."

"PEOPLE WANT A NEW FILM EVERY WEEK," ADDS MANCHANDA. "ALL RIGHT, MORE THAN THAT. BECAUSE IT TAKES CARE OF ONE EVENING. SO IF THERE ARE TWO FILMS, IT CAN TAKE CARE OF TWO EVENINGS FOR THE ENTIRE FAMILY. IF WE COULD TURN OUT 900 *GOOD* FILMS EVERY YEAR, WE'D HAVE 900 SUCCESSFUL FILMS. THAT'S HOW IT IS. THE PEOPLE ARE DYING TO SEE GOOD FILMS. THEY DON'T OUTRIGHT REJECT YOU UNLESS YOU REALLY COME OUT WITH A TRASHY FILM."

"FOR YEARS, FILMS HAVE BEEN THE ONLY MAJOR SOURCE OF ENTERTAINMENT IN THIS COUNTRY," SAYS GULSHAN GROVER, AN INFAMOUS CHARACTER ACTOR KNOWN THROUGHOUT INDIA AS THE BAD GUY IN BOLLYWOOD BLOCK-BUSTERS. "THE FILMS HAVE BEEN THERE FOR 50, 60, 70 YEARS. THE REST IS PRETTY NEW. PLUS IT REACHES EVERY VILLAGE, EVERY NOOK AND CORNER OF THE COUNTRY. AND IT STILL IS CHEAP."

BOLLYWOOD *IS* INDIA'S POP CULTURE. IT HAS ALMOST NO RIVAL, DOMINATING THE SCREEN, THE RADIO, THE TELEVISION, PRINT MEDIA AND THE INTERNET. INDIA'S EQUIVALENT OF TOP-40 RADIO IS COM-PRISED ALMOST COMPLETELY OF FILM SONGS. THESE ARE PRE-RELEASED TO RADIO, BUILDING AN AUDIENCE BEFORE THE FILMS APPEAR, BLASTING OUT OF EVERY TAXI IN TRAFFIC, TRACTOR IN THE FIELD, ROADSIDE FRUIT STAND, NEWS AGENT, AUTO REPAIR STALL, CONSTRUCTION SITE AND PRIVATE HOME IN THE COUNTRY. THE *MASALA*, OR SALSA, PLOT FORMULA CURRENTLY POPULAR AMONG MAINSTREAM FILMMAKERS CALLS FOR SIX SONGS IN EVERY FILM. SO EVERY FILM IN INDIA IS A MUSICAL. THESE SONG SEQUENCES ARE LONG, RUNNING FOR UP TO EIGHT MINUTES, AND ARE OFTEN SHOT IN EXOTIC LOCATIONS. THEY ARE THE FILM'S PRIMARY MARKETING TOOL, AS

SLIGHTLY CUT-DOWN VERSIONS ARE RELEASED AS VIDEOS. THESE MAKE UP ABOUT 70% OF THE PROGRAMMING ON THE VERY INFLUENTIAL NEW MTV INDIA AND V-CHANNEL.

EVEN IN BOMBAY, INDIA'S MOST WESTERNIZED CITY, LIVE MUSIC OTHER THAN INDIAN CLASSICAL MUSIC IS ALMOST NONEXISTENT. THERE ARE FEW ROCK BANDS AND ONLY SLIGHTLY MORE DJS. THE ACTS THAT COME THROUGH TENDS TO BE MASSIVE STADIUM ACTS LIKE MICHAEL JACKSON OR MADONNA, AND THEN ONLY ONCE OR TWICE A YEAR. THEATER EXISTS MOSTLY AS PART OF THE SPECTACLE OF RELIGIOUS FESTIVALS. THERE ARE RARELY ANY RUNWAY FASHION SHOWS OR OTHER EVENTS THAT COMPRISE WHAT IS KNOWN AS POP CULTURE IN THE WEST.

POPULAR ACTORS HAVE JUMPED IN TO CAPITALIZE ON THIS VOID, PUTTING TOGETHER LIVE TOURING SHOWS WHERE THREE OR FOUR HOT FACES WILL SHOW UP ONSTAGE TO LIP-SYNCH THEIR MOST POPULAR FILM SONGS. THESE SHOWS SELL OUT MONTHS IN ADVANCE.

TELEVISION HASN'T GIVEN BOLLYWOOD MUCH OF A RUN FOR ITS MONEY. IT WAS ONLY INTRODUCED TO INDIA IN 1972, AND THEN ONLY AS ONE STATE-RUN CHANNEL WITH MOSTLY CULTURAL PROGRAMMING. NOR HAVE THE 50 NEW SATELLITE CHANNELS. WHEN AUSTRALIAN MEDIA MOGUL RUPERT MURDOCH WIRED ALL OF INDIA WITH CABLE IN 1992, MANY IN BOLLYWOOD SAW IN IT THE DEATH OF THEIR GOOD THING. BUT, AFTER AN INITIAL LULL ATTRIBUTED TO THE NOVELTY OF THE CHANNELS, CINEMA ATTENDANCE HAS RETURNED TO ALL-TIME HIGHS.

"IT'S JUST THE DEMOGRAPHICS OF THE COUNTRY," SAYS AMITABH BACHCHAN, REGALLY COMPOSED OVER THE MILKY TEA KNOWN AS *CHAI* IN HIS JUHU OFFICES. LOOKING SOMEWHAT LIKE BOTH WARREN BEATTY AND AL PACINO, BACHCHAN HAS PLAYED THE ROMANTIC ACTION HERO IN ALMOST A HUNDRED

BOLLYWOOD FILMS SINCE HIS DEBUT IN 1969. YES, A HUNDRED. "WE HAVE 900 MILLION PEOPLE AND HARDLY ANY OTHER SOURCE OF ENTERTAINMENT. WHAT DO YOU EXPECT?

"THE SAME GOES FOR TELEVISION," HE ADDS. "OPRAH, FOR EXAMPLE, WOULD BE REJOICING AT A RATING OF 12 MILLION PEOPLE. WE TAKE CARE OF THAT IN ONE CITY. IT'S A HUGE FORCE. IT'S A HUGE RESPONSIBILITY AS WELL. BECAUSE IT'S NOT AN EASY TASK TO MAKE SOMETHING THAT PLEASES 900 MILLION PEOPLE, OR LET'S SAY AT LEAST HALF OF THEM."

IF THE DREAM IS BOLLYWOOD'S TRUE PRODUCT, THE SOLVENT WHICH CAUSES ITS MULTIPLE MEDIA MANIFESTATIONS AND ITS CONTENT TO BE DRAWN UP INTO THE IDENTITY OF THE PEOPLE, THEN THE ACTORS AND ACTRESSES ARE THE FACE OF THE DREAM. BOLLYWOOD'S RAW SPEED IS REFLECTED THERE.

"FOR SOME PECULIAR REASON, THE INDIAN AUDIENCE IDENTIFIES WITH THE LEADING ACTOR OR HERO ALMOST WITH GOD-LIKE REVERENCE, AND HE HAS A VERY SPECIAL PLACE IN THEIR HEARTS," CROONS BACHCHAN. "IT'S MUCH LIKE SOME OF YOUR POP STARS THERE, OR FAMOUS ATHLETES LIKE MICHAEL JORDAN."

BACHCHAN SHOULD KNOW, HAVING BEEN THE GOD OF INDIAN CINEMA FOR THE WHOLE OF THE 1970s AND MOST OF THE 1980s. LOVINGLY NICKNAMED "THE LAST EMPEROR" BY THE BOISTEROUS BOLLYWOOD PRESS, BACHCHAN IS INDIA'S BRANDO. HIS POPULARITY AND INFLUENCE IS EXPONENTIALLY BEYOND THAT OF YOUNG STARS LIKE AAMIR KHAN AND SHAH RUKH KHAN WHO DRAW THE TOP AUDIENCES TODAY.

THE REFERENCE TO "GOD-LIKE" STATUS IS NO EXAGGERATION. IN CONTRAST TO THE WEST, WHERE EAGER FANS MAKE CELEBRITIES OF THOSE WHO HAVE IMAGE POWER WITHIN THE PARADIGMS OF ULTRA-UBIQUITOUS MEDIA LIKE TV, IN INDIA THE LINE BETWEEN CELEBRITY AND ACTUAL RELIGIOUS OR SPIRITUAL POWER GROWS VERY BLURRY.

"THERE IS AN ACTOR, RAJNI KANT, WHO'S REACHED SUCH A HEIGHT TODAY IN THE TAMIL INDUSTRY THAT, ON SCREEN, YOU CANNOT SHOW HIM BEING SLAPPED," SAYS AAMIR KHAN, SITTING IN HIS TRAILER OUTSIDE FLOOR 10 OF THE SPRAWLING STUDIO COMPLEX KNOWN AS FILM CITY IN BOMBAY'S GORAGAON DISTRICT. HE EXPLAINS THAT FANS IN THE STATE OF TAMIL NADU ACTUALLY BUILD RELIGIOUS SHRINES TO THEIR BIGGEST ACTORS. "THERE WAS A VILLAIN IN ONE OF HIS FILMS WHO SLAPPED HIM. THE VILLAIN WAS GOING IN A CAR, AND

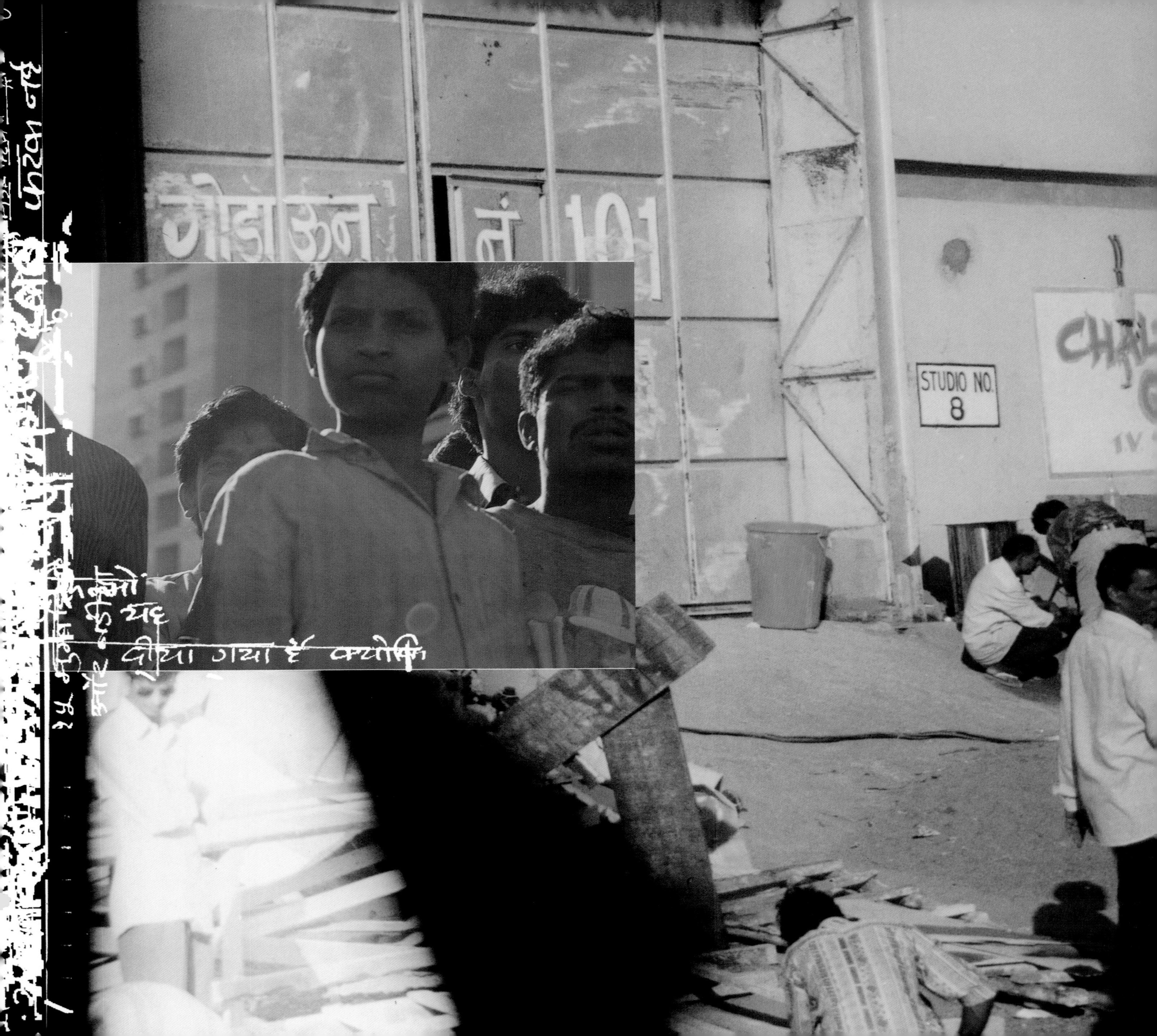
गोडाऊन नं 101
STUDIO NO. 8
दीया गया है क्योंकि

RAJNI'S FANS PULLED HIM OUT OF HIS CAR AND THEY WANTED TO BEAT HIM UP BECAUSE HE SLAPPED RAJNI KANT ONSCREEN."

"IF SOMEBODY PLAYS GOD IN A MOVIE, PEOPLE REALLY CONSIDER THAT PERSON GOD," SAYS GROVER. "THEY'RE GOING TO TOUCH THEIR FEET. SOMEBODY WHO PLAYS EVIL IS BOUND TO HAVE A NEGATIVE EFFECT. PEOPLE ARE FRIGHTENED OF ME, BECAUSE THEY FEEL THAT I AM A GANGSTER, I AM A BAD GUY, I AM A KILLER. A FEMALE FAN MAY GO TO AAMIR KHAN'S ROOM ALONE TO GET AN AUTOGRAPH, BUT TO MY ROOM, SHE'LL COME WITH AN AUNT, WITH A YOUNGER BROTHER, AND WITH TWO OR THREE OTHER FRIENDS. SHE'S FRIGHTENED THAT I MAY SUDDENLY RAPE HER OR SOMETHING, BECAUSE THAT'S WHAT I DO ONSCREEN."

BACHCHAN TIES THIS IDENTIFICATION TO CENTURIES-OLD TRADITIONS IN RELIGIOUS DRAMA. "WE HAVE HAD, THROUGH CENTURIES, THE DEPICTION OF OUR RELIGIOUS EPICS ONSTAGE AT A PARTICULAR TIME OF THE YEAR," HE HYPOTHESIZES. "THE *SHERA*, WHICH IS THE CELEBRATION WHEN LORD RAMA CAME BACK AFTER HIS EXILE, HAS BEEN CELEBRATED AROUND OCTOBER EVERY YEAR. THERE ARE HUGE STAGE PER-FORMANCES PUT UP IN EVERY CORNER OF THE COUN-TRY, IN CITIES AND VILLAGES, AND THEY ENACT THE ENTIRE EPIC. AND MOST OF OUR EPICS, THE *RAMAYANA* IN PARTICULAR, IS REALLY THE STORY OF HOW EVIL WAS OVERCOME BY GOOD. A MANIFESTATION OF THAT CONCEPT IS WHAT INDIAN CINEMA HAS BEEN FOLLOWING. THE GOOD IN INDIAN CINEMA IS RELATED TO THE GOOD OF THE RELIGIOUS EPICS, AND THEREFORE, PERHAPS, THIS FORM OF IDOL WORSHIP. THE HEROES ALWAYS DO THE RIGHT THINGS, THEY ALWAYS BEHAVE CORRECTLY, THEY FIGHT FOR THE DOWNTRODDEN."

THOUGH NOT PART OF ITS STRICTLY ENTERTAINMENT FUNCTION, INDIAN FILMS HAVE OFTEN HARNESSED THIS IMAGE POWER, RELIGIOUS AND OTHERWISE, TO OVERTLY POLITICAL ENDS. AFTER A SERIES OF EXTREMELY INFLUENTIAL FILMS CHAMPIONING THE TAMIL NATIONALIST MOVEMENT THAT TOOK ROOT FOLLOWING PARTITION IN 1947, TAMIL STARS M.G. RAMACHANDRAN AND N.T. RAMA RAO TRADED ON THEIR POPULARITY TO BECOME CHIEF MINISTERS IN THE STATES OF TAMIL NADU AND ANDHRA PRADESH. BACHCHAN HIMSELF WAS ELECTED TO OFFICE IN THE NORTH IN THE 1980S, BUT PROVED TO BE BETTER AT PLAYING A HEROIC POPULIST POLITICIAN THAN ACTUALLY BEING ONE.

THIS MAY BE NO DIFFERENT THAN THE UNITED STATES, WHERE RONALD REAGAN BECAME PRESIDENT AND CLINT EASTWOOD MAYOR OF CARMEL, CA, OR THE U.K., WHERE NATIONAL HERO SEAN CONNERY IS A SPOKESMAN FOR SCOTTISH INDEPENDENCE. OR ITALY, FOR THAT MATTER, WHERE PORN STAR CICCOLINA WAS ELECTED TO PARLIAMENT. UNFORTUNATELY FOR

THE LEAGUES OF MUCH-WORSHIPPED BOLLYWOOD ACTRESSES, HOWEVER, THIS ONSCREEN POWER IS VERY MUCH A BOYS' CLUB IN INDIA. MEANINGFUL LEAD ROLES FOR WOMEN ARE FEW, AND VERY RARELY BUCK STRICT RELIGIOUS BEHAVIORAL STANDARDS. SUBSEQUENTLY, FEW WOMEN RISE TO POSITIONS OF TRUE POWER IN THE INDUSTRY.

ONSCREEN, MAINSTREAM BOLLYWOOD FILMS USE WOMEN AS OBJECTS WHICH GOAD THE HERO INTO ACTION. ART CINEMA DIRECTORS LIKE DEEPA MEHTA HAVE TAKEN ON THESE STEREOTYPES, BUT WITH LITTLE BOX-OFFICE EFFECT INSIDE INDIA. HER FILM *FIRE,* FOR INSTANCE, DEPICTED A LESBIAN RELATIONSHIP BETWEEN TWO OPPRESSED SISTERS-IN-LAW. FILMGOERS RESPONDED NEGATIVELY TO THE MORAL BREAKDOWN OF THE FAMILY, AND FILM CRITICS WHO OTHERWISE SUPPORT MEHTA RESPONDED NEGATIVELY TO THE FILM'S REALISM. THEY'D RATHER HAVE THE UPLIFT OF FLYING HORSEMEN SAILING UNSCATHED THROUGH A MONSOON OF BULLETS IN ACTS OF HEROIC CONQUEST.

BOLLYWOOD ACTRESSES WITH HEAVY ATTITUDES TEND TO BURN UP IN A POPULAR METEORIC FLARE-OUT, BOTH ONSCREEN AND OFF. THE GOOD WIFE BACKS HER MAN, AND EVEN IN THE RARE INSTANCES WHEN SHE MAY OPPOSE HIM, SHE IS NEVER THE ACTOR EXPERIENCING THE PRIMARY CONFLICT. HOT BOLLYWOOD ACTRESSES LIKE MANISHA KOIRALA, KAJOL, KARISMA KAPOOR AND MADHURI DIXIT MAY BE THE FACES THAT LAUNCHED A THOUSAND STICKY WEB SITES, BUT THEIR BARE MIDRIFFS, WET SARIS AND HIP-DISLOCATING PELVIC THRUSTS HAVE SEEMINGLY EARNED THEM ONLY THE RIGHT TO BE OBJECTS AROUND WHICH MALE-DRIVEN PLOTS ARE BUILT.

"I MOSTLY DO FILMS FOR THE A CENTERS, THE OVERSEAS AND CITY MARKETS," NOTES FARAH KHAN, A FEMALE CHOREOGRAPHER NOW BEST KNOWN FOR THE HIT SONG "CHAIYYA CHAIYYA" FROM THE FILM *DIL SE,* IN WHICH SHAH RUKH KHAN AND INDIAN SUPERMODEL MALAIKA AURORA LEAD A GROUP DANCE NUMBER ATOP A MOVING TRAIN. INDIAN MARKETS ARE SPLIT INTO A, B, AND C: A CENTERS ARE BIG CITY MARKETS, MOST LIKELY TO EXPORT OVERSEAS, B ARE LARGE TOWNS, AND C ARE RURAL VILLAGES. IN A MARKETS, SHE SAYS, "THE SONGS ARE A LITTLE MORE YOUTH-ORIENTED AND THEY'RE A LITTLE MORE MODERN. THESE DON'T REALLY DO WELL IN THE RURAL AREAS. THEY STILL WANT GIRLS LIFTING THEIR SKIRTS UP AND WOMEN UNDER THE WATERFALL, DOING ONE LITTLE JIG. YOU KNOW YOUR FILM WILL SELL ACCORDING TO WHO YOUR MALE STAR IS. IT DOESN'T MATTER WHO YOUR HEROINE IS. IT MAY MAKE A DIFFERENCE OF A FEW LAKHS [100,000 RUPEES] HERE AND THERE, BUT NOT REALLY."

SUCH PROSCRIBED ROLES ARE PART OF A BOLLYWOOD FORMULA SYSTEM THAT DEMANDS THE SAME
FROM BOTH ITS MEN AND WOMEN: WHEN YOU'RE HOT, YOU MAKE MORE FILMS THAN WOULD SEEM
HUMANLY POSSIBLE.

"I'VE WORKED ON 300 FILMS," SAYS GULSHAN GROVER. "RIGHT NOW, I'M WORKING IN 15 FILMS.
I HAVE DONE FIVE INTERNATIONAL FILMS: AMERICAN, ITALIAN, FRENCH, GERMAN. THERE WAS A
TIME IN MY CAREER, ABOUT FOUR YEARS BACK, WHEN THERE WAS A MAJOR BOOM, PRODUCTION
WAS AT ITS HIGHEST, I WAS WORKING ON 60 FILMS."

EVERY TOP INDIAN ACTOR TELLS THE SAME STORY. THERE WAS A TIME IN THE 1980s WHEN LEAD
ACTORS WERE SIGNING FROM 10 TO 40 CONCURRENT FILMS, THE AVERAGE BEING 20. NEARLY ALL
OF THESE FILMS WERE IN PRODUCTION SIMULTANEOUSLY, AS ONLY HAPPENS IN INDIA, WITH
ACTORS AND EVEN DIRECTORS WORKING THREE SHIFTS A DAY, ON THREE DIFFERENT FILMS.

"I'VE DONE ABOUT 15 AT SOME POINT IN TIME, WORKING ON THREE FILMS IN THE SAME DAY,"
SAYS BACHCHAN. "IT'S A LOT TO DO WITH ECONOMICS. WE DON'T HAVE INSTITUTIONALIZED
FINANCE. YOU'RE NEVER ABLE TO PLAN YOUR ENTIRE FILM BECAUSE YOU NEVER HAVE THE ENTIRE
MONEY IN YOUR HAND. YOU MAY SHOOT FOR A WEEK AND BE SITTING FOR SIX MONTHS. BUT THE
ARTIST DOESN'T LIKE TO BE WASTED FOR SIX MONTHS, SO HE PICKS UP OTHER PROJECTS. WE'D BE
VERY HAPPY TO WORK ON A PROJECT FROM START TO FINISH. BUT WE'RE FORCED TO TAKE ON
OTHER PROJECTS JUST FOR MERE SURVIVAL."

IN ORDER TO BOUNCE FROM ONE PROJECT TO THE NEXT, STEREOTYPING IS THE RULE. MANY FILMS HAVE FAILED OR BEEN RECUT BECAUSE THE HERO SIGNIFICANTLY CHANGED HIS LOOK FROM THE LAST FILM. ONE OF BACHCHAN'S FILMS HAD TO BE REDUBBED AFTER HE TRIED TO CHANGE HIS VOICE À LA BRANDO IN *THE GODFATHER* AND AUDIENCES REACTED BY SETTING FIRE TO THEATERS, THINKING THAT THE SOUND SYSTEMS HAD BEEN PURPOSELY SABOTAGED TO HURT THEIR HERO. THIS INFLEXIBILITY ALSO WORKS TO SOME PEOPLE'S ADVANTAGE.

"I AM NOT A REJECT HERO, I'M A VILLAIN OUT OF CHOICE!" LAUGHS GROVER. "I HATE THE HERO PART BECAUSE I HATE DANCING AND I'M NOT GONNA RUN AROUND THE TREE AND DO ALL THOSE SILLY THINGS. IT WAS A WISE POLICY ON MY PART TO BE A VILLAIN. I'M HUGELY SUCCESSFUL IN PLAYING THE BAD GUY."

WHEN AAMIR KHAN MADE HIS FIRST FILM AS LEAD, IN MANSOOR KHAN'S 1988 DEBUT SMASH *QAYAMAT SE QAYAMAT TAK*, HE FELL IN STEP, SIGNING EIGHT FILMS OVERNIGHT. BUT HE AND HIS COUSIN MANSOOR WERE PART OF A NEW GENERATION OF FILMMAKERS WHOSE IMPACT HAS COME TO REPRESENT THE SUBTLE MATURATION OF THE INDUSTRY, INCLUDING SOORAJ BARJATYA, WITH THE INFLUENTIAL HIT *MAINE PYAR KIYA*, ADITYA CHOPRA, DHARMESH DARSHEN, RAJ KUMAR SANTOSHI, AND INDRA KUMAR. ALL CHILDREN OF THE BIGGEST BOLLYWOOD DYNASTIES, THESE YOUNG FILMMAKERS WANTED A CHANGE. THEY REJECTED THE ACTION AND FLUFF OF BOLLYWOOD'S 1977 TO 1988 "DISCO ERA"— IN FACT, THE HEYDAY OF AMITABH BACHCHAN. THEY WERE ALSO FORCED TO DEAL WITH THE SUDDEN DISAPPEARANCE OF TRENDY ONE-TIME PRODUCERS WHO ONCE POURED THEIR INDUSTRIAL MONEY INTO FILMS LIKE GAMBLERS. SO THIS NEW GENERATION HAVE SLOWED THE HURTLING TRAIN SOMEWHAT. BUT ONLY A LITTLE.

"FROM 40 AND 50 FILMS, ACTORS ARE NOW DOING AN AVERAGE OF EIGHT," SAYS AAMIR. AFTER HIS FIRST HIT, AAMIR BALKED AT HIS OWN FAME. HE REFUSED TO SIGN FILMS, HE WOULDN'T WORK ON SUNDAY, HE'D ONLY DO ONE EIGHT-HOUR SHIFT A DAY. THE BIZ THOUGHT HE WAS NUTS, THEN CAPITULATED TO HIS STYLE. "I HAVE CONTRIBUTED TO THAT HAPPENING, THOUGH EVEN EIGHT FILMS IS TOO MUCH. BUT AT LEAST IT HAS COME DOWN TO EIGHT."

THOUGH THE FEVERISH PACE OF THE DISCO ERA HAS COOLED SOMEWHAT, BOLLYWOOD'S TIME-TESTED FORMULAS HAVE REMAINED ESSENTIALLY UNTOUCHED. IN FACT, ACCORDING TO MANSOOR KHAN AND OTHERS, THE EMOTIONAL REQUIREMENTS OF INDIA'S CINEMA AUDIENCE HAVE ONLY GROWN MORE STRICT IN THE FACE OF AN INCREASINGLY INVASIVE GLOBAL CULTURE. MELODRAMA IS NOT A NEGATIVE WORD IN INDIA; IN FACT, IT IS A COMFORT AND A STANDARD.

"I'M NOW INTO MY 30TH YEAR. THE PATTERN HASN'T CHANGED AT ALL," SAYS BACHCHAN BLITHELY. "INDIAN AUDIENCES LIKE TO SEE THE VICTORY OF GOOD OVER EVIL. THEY LIKE TO IDOLIZE THEIR LEADING MAN, THEIR HERO. THEY LIKE TO HAVE SOME ENTERTAINMENT AND MUSIC, A BIT OF ACTION, SOME EMOTIONS. REALLY A VERY HEALTHY MIX OF ALL FACETS OF LIFE." HE SMILES, THEN ADDS, "THE FASCINATION, OF COURSE, BEING THAT POETIC JUSTICE IN INDIAN FILMS IS DELIVERED WITHIN THREE HOURS. WHEN IT TAKES A LIFETIME IN REAL LIFE."

MANY OF THE NEW BREED SAY THAT BACHCHAN AND HIS CRONIES ARE OUT OF TOUCH, THAT THEY ARE THE VERY REASON THE *MASALA* FORMAT IS LOSING STEAM. BUT THEN, THE BIGGEST FILM IN INDIA IN 1998 WAS, IN MANY WAYS, BACHCHAN'S VINDICATION. FOR THE FIRST TIME EVER, THE TOP FILM WAS NOT AN INDIAN PRODUCTION. IT WAS *TITANIC*.

"*TITANIC* IS BASICALLY SEEN AS A HINDI FILM," SAYS SUNIL MANCHANDA. "IT HAS ALL THE MELODRAMA AND PLOT OF A HINDI FILM, WITH THE ADVANTAGE OF THE AMAZING EFFECTS REGARDING THE BOAT AND SO FORTH." IT WAS ALSO ASSOCIATED WITH A HIT SONG BY CELINE DION, WHICH WAS HEARD EVERYWHERE. FEW HOLLYWOOD FILMS STILL HIT THIS OLD MGM-STYLE MARK THESE DAYS, WHICH IS ONE REASON THAT INDIA REMAINS ONE OF THE FEW PLACES IN THE WORLD WHERE HOLLYWOOD HAS VERY LITTLE IMPACT.

"IT'S THE *MASALA* FORMAT," MANCHANDA CONTINUES. "RICH MAN, POOR GIRL, OR POOR MAN, RICH GIRL, FALLING IN LOVE, FAMILY AGAINST IT — ROMEO AND JULIET. OR YOU HAD TWO GIRLS GETTING LOST AND MEETING EACH OTHER JUST BEFORE THEY KILLED EACH OTHER. OR TWO FRIENDS FALLING FOR THE SAME WOMAN AND THEN FIGHTING OR SPLITTING, AND ONE OF THEM DYING IN THE END FOR THE OTHER. AND FOR ALMOST 20 YEARS, WE HAD TO HAVE A VILLAIN WHO EITHER RAPED YOUR WIFE OR SISTER OR KIDNAPPED YOUR DAUGHTER OR KILLED YOUR FAMILY AND YOU WERE LEFT HIDING IN THE CUPBOARD AND YOU GREW UP AND TOOK REVENGE."

STAPLE VALUES HAVE REMAINED THE SAME SINCE
THE 1950s, AND REFLECT INDIA'S TRUE SOCIAL FABRIC:
THE SANCTITY OF THE FAMILY, WHICH IN INDIA MEANS AN
EXTENDED NUCLEAR GROUP ALL TENDING TO REMAIN
TOGETHER IN THE SAME BUILDING OR NEIGHBORHOOD
FOR MANY GENERATIONS; RELIGIOUS CODE; CASTE OR
SOCIAL BARRIERS; MALE BONDING; AND MAD ROMANTIC
LOVE; ALL DEFENDED BY EQUALLY MAD VIOLENCE
WHENEVER ANY OF THESE ARE THREATENED.

THE SPEED WITH WHICH BOLLYWOOD'S FILMS PENETRATE
INDIAN SOCIETY DOES NOT INDICATE CHANGING NATIONAL
STYLES, LANGUAGE OR CULTURAL ASSUMPTIONS. NOR
DOES IT PROMOTE ANY CHANGE. RATHER, IT REAFFIRMS
THE STATUS QUO. THESE FILMS DON'T LEAD THE INDIAN
IMAGINATION; THEY FOLLOW. THAT'S WHY THEY'RE SO MAS-
SIVELY SUCCESSFUL. THEY ARE SO INTEGRAL TO INDIAN
LIFE THEY'RE MOSTLY CHEMICAL IN EFFECT: AN ADRENAL
SURGE OF EMOTIONS CARRIES A FILM AND ITS CHARAC-
TERS TO THE CENTER OF INDIAN HISTORY.

AS PAUL VIRILIO WROTE IN THE *AESTHETICS OF
DISAPPEARANCE:* "SPEED TREATS VISION LIKE ITS BASIC
ELEMENT; WITH ACCELERATION, TO TRAVEL IS LIKE FILMING,
NOT SO MUCH PRODUCING IMAGES AS NEW MNEMONIC
TRACES, UNLIKELY, SUPERNATURAL. IN SUCH A CONTEXT
DEATH ITSELF CAN NO LONGER BE FELT AS MORTAL; IT
BECOMES AS IN WILLIAM BURROUGHS, A SIMPLE TECHNICAL
ACCIDENT. THE FINAL SEPARATION OF THE SOUND FROM
THE PICTURE TRACK. WHETHER THE TITANIC OR ZEPPELIN
THE FATAL CATASTROPHE SEEMS TO PASSENGERS OF THE
GIANT VEHICLE LIKE A SENSELESS, UNREAL HYPOTHESIS,
AND WHILE THE SHIP SINKS THEY CONTINUE TO DANCE TO
THE SOUND OF THE ORCHESTRA."

"WE ARE AN UNEDUCATED PEOPLE," POINTS OUT FARAH
KHAN. "OUR LITERACY RATE IS NOT VERY HIGH. WE NEED
TO BE TOLD EVERYTHING. WE CANNOT MAKE *E.T.*,
BECAUSE A RICKSHAW *WALLAH* OR A TAXI DRIVER DON'T
KNOW WHAT IS AN ALIEN IN INDIA. A PSYCHOLOGICAL
THRILLER LIKE *SEVEN*, IT'S TOO INTELLIGENT FOR HIM. OR
USUAL SUSPECTS. YOU HAVE TO HAVE YOUR SIX SONGS."

THROUGH BOLLYWOOD, INDIA HAS ADAPTED ITS
HARDWIRED MILLENNIA-OLD TRADITIONS TO A CREEPING
GLOBAL CULTURE THAT DEMANDS FLUID LOYALTIES, AN
ABSENCE OF RIGID SOCIAL STRUCTURE, AND A SUBMIS-
SION TO INTERNATIONAL MARKET FORCES AND STAN-
DARDS. IN INDIA, THE MOVIES FLASH BY WITH BLINDING

SPEED, PRESENTING A MINIMUM OF THREE NEW AND IMMERSIVE REPRESENTATIONS OF THE UNIVERSE EVERY DAY. THROUGH THEM, THE MOVIEGOER CONSTANTLY REINVENTS HIS OR HER OWN DREAM LIFE. THEY FLY IN THEIR IMAGINATIONS. NO MATTER THAT THEY ARE FORCED ALWAYS TO RETURN, EVEN IN THOSE DREAMS, TO THE RIGID STANDARDS OF AN INDIA THAT HAS ALWAYS BEEN. AT LEAST THEY ARE FLYING. AND THAT IS SOME SEMBLANCE OF ESCAPE.

"INDIAN AUDIENCES LIKE TO MOVE AWAY FROM REALITY," SAYS MANCHANDA. "SATYAJIT RAY, WHO WAS CONSIDERED AN INTERNATIONALLY VERY FAMOUS DIRECTOR, HIS MOVIES NEVER DID WELL IN INDIA BECAUSE HE SHOWED A LOT OF POVERTY. EVERYONE OVER HERE WANTS TO MOVE AWAY FROM THAT BECAUSE IT'S PRETTY DEPRESSING."

"FILMS TAKE PEOPLE ON A JOURNEY," SMILES GROVER. "THEY'RE BASICALLY LARGER THAN LIFE: BEAUTIFUL PEOPLE, BEAUTIFUL SETTING, BEAUTIFUL WOMEN, SONGS. THE INDIAN PUBLIC HAS TOO MANY PROBLEMS. THIS IS A DREAM WORLD. IT'S LIKE TAKING YOU IN A TRANCE: 'PUT THE LIGHTS OFF. LET ME TAKE YOU AWAY.'"

दिल
बन्द हूँ (आखें बन्द) जो चीज़ में कर
कोई नहीं कर सकता
बॉलीवुड, यह नाम
के घर को दिया गया
स्टूडियो जो
बनती हैं।

→ jet trails

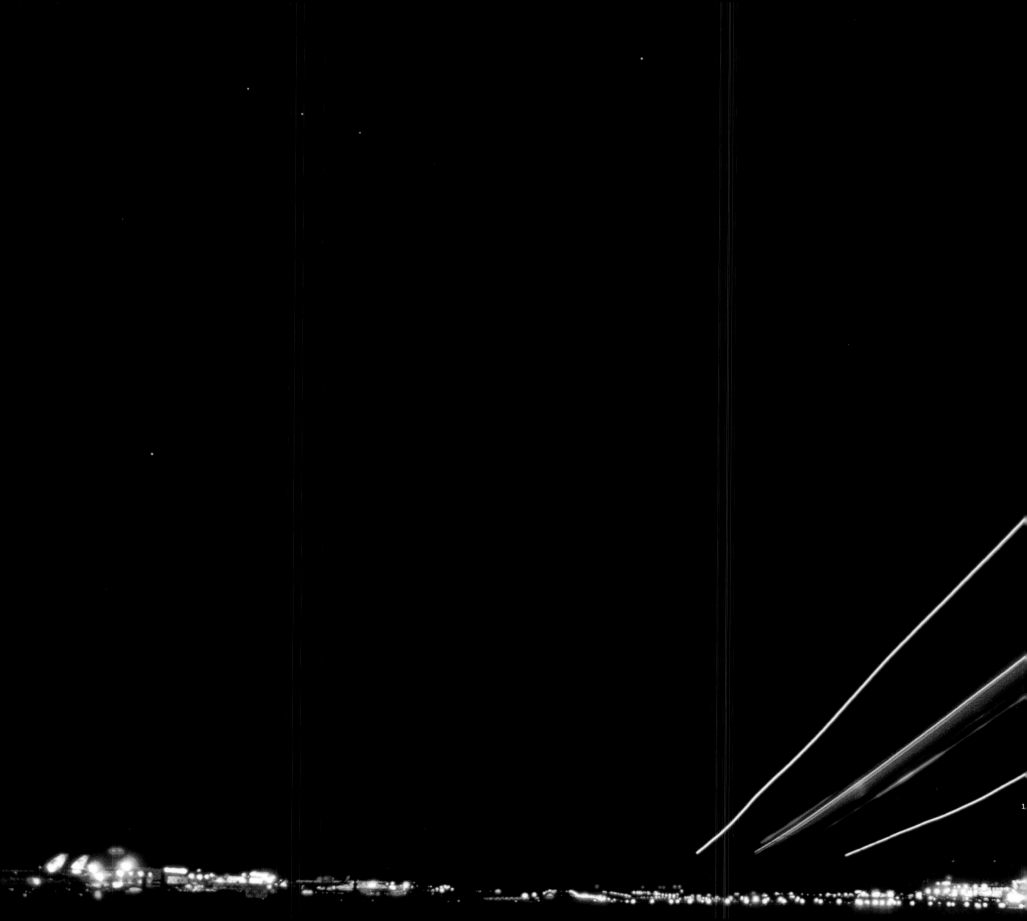

→ identity

→ identity

t trails

8　SPEED

AS
IDENTITY

LONG-HAUL TRUCKERS LOST IN PLACE

"NOW THAT THE CARS ARE GONE BY AND ALL THE RESTLESS WORLD WITH THEM, AND THE FISHES IN THE POND NO LONGER FEEL THEIR RUMBLING, I AM MORE ALONE THAN EVER." ↪ THOREAU, *WALDEN*

"TRANSPORTATION EXISTS TO OVERCOME GEOGRAPHY." ↪ U.S. BUREAU OF TRANSPORTATION STATISTICS

→ Time slips away behind a pair of mirrored aviator shades. It forms a straight white line and shoots into the distance. Hard afternoon sun drains off the desert and filters through the blinds into the coffeeshop at the 76 Truckstop in Ontario, Califo Sitting men fill the room with their silence, sometimes two to a booth, more often alone. A waitress in a dirty pink uniform wanders through with a pot of scalding coffee. Dust motes swirl in shafts of refrigerated sun. Cigarette smoke blows sl past jeans and T-shirts leaned up against the window outside. Out in the lot, 400 or so huge diesel tractors throb in the heat shimmer of 110-degree asphalt.   The only motion here is in the eyes. Behind every set of reading glasses and r colored Oakley sportshades, over every toothpick pinched between pursed lips, aimed at every logbook, the eyes are fixed on some point in the distance. On a stretch of black asphalt. Constantly dissolving beneath the wheels. Every OTR (c The Road, or long haul) driver in this coffeeshop is moving *all the time.*   In this cosmography, time is an absolute, not in the form of hours, but as miles of asphalt: the distance from Point A to Point B. Time makes perfect sense when mo between those two points. Truckers don't get paid by the hour, but by the mile. And time opposes the effort. It can't be beat, so it has to be made immaterial. Moving over the road is not only a strategy for staying on time; movement itself is a stra getting outside of time.   So truckers are a rolling metaphor for America itself: a constantly failing attempt to make a clean escape from time, which, in failing, gives time perfect meaning.   Americans, in particular, hate the very idea of e. They are at war with it. Their ahistorical nature is well documented; the passing of time is commodified as a warm-fuzzy nostalgia. That is because the restlessness built into the mythological terrain of America is one of *becoming*. Americans eve in the constant reinvention symbolized by the frontier. No one wants to be known as what they are, but what they are going to be. Very soon. Any day now. The entire nation prays for, and bets on, that event which will transform their lives, which can be summed up in a bumper sticker saying, "Please be patient, God isn't finished with me yet."   And to what end? Significantly, the bumper-sticker dreamer longs for some quasi-permanent harmony with time; a calling or mission renders one's every action, and thus every passing moment, as meaningful. A total commitment to lifestyle that makes time something other than time.   Meanwhile, the clock measures everyone's progress. But the American is never ready. it is a bullet to be dodged.   The strategy is constant motion. Aren't you with it? Any good junkie knows. Truckers, too. Constant motion is a disguise, the illusion of becoming. Street sweepers enforce the American way. Can't park there on

53
dentity

Mondays. Stasis really does equal death. However, simple motion does not necessarily equal life. Motion only makes sense of the Problem of Time — why the sun flies across the heavens; why that only happens so many times and then we d
what happens to other people and our stuff during the periods when we're not here; and so on. Artist Laurie Anderson once told me the same thing about the Bible.   Brian and Betty Jo Burton sit in stony contemplation at the 76. She stirs
coffee. He chews plug and tips his cowboy hat forward and back. They should look worn out: they've logged 259,000 miles over the road in the last year. Instead, they look serene. You've never seen a couple look more calm, nor two people
committed to keeping it that way. They drive together about 325 days a year, Brian by day and Betty Jo by night. Their universe is five feet of hallway between the wheel and the bunk.   "When we're constantly going, we see each other abo
two hours a day," says Betty.   "If that much," Brian drawls in a heavy southern Illinois accent. "'Cause we really get to runnin', only time we see each other is..."   "Passin' in the halls," she laughs.   They never used to think about tim
It was all about getting produce and ice cream down the line as fast as possible. Or those 2nd-Day FedEx's that never met the plane. They live according to the dictates of speed, measured not so much by velocity but by constant deadlines a

154

ar-constant motion.   But he's been on the road for ten years now, and Betty Jo for seven, and it's starting to wear. They want to slow down. They want to let time pass unmeasured, instead of squeezing it into a line of mile markers.   "Life sses you by," says Betty.   "You're in the fast lane, runnin' with life, and life passes you and you don't know it," nods Brian.   Betty fixes me with a steady look. "The only thing we actually know out here is from Point A to Point B. Everything sides Point A and Point B is a mystery to us. We don't go to movies because we ain't got time. We don't do anything. When we're home, we've got all this other stuff to get done, plus we end up tryin' to get the truck situated to go back out on road. There's just not enough time."   The slowness of the other drivers sitting quietly over their lunches belies the asphalt running through their minds. Brian says he can't wait to stop, to get at farming the 40 acres they bought, but Betty has some reservations.   "I think I'm just a person that needs to be on the go," she says. "I can't sit here. I get edgy. Sit in the truckstop too long, it's like, 'Get me out of here!'   "You go home and it's like you're constantly moving, so u gotta get back into the swing of things. You can't wait to get out here. Not to mention there's nobody to fight with out here, except us. The family members and everything — at home, you don't have their problems. So when they start fightin', it's time to go." Brian disagrees. "Any more, it's almost like you gotta use a bull whip to get me to go back out the door," he says. "You, yeah," nods Betty Jo. "Me, it's kind of different. After I'm home for a week, I get an edge to get g again. I don't want to. But it's that constant runnin' there that I can't..." "Can't make my livin' sittin' still," adds Brian, speaking for both. Prairie Dawg and Sweet Texas send e-mail from the road. Most every truckstop has an online ki now, and lots of truckers carry laptops. He went on the road four years ago, when a bad divorce cost him his job as a machinist, his house, his kids, and his former life in St. Louis. Her story wasn't much better. Now they haul obsessively, mo "hot loads" of explosives back and forth across the country. Prairie Dawg writes with a workman's economy that expands, at times, into sunset visions. "I am not a religious man," he writes, "but there are times when I have to th the Lord when I get to the end of my run that I have another day to see the world from the windshield of my truck." The road is dislocation. It is windshield cinema. The eyes are in a constant state of suspension. Any fixed point is dangerous to hold on the retina. Sleep or daydreaming means death. Truckers are preoccupied with images of death, and with moving past it. The eye is the window to the soul. Trucking demands that whatever is in that window must fly through it

SUPREME
RIVERSIDE CA

15

The eye must continually empty or be distracted to death. This is the Tao of Kerouac and the drifter and the Deadhead. Of Steinbeck, of Theroux. Of *Two-Lane Blacktop* or *Easy Rider* or *My Private Idaho* or *Vanishing Point*. This is the Tao of frontier, the great American dream of disappearance.   In his fifth dispatch, Prairie Dawg tags the road's seductive promise: "One of the hardest things to learn on the road, for some of us, is to like yourself. The loneliness is enough overwhelm you. I started finding myself going into restaurants just to be around people. I was hungry for the company. When I should have been out in the truck sleeping, I was sitting around drinking coffee just to be around people. While I was ing I found myself thinking a lot about my life. Pretty soon you get to know yourself real well. I accepted who I am and what I stand for and promised myself that I wouldn't lose it to the road. A lot of drivers out here lose themselves to the road. not sure why, maybe they couldn't accept themselves for who they were. The only thing they talk about is trucks and the life out here. It's like they have become a machine that is part of the truck itself."   Brian: It's called White Line Theory. ty: It's not wanting to deal with responsibilities back at home. Your only responsibility is that truck, and getting loads there. It's a routine.   Brian: White Line Theory: You ain't happy unless you're seeing that line go by. The only thing you got

57
dentity

to deal with then is what's in the cab with you.   Betty: Yeah. If a shipper makes you mad or anything, you pick up their load and you leave. You never have to see them again. The receiver's the same way. You don't have to deal with their proble
You don't gotta deal with your own. There's a lot of times when there's aggravation at home...   Brian: Then it is time to leave. (laughs)   Betty: (laughs) Yeah. It's easier getting in the truck and leaving than dealing with it.   "There's a s
ing: 'Once you get diesel in your blood, you're done,'" chuckles Bob Nunnally, taking a break from laundry chores at the big Rip Griffin truckstop in Barstow, California. Dressed hat to boots in sharp cowboy gear, Bob has been driving "on and
since coming out of the U.S. military in 1967. "I tried retiring one time, back in 1989, for three years. Every time a truck would go by the house, I always had that feeling that I should be somewhere else. I'm one of the few that doesn't have a
and children. Fifty-two years old, I've never been married. I'd be one of these guys you hear about, been divorced five or six times. Once you get out here and start running, you're never home."   Trucking is not about arriving. Arriving is soci
awkward and risky. Leaving, however, is romantic. Riding off into the sunset is the ultimate expression of cowboy culture. Like *Shane*.   "It doesn't make any difference where I am, I always want to be somewhere else," nods Dave Sweetn

15

host before I have the question out of my mouth. "I love my wife dearly, but after I've been home for that five-, six-, seven-day span, I'm ready to head for Dallas. Not because I particularly love Dallas or Cleveland or any place else...it's not the living that's important, it's the going." Sweetman hauls vintage and exotic cars for Horseless Carriage. He's 47, childless by choice ("I would not want to raise a family over the telephone"), and started hauling in the army in 1969. He owns a 35,000 1997 Kenworth T-600 with a 475-hp Caterpillar engine and a tricked-out sleeper cab, and gets a new one every four or five years. He's an owner-operator at the very top of his profession. He owns a Ferrari and a condo on a tony hillside overlooking Dana Point, CA. But his struggle with time and identity issues are exactly the same as his company-driver counterpart, the JB Hunt pool driver making 41 cents a mile. He tries to connect with a network of friends wherever he goes, writes for magazines, participates in a "Trucker Buddy" program with schools and a safety program with Chevron. All are strategies against loneliness and the trucker's loner image. "It keeps you from being drawn too far into getting lost on the road," he says. "When I got divorced, I didn't have a house. I didn't have a car. I had nothing. I had a semi-truck. I'm sure a psychologist would look at that and say, 'Oh, well, that was just the rebellion stage, 'cause you were hurt from a bad

relationship.' All I wanted to do was go from place to place and have nothing to hold me back. It wasn't that I was running away *from* anything, it was more like I was running toward something. I just didn't know what it was."   A new relationsh
with time? Speed and motion became Sweetman's strategy to rebuild meaning. "Lost on the road" means losing volition or identity to the demands of the odometer. Just get the miles in. Don't worry about what you know, what it means, what it w
that you once wanted or believed in, or any events that occur outside the white lines. It doesn't even matter who you are. Just believe in the destination as a mission. Let it define you. Motion is identity.   "I don't wear a watch because tim
irrelevant," says Scott Blake, 24, sitting in the coffeeshop at Rip Griffin in Barstow. "I don't have no time."   Mileage is a perfect illusion to mask the process of becoming. In the career arc of the trucker, he eventually comes to know hims
by...mileage. More than the years, the jobs held and lost, homes or spouses or financial goals longed for, gained, traded in. Every trucker tells me it's hard to remember what day it is without the log book. The log is history. *Festino ergo sum*. I hu
therefore I am. By a constant emptying of miles, a place-dependent identity is transformed (lost on the road) into an identity of arrival and departure.   Speed is history. Speed is self.   More people are trucking every day. F

.99

16

n being some relic of the pre-online world, the trucking industry is growing faster than drivers can be found and trucks built. The 2,897,000 drivers in 1994 will swell to 3,196,000 by 2005, a 10.3% increase.[1] According to the American Trucking ssociation, one out of every 14 civilian jobs is trucking-related.   According to the 1993 Commodity Flow Survey conducted by the U.S. Census Bureau, freight transportation has grown an average of 2 percent annually from 1970 to 1996, en it reached 3.7 trillion ton-miles, and that's why you see more trucks on the road.[2] In 1993, trucks moved 72 percent of all freight by value and 53 percent by tonnage — more than rail, intermodal (combinations of rail and truck, boat and rail, boat d truck, etc.), air and "other and unknown." This is a higher percentage than ever. Most of the high-volume, low-cost stuff like coal or ore tend to move by rail, but the higher the value of the goods, the more likely they move by truck.   U.S. reau of Transportation Statistics analyses also point out that Just-In-Time inventory systems and Information Technology used to coordinate catalogue sales (for instance) place a premium on speed, shipping smaller quantities of higher-priced ds much faster than trains and often faster than scheduled air delivery, thus favoring the use of trucks.   This is part of an overall transportation boom. Between 1980 and 1996, U.S. domestic air travel has doubled to 538 million "emplanements" (one person flying one scheduled passenger flight). Passenger-miles (car, plane, bus, train, etc.) increased more than 50 percent to 4.4 trillion annually, and ton-miles of freight increased 25 percent. The average household making $50K per year now takes an unbelievable 6.3 long distance trips annually. And space shrank on the road: highway lane-miles increased 0.2 percent while vehicle-miles increased 3.1 percent.   Factoring in heavy job attrition, "turnover" hires, and indus-try growth, trucking figures to hire 4,425,000 drivers between 1994 and 2005.   Because of the numbers involved, trucking could be considered a nomadic subculture. After being glorified in the 1970s by such movies as *Smoky and the Bandit* and television shows like *BJ and the Bear* and *Movin' On,* or even one-hit-wonder C. W. McCall's tune, "Convoy," trucking culture has shed its romantic cowboy image (smash-up action movies like 1998's *Black Dog* ring the change) and settled into the monotonous grind of steady displacement. In other words, riding off into the sunset is now a professional and permanent state for a huge number of Americans. Nomadism is on the rise.   "The 'search for identity,'" writes Paul Shepard, "is not only a social but an ecological problem having to do with a sense of place and time in the context of all life."[3]   Who are we when we can no longer say, "Where I'm from...?" It only takes a couple of years on the road, or in some cases months,

idea of "home" to be romanticized beyond any real interaction with a house or a neighborhood as a continuum of self. In this sense, truckers experience a more extreme version of the loss of sense of place that has accompanied the malling merica. A strong sense of alienation from place has been decried as a major consequence of a global franchise economy by ecologists such as Shepard, sociologists, and even child psychologists.[4] Wendell Berry writes in *The Unsettling merica*: "Once we see our place, our part of the world, as *surrounding* us, we have already made a profound division between it and ourselves." But it's an everyday reality on the road. Home, the place where one truly interacts with oneself in s of a dynamic interaction with the Other (loved ones, animals, structures, plants, dirt, weather), becomes static. It's present only as hypertrophied memory.   And held in place by the illusion of movement. American-style convenience, oard argues, is a poor substitute for a culture or "true *cultus* with its significant ceremony, relevant mythical cosmos, and artifacts." Will a mix of nostalgia and speed do? Who's to say that a *cultus* of constant motion is not rising? Perhaps our stance to speed has blinded us in the same way that our grand romance with progress has turned Anytown, Earth, into Disneyland. Shepard doesn't see us giving value to solitude and integrating our frenetic motion with evolutionary goals,

like some great manifesto by the Futurists. "Instead of these," he says (and we elect him spokesman because he says it more succinctly than the others), "what are foisted on the puzzled and troubled soul as Culture, Security and Escape are m[...] art museums, more psychiatry, and more automobiles." But exactly. We are all cruising along in the trucker's wake.   Bob Nunnally has a farm in Harrison, Pennsylvania. He has a college degree and wore a suit and tie for the Ford M[...] Company for 20 years, driving part time all the while. He speaks fondly of his home and his three dogs, two cockatiels, and four horses. But he spends six to ten weeks at a pop away from them. That place doesn't define him, or his day-to-[...] behavior, as much as the Rip Griffin truckstop. Or driving away from it.   "Johnny Cash sang an old song that says, a driver has nothing in common with the working man that's home every day at five. They get up, they go to work, they're h[...] by five. We're not. We're hauling our home down the road, more or less. That's where we live."   Wendell Berry writes about "specializations" that pull one away from a generalized knowledge of life or a place. For a trucker, the image[...] permanence that make up memory become images of passing, of having been there once and left. Or, conversely, they become images held static by displacement, like a photograph of an old girlfriend treasured by a man in jail. The trucker ma[...]

16

e — the passing of seasons, years, people — by the route they were driving at the time. The lot they were sleeping in when it happened. The model truck they were operating that year. How does it affect a nation to have a growing number of ctically invisible citizens circulating through the culture and never stopping, never settling in a knowable local routine, whose paid function is to move at top allowable speed at all times? Perhaps truckers actually choose the road as a rational ponse to a culture already uprooted and homogenized, a way to make sense of their restlessness just as miles make sense of time. Constant motion means losing control of place. Diane Wood went out on the road three years ago, already er fifties, and saw her mother sell the family farm in Illinois. "Oh, God, it was beautiful," she laments. We sit in the Burger King at the TA truckstop in Ontario, California. "Had a little house on it, big humongous yard. She had pear trees, peach trees, ble trees, gooseberries. Now all those trees are gone and the guy who lives next door, his family tore down all the trees and built a huge semi-barn, to put his semi in when he's home. He drives for Warner. They ruined it." Paul Virilio argues t being out of place is also being out of time, and both are a threat to identity. In *Speed and Politics*, he writes: "Social conflicts arise from rivalries between those who occupy and preserve an ecosystem as the place that specifies them as a family or group, and that therefore deserves every sacrifice, including sudden death. For if 'to be is to inhabit' (in ancient German, *buan*) not to inhabit is no longer to exist. Sudden death is preferable to the slow death of he who is no lo[nger] welcome, of the reject, of the man deprived of a specific place *and thus of his identity*." Scratching at standard models to help him make transition to identity, Nunnally sustains himself on that good ol' nostalgia: "It's the last of the Amer[ican] cowboy," he says. "The American cowboy had no place. He drifted. You look at your drivers today, it's the same thing, 'cept instead of drifting on horseback from cattle drive to cattle drive, you drive from city to city." "Everybody's born a little bit of Gypsy," says Diane Wood. "And once you get the taste of being a Gypsy, you kind of like it." "I look at it as a permanent vacation," says Scott Blake. He hauls double-wide trailer homes. "You're the last of the pioneers. You know [the] land almost better than your government. I come out here every day with a smile. Any way you want to go, you can go there and get paid to do it." "I love what I do a great deal," says Dave Sweetman. "I'm better able to find myself. Doe[s] that sound a little sixties-ish?" Brian from Alberta adds: "I used to work at an office for seven years, and four walls got me down. You're always out, gone different places. It's cold in the winter in Canada, it's warm coming to California. Th[e]

we do it. It's fun."   Mythology, it seems, is part of the business. This nomadic culture longs for symbols of permanence, but more accurately defines itself by restlessness, and by the motion that is its only cure.   "I'm sitting here now,
a pick-up in L.A. tomorrow morning and it's going to Raymond, New Hampshire," Nunnally drawls. "I'm going 3,000 miles the other side of the country because, right now, sitting is driving me crazy."   The longing for mythology itself holds
potential for an emerging Acceleration Culture. Truckers' lore is deepening. They repeat certain mantras: Sitting still makes you crazy. Time doesn't exist without a log book. You become part of the machine. Sleep better in the truck than at home.
wife told me one time that if I ever retire — and I probably never will, because it would be too boring otherwise — how would I be able to sleep at night without that vibration of the engine?" says Sweetman. "I sleep better in this truck than I do in
own bed at home."   Mobile society is powered by a compulsion to move, and is comforted by the signifiers of movement. They cannot sleep without the droning of a reefer unit or an idling Caterpillar. Not unlike the rest of America, asleep in
of the TV, the vehicle of their everyday motion. In a country where being able to drive is a birthright, trucking is both the dream of freedom and the dream crushed. "There are a lot of closet truck drivers out there," says Sweetman. Not only

ntity

does the choice to drive a truck seem more driven by an urge to leave than by a desire to arrive, but the constant state of motion is also accompanied by a constant state of loss.   "It's made me lonely," says Wood. "I've got a constant pain I'm lonely, so that takes down a lot of area, that word 'lonely' does, all by itself."   "You can turn yourself into a hermit without a whole lot of trouble," notes Sweetman, gesturing around the interior of his truck. "I have a microwave and a vection oven. I have a fridge. I have a freezer. I have a satellite dish. I have a color TV, a VCR. I have a shower. I have a potty. I've got a highway master's satellite GPS tracking system, and cellular phones, and all the bells and switches and kn and dials and gauges...it's a little bit inviting. I can completely cut myself off from the human world except for dealing with my customers, if I want to." He immediately adds, "I don't want to."   "You got to be stable within yourself in ord pick up and go," says Wood.   "You lose your life," says a driver named Russell, adding, "I would be doing something else, sure. Get treated too much like a second-class citizen. Truck driver, you're nothing."   Acceleration culture is culture of the permanent outsider. Nomads everywhere are ostracized because lack of investment in place gives them an air of unaccountability. The trucker is America's Bedouin. The first obstacle is simply the physical size of the truck. Reside

reets are off limits. Drivers of "four wheelers" (passenger cars) hate them. Only Wal-Marts let them on their lots to shop. Worse, though, is the age-old fear of the drifter. The migrant. The homeless.   "The first thing I noticed when I became driver was being shunned," writes Prairie Dawg. "Society has gotten this image of truck drivers being a low-life animal. I went out to a country nightclub and asked this woman to dance. As we were two-stepping around the dance floor, she asked e what I did for a living. When I told her that I was in school to be a driver she walked off the floor and left me standing there."   Soon, though, the dance itself will be whatever the nomad makes it. Because Acceleration Culture will decide what is pular. It'll be considered real, *muy autentico*. As shopping becomes a sole source of national identity, transforming online communities into nodes of exploding demand for goods delivered to homes located in a totally different geography, truckers e going to move it all, faster and faster. In a very short hop into the future, truckers may be among the few who must interact with that geography, our old geography, at all.   But right now, the culture isn't in place. And there are physical limits to w much motion and stripping the old identity can take. For the trucker, the spastic dream of escape, of speeding, of being a "mover and shaker," of divorce from the sweat and labor of Genesis, is often finally supplanted by the dream of Old Time,

169
identity

of that terrain before the eye learned to perceive the motion of the steam engine and the Industrial Revolution of the 1830s.   "I've worked horses, I've worked the river, I've drove trucks, and I've farmed. I'm goin' back to what I know: the farm," says Brian Burton. "Raising horses because it's slowed down. I can watch life go by."   "Yeah," says Betty Jo, "time to slow down, watch the world just pass you by instead of you passing the world by."   "Sit back on the front porch swing, kick a pig while you still got the legs to do it," says Brian. "Listen to the raccoons fly around on the roof of the house while you're tryin' to sleep.   "Eventually, all that stuff will be gone," Betty adds ruefully.   "There also comes a point in your life where you need to slow down," says Sweetman. "That doesn't mean that you drag along at fifty miles an hour, because, in this business, time is money."   "I'm looking at that one of these days," nods Diane Wood. "Get a little job and stay home and that'll be it. It used to be the American Dream. Nice house, nice car, good job, 3.2 kids. But right now, this is my life."

1 Gallup Organization, for the American Trucking Association Foundation, "Empty Seats and Musical Chairs: Critical Success Factors in Truck Driver Retention," Oct. 1997.
2 U.S. Dept. of Transportation, Bureau of Transportation Statistics, "Transportation Statistics Annual Report 1998: Long-Distance Travel and Freight," BTS98-S-01, (Washington, D.C., 1998).
3 Paul Shepard, "Ecology and Man — A Viewpoint," in The Subversive Science: Essays Toward an Ecology of Man, ed. Paul Shepard and Daniel McKinley (Boston: Houghton Mifflin, 1969), 9.
4 Paul Shepard, "Place in American Culture," North American Review 262 (Fall 1977): 22-32.

→chinese funeral objects

CHINESE FUNERAL OBJECTS

 Paper funeral objects which accompany the Chinese into the grave
take speed and convenience into the afterlife.

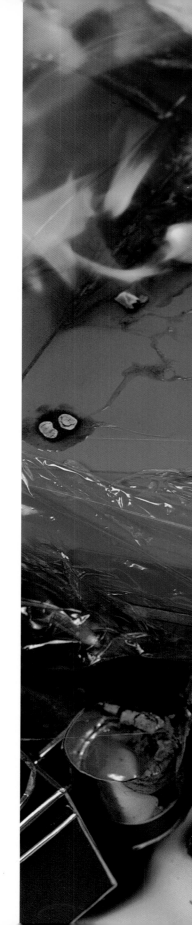

75
hinese
ineral
bjects

9 SPEED

AS
VEHICLE

IMAGINATION AND THE WORLD SUPERSONIC LAND SPEED RECORD

→ The sun leaks over the Selenite Mountains to the east and the horizon shifts, seems to shorten by several miles, as a huge pyramid of talcum-fine lake bed dust erupts from a spot made invisible by the curvature of the earth. Then the dust becomes a line across the slate-flat heart of the 30-mile alkaloid playa of Nevada's Black Rock Desert, and then a line moving so fast it becomes difficult to follow, and finally a black nose cone pokes through the heat shimmer and flash of afterburners and the witnesses on the media island are hit by the 175-decibel roar of twin Rolls-Royce Spey 205 turbo-jet engines as Royal Air Force squadron commander Andy Green plows by in the 10-ton *Thrust SuperSonic Car*, moving at 517 mph like he's rolling a Cadillac to the corner for bread.   On another day two weeks later, the gargantuan Thrust "car" pierces the sound barrier here without too much trouble on its way to a new supersonic world land speed record of 763.035 mph (Mach 1.020) — a barrier which, like Chuck Yeager flying the X-1 rocket plane exactly 50 years (to the day) earlier, most experts said could not be crossed.   This used to be a contest in which men drove the fastest cars on earth, but it's not anymore. In order to relate this to the car in your garage, and what it is becoming, we need to see it in Doobyvision.   The Imagination Station is an art installation, of sorts, overlooking Black Rock's bonemeal flats. This one-man hut was erected in the foothills outside the wind-scored watering hole of Gerlach (pop. 350) by a true outsider artist named DeWayne "Dooby" Williams, also known as the Guru of Gerlach. It sits on Guru Ave., a mile-long dirt loop just off route 34 along which Dooby set hundreds of headstone-like rocks etched with bits of wisdom and remembrance such as "life is nothing but a big joke kick back and watch the show" and "the guru will guide you anywhere you want to go" and "the heart of art is a cute butt."   Sitting in the single rusted chair inside the Imagination Station, the eye travels out through seven screenless television bodies hung as windows in its tamarisk-and-pigwire walls — out to where the Jackson range and the Black Rock itself pokes up through the heat shimmer, and then further out, to an unmarked but oft-visited spring where hearts empty out and the person you want to be is waiting. The terrain of transformation.   The seven TV windows offer different views of an expanse which humans have not changed much, but which changes them instead. Above each gutted TV hangs a clock, hands fixed or missing, electric cords plugged into wood poles or banging in the sage-soaked wind. A rock at the entrance reads: "The Desert Broadcasting System."   Doobyvision sends the eye out over this magical terrain at the speed of imagination. That is the terrain over which the world land speed record racers must drive now. The latest showdown on the playa between Englishman Richard Noble's Thrust team and all-American daredevil Craig Breedlove's Spirit of America crew has broken with the past. The age of hot-rodding is over. The fierce competition between these two camps has accelerated transportation technology beyond the garage, beyond the 30-mile run-out of this dormant lake, beyond their own meta-drag race. In many ways, they've rendered the world land speed record moot by a quantum leap in design that exposes not just new possibilities for fast cars, but rather a new end-goal altogether: travel at the

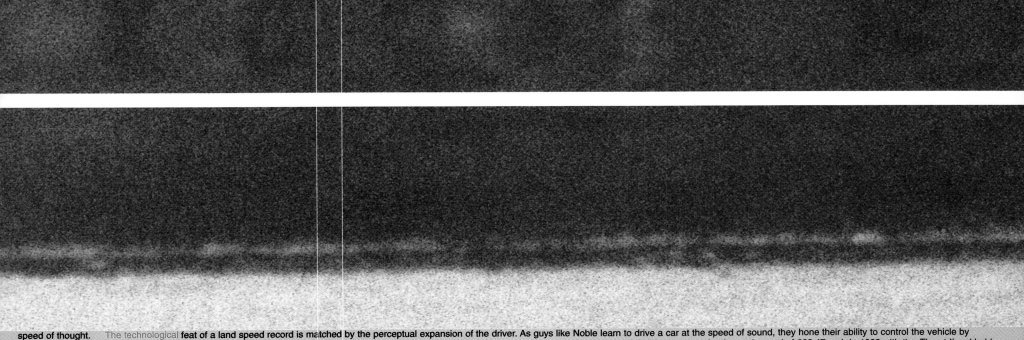

speed of thought.   The technological feat of a land speed record is matched by the perceptual expansion of the driver. As guys like Noble learn to drive a car at the speed of sound, they hone their ability to control the vehicle by reconfiguring their sense of time.   "It's very interesting," says Richard Noble, visionary behind the *Thrust SSC* and its predecessors *Thrust I* and *II*. Noble set a new land speed record of 633.47 mph in 1983 with the *Thrust II* and held it for 14 years until Andy Green drove the new *Thrust SSC* to beat it by 130 mph in 1997. "When I was driving [*Thrust II*], I was driving on a very regular basis. What happens is that your mental processes speed right up, just like when you're about to have an auto crash. Everything happens in very, very slow motion. You're actually holding the wheel between finger and thumb — it's a very delicate sort of thing. There is plenty of time for everything. It's very relaxing. On the last [record attempt], I was actually hammering the side of the car saying, 'Get on with it! Hurry up!' 34,000 horsepower, ya know? I suppose I'd gotten to a stage of development where I was ahead of the car."   Being ahead of the car reflects our Darwinian urge to accelerate. We travel, communicate, and even live so much faster in our minds than the body allows. But that is slightly less true if you happen to be driving a land speed record car, where the blinding speed is actual, registered by real dirt moving beneath your wheels, and control has perfectly correlating consequences. Mostly we struggle with the perceptual gap. Unconsciously or not, we want the body to move as fast as our ever-faster electronic reality. This modern version of the classic mind/body split fuels "the need for speed" and helps explain the quest for the unlimited land speed record.   These jet cars, in particular, are somewhat analogous to spacecraft in that they represent an evolution in moving the body through real distances. They clearly mimic communications technology in delivering us from the limitations of the body, but they also reaffirm the body by actually hurling it through space. And in the most ordinary way: in a car.   "*Thrust II* was probably one of the most stable and best land speed cars of all," Noble chuckles, obviously discounting the new *Thrust SSC*. "It went over 600 mph 11 times. It got so reliable that it was our 600 mile-an-hour taxi. Seriously. That's what you've gotta do with them, of course. You've gotta keep making them more and more reliable until eventually you get to a point where 600, 650, 700 mph is just commonplace."   "I think the sense of time is probably the same, it's just that the amount of data that you take in within that time frame is altered," says Noble's principle competition, Craig Breedlove. "It takes a while afterwards to be able to download it. It's amazing how much information you actually pull in and how much you can [retrieve]."   The 600+ mph car has become commonplace among an elite corps of land speed record chasers, including Noble, Breedlove, Art Arfons and his jet-powered *Green Monster*, the late Gary Gabelich with his rocket-powered *Blue Flame*, Ed Shadle and Keith Zanghi's *North American Eagle*, Stan Barrett's 739.666 mph Budweiser rocket car (an unofficial record set at Edwards Air Force Base, December 17, 1979), and Rosco McGlashan's jet-engined *Aussie Invader III.* But the vehicle Noble brought to Black Rock in 1997 bent the perceptual curve into utterly alien territory.

The *Thrust* SSC is a gloss-black monster twice the weight and power of any other known speed record car. It runs a pair of Rolls-Royce Spey 202 or 205 turbojet engines used in the English Royal Air Force (RAF) Phantom fighter jet. The car sucks aviation fuel at 4.8 U.S. gallons per second and generates about 50,000 lbs of thrust with afterburners and a rough maximum of 110,000 horsepower. (Noble points out that this equals about 1,000 Ford Escorts, or 145 Formula One racing cars.) It's stopped by disc brakes and parachutes. Driver Andy Green sits well forward between the two tubular engines, steering with the rear wheels. Computers control an extremely active suspension, making adjustments every microsecond from telemetry gathered by sensors all over the car. The suspension is designed for high downforce, slamming the thing to the ground like a jet-powered brick when buffeted by shock waves at the sound barrier — roughly 760 mph, at this temperature and altitude — and beyond, to its top design speed of 850 mph.   To put that in perspective, 315-mph top fuel dragsters run the quarter-mile in 4.45 seconds, at top speed. *Thrust* does the whole mile in 4.3, dragging the dream of driving fast straight out of the garage and into a world of money and technical expertise where very few can follow.   Including, maybe, American land speeder and people's hot-rodder Craig Breedlove. Breedlove is the original jet-car designer. He bought his first surplus General Electric J-47 turbojet engine in 1961, when he was 24 years old, and in July 1963 the *Spirit of America* was the first to break the 400 mph barrier with a new record of 407 mph. Now 62 and a grandfather, Breedlove has held the record five times. He was the first driver through 500 mph (1964) and 600 mph (1965) and has had his eyes on the sound barrier since the '60s. He built the *Spirit of America Sonic I* in 1965, based on a newer-model GE J-79 engine, but retired it at 600.601 mph. Inspired by Gabelich's *Blue Flame*, he then designed a rocket car that burned hydrazine (his rocket dragster also used a lunar module engine, reifying the link between land speed and space travel), but suddenly imposed government restrictions on that highly volatile space-race fuel forced him to shelve the car in the early '80s. Now he's built a third-generation *Spirit of America* he thinks can push 800 mph.   If it's the same car he brought to Black Rock to run against *Thrust* in 1997, however, he may have to rethink it. Stability problems have plagued the car since it first made record attempts in 1996. Basically, it's the same tricycle design he's been using since 1963 — one (now a dual) carbon/glass wheel up front, two set far apart in the rear. This *Spirit of America* runs a single Modified J79 GE-8D-11B-17 jet engine from a U.S. Navy F-4 Phantom fighter. This engine puts out 22,650 lbs of thrust and 45,200 horsepower with afterburner and water injection. It burns plain ol' Shell 92-octane premium gasoline. Breedlove drives the car himself, crammed into a cockpit 20 inches wide and three feet long at the nose of the 44-foot craft. He steers by the front wheels and the downforce is calibrated to be the minimum necessary. Fully loaded with fuel, *Spirit of America* weighs 9,000 pounds.   Breedlove is the kind of driver that Americans identify with. He puts his helmet on and the hammer down. Because of the difficulty in simulating the ground moving under the car in the wind tunnel, his

car is built with only computer modeling. In a sense, it's a completely untested design. In November 1996, that almost cost him his life. He ran the new *Spirit of America* up to an unofficial speed of 675 mph out on the Black Rock playa when it was hit by a sudden gust of crosswind and went into a long, hairy U-turn. Unable to correct it, Breedlove rode it out until the car flipped on its side and ground to a halt in a seven-mile-long skid, his head only inches from the grinding desert surface.   This death-sledding gave him pause, but not the Fear. Thinking about it, he offers a dose of his trademark feelgood: "If you hit a few bumps along the way, that's just what doing this is, and you've got to dust yourself off and get on the next horse, you know? You're not going to break all the horses."   The *SOA* engineering team, led by a 30-year-old rocket and robotics developer named Dezsö (say "Dezshur") Molnar, who proudly tells me, "I don't know a thing about jet engines," determined that the car flipped because of transonic instability. That means that parts of the car went supersonic while other parts did not — especially the underside, where air accelerates as it's squeezed between the aluminum shell and the ground.   With some aerodynamic redesign, this is the same car Breedlove is running now. It quickly met with other hardships. In an unprecedented meeting of technology and testos- terone, Breedlove and Noble agreed to run head-to-head for the record in 1997, with both teams on the desert at the same time. On his second day of low-speed shakedown runs, Breedlove took his car straight to 328 mph, but the engine apparently sucked in some kind of FOD — foreign object damage — shredding its compressor blades. While the *Thrust* car ran smoothly to 624 mph the following day, Breedlove was back in his shop in Rio Vista, California, making a public appeal for money to put a new engine in his car. To add insult to injury, the *Thrust* crew had to tow the *Spirit of America* transport vehicle out of the playa mud in the middle of the night. By the time Breedlove did make it back to Black Rock with a new engine, he was essentially too late, too slow, and his team too raggedy.   "Performance is not a problem," says good-natured *Thrust SSC* designer Ron Ayers, the man who single-handedly outmoded land speed records forever. As we talk on a flatbed truck next to *Thrust*'s inflatable quonset hut, he squints at the Breedlove camp a few miles away across the playa. "You just put a big enough engine in a small enough chassis and you can go as fast as you like, God help you.   "I reversed the usual logic and said, 'What is the most *stable* shape we can have, and then see how fast you can make it go.'"   The shape Ayers dreamed up is exactly the reverse of every car that came before. Two wide-set wheels up front, long tail out the back. Weight forward. Somewhat like Buckminster Fuller's vaunted Dymaxion car. Two engines instead of one. Ayers drew it from gut instinct, designed it using a quarter-million British pounds' worth of donated Cray supercomputer time, and tested it exhaustively on a rocket sled. He also saw to it that the results were well published in journals and on the excellent *Thrust* web site (sponsored by Digital). Even Breedlove could have used them.   "Imagine if you're throwing a dart: you have the heavy bit at the front and the feathers at the back, otherwise it'll turn 'round in mid-air," says Ayers. "A high-speed car's got to be the

same. By comparison, a single engine can only go out the back. Anywhere else and you burn the driver's head off. So, two engines for stability, not performance." He smiles mischievously, an old man on vacation. "But the extra engine does no harm for performance at all."   Dooby's Imagination Station is an origination point for instantaneous transmission of self and extension of vision. Peering through the empty TVs, you're reminded that the waste dump of stock images representing electronic culture — TV, web, film, radio, and all future-sounding combinations of same — are really only a microscopic part of the Big Picture. They don't represent the *possibilities* at all. Out here you know the movement of geologic time instead of the loud ticking of human fear. From here you can see what you are and what you want to be and the infinity between them — which, seeing both sides, you can cross at will. Through an endless succession of technical hurdles such as the ominously worded "sound barrier," Noble and Co. are chasing an idealized image of themselves and acting out a culture-wide desire for transformation that borders on desperation. They are accelerating toward an imagined self. Along the way they are closing, technologically, in on the speed barrier that now dominates our worldview: the speed of light.   "If most drivers are still not yet capable of utilizing a complex electronic language, of combining the transportation of bodies and of information," Paul Virilio wrote in *The Aesthetics of Disappearance,* "at least the headlights and parking lights seem already a means of primary emission, a sort of formulation of desire and of a new presence that drivers are happy to abuse."   The form and terrain of this "new presence" is precisely the subtext to the land speed record. Electrons travel through wires and fiber optic cable at the speed of light. This is the speed of a digital universe. Electrons also carry information through the human nervous system at near-light speeds. This is the speed with which the brain thinks: the speed of thought. The nervous system is of course the paradigm for the electronic or online universe; whole economies pour back and forth through the pipe, reestablishing themselves at each terminus to take on a similar but different life. Online life has also made it commonplace to project our emotional and fantasy selves through telepresence. Instantly. Which once only happened in the mind.   Some top conceptual thinkers entertained the consequences of the "new presence" in November 1996 at the fourth annual Doors of Perception conference — a popular Netherlands-based confab ruminating on sticky new media subjects. The subject was "Speed." The presentations, given by more than 40 speakers ranging from architect Rem Koolhaas to environmental guru Wolfgang Sachs to Disney's Danny Hillis, coalesced around two main points: first, that the vectors of technology and natural resources are out of synch and diverging, leading to an industrial ethic that designs and markets products much faster than natural resources can actually be grown, mined, or recycled to make them; and second, that this is happening on a personal level as well, where our rapidly changing, media-oriented lives are diminishing the physical reality of our bodies. Both phenomena, the conferees suggested, raise the specter of societal schizophrenia and general environmental collapse.   Despite the apocalyptic

763.035 mph (mach 1.020)

overtones,the "Speed" conference posed one of the most important questions of our age: as we trill across the electronic and mental structures of cyberspace, what happens to this bag of bones we drag around attached to our heads? "For the modern mind, space and time are the basic forms of hindrance," lectured Sachs, a member of the Wuppertal Institute environmental think tank and co-founder of Sustainable Germany. "Anything that is away is too far away. The fact that places are separated by distances is seen as a bother. And anything that lasts, lasts simply too long. The fact that activities require time is seen as a waste. As a consequence, a continuous battle is waged against the constraints of space and time; acceleration is therefore the imperative which rules technological innovation as well as the little gestures of everyday life." Land speed records are a kind of gleeful road rage in the face of this hypho-thetical schizophrenia. Guys like Breedlove are experiencing new perceptual models that abide somewhere between the currently polar realities of physical presence and virtual presence. Noble calls this a "new era" of speed machines. "If I could describe being the head of a bird, and the car as an extension of your being, you'd be like the brain inside of the bird because you are part of the vehicle," says Breedlove. "Through the input that comes through the steering wheel, through your back, and through the sensory input you get inside the cockpit, the vehicle becomes an extension of yourself, and you operate it from that level. You are the guidance. You are so integrated with the hardware, it's like there's an absolute synergy between man and machine. Pilots experience that, too. They become like the head of a bird. They feel the wingtips as if they're up there flying with feathers." Dooby knew what he was looking at. Black Rock is the terrain of transformation. The mind races over the horizon where, only a few miles away, the absolute flatness of the place meets the curve of the earth. The lake is dry, but not permanently; the sediment is reportedly 10,000 feet deep in spots, and the water in it is subject to tides. One morning, while a small group of people stood around staring at that horizon waiting for Breedlove's car to run, U.S. Bureau of Land Management Ranger Richard Meyer started running down all the plans that had come across his desk regarding this playa. A San Francisco rock promotor wanted to fence 13 square miles of it, astroturf it, throw a huge music festival and then "donate" the materials to the state (i.e., abandon it). A frog farmer proposed wetting the place and shipping out frog legs by train to Reno and beyond. A Korean man wanted 5 square miles "for purposes he couldn't detail, but which were vital to the continued security of Korea and U.S.-Korean relations." Then there's the fly-in brothel idea that keeps popping up. Prostitution is legal in Nevada. In fact, planes land with impunity out here, picking up and delivering God knows what. Meyer warns, "If a plane lands at night, and there are people there to meet it, I don't advise investigating." The Burning Man festival happened here again only the week before the land speeders arrived, an experiment in instant, free, vaguely technopagan community. The Fly Geyser hot springs are still gray with the baptismal slough of their thousands of bodies. A few of the leftover seekers drift in and out of Bruno's hotel bar and diner in Gerlach looking

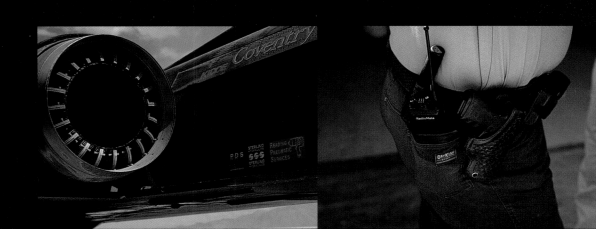

either chemically burnt or possibly enjoying a sort of satori. Bruno's slogan is "Where the Pavement Ends and the West Begins," and that's why people come here. Gambling and prostitution are legal; marriage, gun and corporation laws are slack; get-rich-quick schemes rule the psyche of the place. Nevada is the bitter filter at the end of the American dream; it all strains through here.   The land speed record teams, too, during the month or so they are trying to get the cars perfectly dialed-in, begin to fall into idealized forms. Astoundingly, they are exactly what you might predict. Craig Breedlove and his garage rat *Spirit of America* team fall into an anarchic, brooding, *Rebel Without a Cause* mode, which exactly mirrors the outsider fantasy of the homegrown hotrodder culture from whence they came. Richard Noble and his squad of moonlighting RAF careerists, on the contrary, cop an attitude of hyperefficient sacrifice worthy of *The Bridge Over River Kwai*. One expects them to bust out whistling that annoying theme song any second! The aptly named Breedlove slinks around in his Mustang convertible, custom Buell motorbike and leather coat, taking surreptitious twilight dips in the hot springs with a trio of sexy cheerleaders imported to work his *Spirit of America* media center. A classic old playboy, he's swingin' at the speed of sound. Noble, meanwhile, buzzes about in his crappy rented Dodge Neon, lives like a hermit, and rallies his crew to a military timetable that would do Mussolini proud. When the *Thrust SSC* is running, they take away our car keys to eliminate traffic.   Noble's superior fundraising effort allows him to assemble a small assault force of equipment to bring to the desert, anticipating the possibilities of transformation there. Gloss-painted semi trailers roll out of an Antonov heavy-lift aircraft that transports the whole kit across the world. A pair of Pegasus microlight aircraft police the desert to keep wanderers off *Thrust*'s path. There's a Jaguar firechase car and a paramedic team with a Turbo Commander plane, an army's worth of extra engines, inflatable hangers, tow tractors, trailers, a satellite internet link and 40 days of budget. Guards on the perimeter. "Please stay outside the rope." The whole thing is knit together by a voice emanating from radios on every belt, every car, every plane, a reassuring British woman cooing straight out of James Bond: "Engines are lit. One minute *and counting.*"   So military are they, in fact, that the only man in the world to ever drive faster than the speed of sound has nothing to say about it. "This is my job," says driver Andy Green, upper lip stiff as a corpse. "It's no different from flying jet aircraft, except for the proximity to the ground." Smiling, he deflects questions about perception and fear. "I'm trained not to fear. It's all about the car."   The Americans, on the contrary, have no run schedule, no security, and no apparent rules against drinking on the job. People wander in and out of the quonset hut at will. In fact, advice seems to be flowing freely from a couple of habitual hangers-on who should maybe be in jail. Molnar sprints around in a panic. There's no radio protocol. Breedlove's instinct for publicity, however, has Noble beat by a mile: his SOA Media Center, the converted old post office where locals can buy a T-shirt and a poster and pose for a picture with sexy girls, is a big hit in a town with about 20 public buildings, five of which are bars.   Every night, when the Spirit of

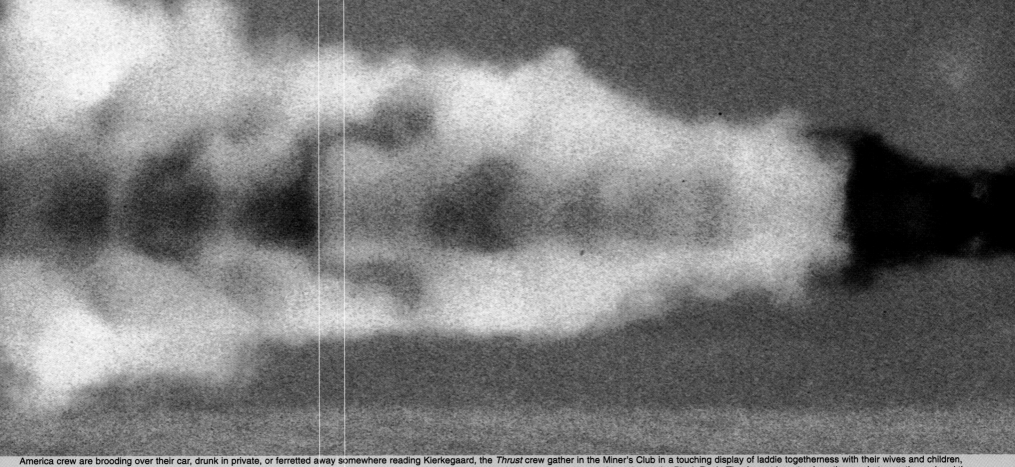

America crew are brooding over their car, drunk in private, or ferretted away somewhere reading Kierkegaard, the *Thrust* crew gather in the Miner's Club in a touching display of laddie togetherness with their wives and children, destroying Coors Light and telling jokes with all the gusto they can manage.   The appearance of these national archetypes seems a natural reaction to the Black Rock. They're out here to close the gap between the real and the ideal, trying to wrestle a life-changing transformation from its harsh dust storms and unforgiving sun and disorienting flatness. Perhaps, in the face of the desert itself, the new presence doesn't seem quite as attainable as the old. Nostalgia is the enemy of acceleration. Or maybe nostalgia is just an acceleration straight toward old traditional goals. Neither whiz-bang technology nor blinding speed necessarily indicate a breakthrough evolution in and of themselves.   Guru Ave. is, by its own signage, "the Wonder Road," "A Story with No Beginning and No End," "Destination Unknown." Dooby was one of those men brave enough, like Edward Abbey maybe, to let the desert wind into his heart and live with the harrowing sounds it made there. The rest of us, the great majority anyway, are looking to get out of that wind as fast as possible, to arrive somewhere. To close the door against it and achieve a result. We not only lust for a newness, but somehow have the gall to imagine it as *permanent,* like a next plateau in experience. Which is why we're so fascinated by a man driving a car faster than sound. It's a step toward a grand arrival. What's next? One thousand miles per hour? It's a given. Two thousand? Why even bother? The secret, Dooby knew, is instantaneous mind travel with no hegemony on possible destinations (such as the cast-iron hegemony of the TV). And who's to say the voyages in his little hut don't involve actual motion? Every quantum leap in speed made by folks like the *Thrust* team closes the gap between technologies high and closed-ended — like the car — and low and open-ended — like the Imagination Station. The new presence is telepresence.

→ bikini

▌→ bikini

→ b²

BIKINI ATOLL, PRESENT

Forty-two years after the last of 23 U.S. nuclear weapon tests laid waste to the island of Bikini in1958, life rushes back undeterred. Washed by the warm South Pacific, the lagoon now shows normal background radiation levels. Bikinians are pushing for treatment of radioactive soil in order to reinhabit their home.

photo © National Geographic Society

18

→end

FOR BETSY SMITH, MEG CRANSTON, AND
SPENSER KUIPERS.

"GOD SPEED THEE AND THY CLOSE" ↳ MILTON

FOR THE HARD WORK AND FRIENDSHIP THAT
MADE THIS BOOK FLY, DOUG AND DEAN
CANNOT ADEQUATELY THANK THE BAFC, ERIC
MATTHIES, HAINES HALL, PATRICK SIMPSON,
WING KO, KATIE MARZOLO, TAKUJI MASUDA,
GUSTAV KOVEN, BIPASHA SHOM, GINO
PANARO, SCOTT HENRICKSEN, FRANCESCO
BONAMI, DAVID GLEAN AND THE STAFF AT
SPOTWELDERS, EVERYONE AT ROCK PAPER
SCISSORS AND P.O.P., JACK AT FREEDOM
TRAVEL AND JANINE AT TRAVEL SOURCE,
ADAM LEVITE, FRANCINE HERMELIN,
EDWARD TAYLOR AND THE DESIGN STAFF
AT ASSOCIATES IN SCIENCE, RAYGUN
PUBLISHING, ROBERT AND MARILYN AITKEN,
BRUCE KUIPERS, AND TOM AND NANCY
WILSON.

PARTICULAR THANKS TO SLOAN HARRIS AND
DAVID UNGER AT INTERNATIONAL CREATIVE
MANAGEMENT, KAREN RINALDI AT
BLOOMSBURY USA, BOB MECOY AT CROWN,
303 GALLERY AND LISA SPELLMAN, NORA
TOBBE AND JENNY LIU, DAVID BOWIE AND
IMAN, AND BULLET INTERNS ROBIN BENWAY,
TONYA CULLEY, SEAN DACK, BRIAN DOYLE,
KELLY HOWSLEY AND DAVID TAKENAKA.
SPECIAL THANKS TO AMY SCHOLDER FOR
ASSISTANCE EDITING THIS MANUSCRIPT, AND
TO DAVID CARSON, CHRISTA SKINNER AND
CORINNA PU AT DAVID CARSON DESIGN FOR
GRAPHIC DESIGN EARLY IN THIS PROJECT.

THE AUTHORS ARE ESPECIALLY INDEBTED TO
THE PERSONS APPEARING IN THIS BOOK AND
AIDING IN RESEARCH ON LOCATION, IN PAR-
TICULAR: COL. JOSEPH W. KITTINGER JR., USAF
(RET.) AND [IN JAPAN] TAKA ISHII AT TAKA ISHII
GALLERY, JUNKO SHIMADA AT GALLERY SIDE
2, JOHNNY WALKER, NOBU KITAMOURA AT
HYSTERIC GLAMOUR, HIROSHI INADA AND
AKEMI NAKAMURA AT CUT, TAKUO HIRAMOTO
AT MTV JAPAN, LUCAS B.B. AT TOKION, RYU
MURAKAMI, TAKUJI MASUDA AT SUPER X
MEDIA, NANACO SATO, TIFFANY GODOY AT
COMPOSITE, SUZANNAH TARTAN, ANNE
MCKNIGHT, TAKAHARU KARASHIMA AND
EMIKO NAKAYAMA; [IN SOUTH DAKOTA]
OFFICERS JOE CROSS AND TIM MCGRADY,
WANBLEE; OFFICER EDWARD YOUNG,
ROSEBUD; CAPTAIN CHRIS GRANT, RAPID CITY
PD; PATROL SERGEANT MIKE WALTERS, DARE
OFFICER CHUCK LECOMPT AND OFFICER
PATSY MARSHALL, EAGLE BUTTE; ELAINE
GIBBONS, PINE RIDGE; [IN LAS VEGAS] DAVE
HICKEY, JAY MOSS AT KAUFMAN & BROAD,
MIMOSA JONES AT ENTERTAINMENT

DEVELOPMENT CORP., P. MOSS AT THE
DOUBLE DOWN, SUSIE TAYLOR AT CATHOLIC
CHARITIES, ROGER RASCH AND JEFF VILLARD
OF LAS VEGAS METRO POLICE HELP TEAM,
PETER RUCHMAN AND HOWARD SCHWARTZ
AT GAMBLER'S BOOK CLUB; [IN OKLAHOMA]
BILLY WILLIAMSON AT ITI FILMS, ARLAN
MANATOWA AT LONG BRANCH STUDIOS, HOLLY
NEUMAN AND THE NATIONAL AUCTIONEERS
ASSOCIATION, AND AUCTIONEERS TROY
LIPPARD, TRACY SULLIVAN, C.D. "BUTCH"
BOOKER, MARTY ROGERS, ELI DETWEILER,
LARRY GARNER, GINGER CASTLE, PAM ROSE,
BETH ROSE, KAREN ROSE, BRENT EARLYWINE,
GARY COFFEE, AND DARLENE DAVIS; [AT
DEMOLITION DERBY] WALTER AND ALLISON
VANWINGERDEN AND THE VANWINGERDEN
FAMILY, ALSO GRAND ROYAL MAGAZINE, ERIC
GLADSTONE, SPIKE JONZE, AND DAN MESSER;
[IN INDIA] ANIL SHARMA AT DESI DESPERADO
CREATIONS, SHEENA SIPPY, HEMA PATEL,
MANMOHAN SHETTY AT ADLABS, RAJESH
JIANDANI AT KODAK, TABREZ NOORANI, AIDA
NOORANI, THE STAFF AT JUHU BEACH HOTEL,
DEPAK NAYAR, KALYANASUNDARAM AND
MISHAL VARMA AT MTV INDIA, SUNIL
MANCHANDA AT MAD ENTERTAINMENT, AAMIR
KHAN, GULSHAN GROVER, AMITABH
BACHCHAN, MANSOOR KHAN, INDRA KUMAR,
FARAH KHAN; [TRUCKERS] DAVE SWEETMAN,
ROBERT AND MELISSA HAYES, BRIAN AND
BETTY JO BURTON, DIANE WOOD, SCOTT
BLAKE, BOB NUNNALLY; [AT BLACK ROCK
DESERT, NEVADA] CRAIG BREEDLOVE, CHERIE
DANSON, RICHARD NOBLE, AND CHERYL
MCGLASHAN.

THIS BOOK WOULD NOT HAVE BEEN POSSIIBLE
WITHOUT THE GENEROUS CONTRIBUTIONS OF
I AM A BULLET SPONSORS: SAMY'S CAMERA
AND STEVE RAAM; OIL FACTORY AND BILLY
POVEDA, JAY WAKEFIELD AND HEIDI HERZON;
SPECIAL PHOTOGRAHIC PRINTING ON DEMOLI-
TION DERBY CHAPTER BY MUSE {X} IMAGING
AND JANE HART AND RANDY GREEN; ALL
PRINTS FROM BOLLYWOOD PROVIDED BY
FLESHTONE COLOR LAB, LOS ANGELES, AND
PAUL KELEMAN.

PHOTO CAPTIONS

→ 006
TESTING A NEW HIGH-ALTITUDE PARACHUTE IN AUGUST 1960, U.S. AIR FORCE CAPTAIN JOSEPH W. KITTINGER, JR., STEPS OUT OF THE BALLOON *EXCELSIOR III* AT 102,800 FEET. KITTINGER FALLS FOR 13 MINUTES AND 45 SECONDS AT SUPERSONIC SPEEDS.

009/010
ACCELERATING AT 32 FEET PER SECOND PER SECOND IN ALMOST PURE VACUUM, KITTINGER FEELS LIKE A MAN IN SUSPENDED ANIMATION. FILM FROM THE GONDOLA SHOWS HIM FALLING AWAY AT 50, 100, AND 165 FEET TOWARD RAIN CLOUDS BELOW AT 21,000 FEET.

014
KITTINGER BREATHES OXYGEN AS HE'S FITTED OUT IN A STANDARD-ISSUE AIR FORCE PARTIAL-PRESSURE SUIT. HE WORE THIS TO PROVE PILOTS COULD BAIL OUT FROM THE EDGE OF THE ATMOSPHERE.

014/015
KITTINGER CHECKS INSTRUMENTS IN THE OPEN, UNPRESSURIZED GONDOLA AT NEW MEXICO'S HOLLOMAN AIR FORCE BASE.

015
EXCELSIOR III RISING THROUGH 40,000 FEET IN A PHOTO TAKEN FROM A JET BOMBER.

016
SPRAWLED IN RAIN-SOAKED NEW MEXICAN SAND AND SAGE, KITTINGER QUIPS, "I'M VERY GLAD TO BE BACK WITH YOU ALL."

022
HITOMI KAMATA AND CHIORI NAKAJIMA IN SHIBUYA PEDESTRIAN ZONE

024
EYE YAMATAKA OF THE BOREDOMS

026
ROCKABILLY DANCERS AT THE CARPARK ON THE HIGH-WAY TO YOKOHAMA

029
HYSTERIC GLAMOUR DESIGNER NOBU KITAMOURA (R) IN STUDIO

038
(TOP) AYUCHI WATANABE IN LOVE HOTEL

039
(LOWER) RYU MURAKAMI

040/041
BOSOZOKU AT THE CARPARK ON THE HIGHWAY TO YOKOHAMA

042
CUT MAGAZINE EDITOR HIROSHI INADA IN POD HOTEL

044
BOREDOMS CONCERT, TOKYO

047
A-DOG IN WANBLEE

055
BOOM-BOOM

059
YOUNG WANBLEE SIOUX IN A POLICE-SPONSORED BOXING CLUB MEANT TO KEEP THEM OUT OF GANGS

064/065
CRAIG LITTLE THUNDER

066
LARRY ROMERO

085
LIMO DRIVER IN FRONT OF CAESAR'S PALACE

091
MS. BETTYE AND GRANDCHILDREN

094
(R) KERRY POPE ON FREMONT STREET

096
C.D. "BUTCH" BOOKER

098
MARTY ROGERS

099
GINGER CASTLE

100
ELI DETWEILER

108
(LOWER) UNIDENTIFIED CREW MEMBER AT THE TULARE COUNTY FAIR DEMOLITION DERBY

109
(CENTER) WALT VANWINGERDEN

110
WALT VANWINGERDEN'S 1966 CHRYSLER 300

124
ON THE SET OF *DAAG* ("THE FIRE") AT KAMALISTAN

132/133
ON THE GROUNDS AT FILMISTAN

134/135
OUTSIDE FLOOR 8, FILM CITY

136/137
LIGHTING TECHNICIANS IN THE RAFTERS ON THE SET OF *MAAN* ("SOUL") AT FILMISTAN

139
(R) GULSHAN GROVER

140
(INSET) AAMIR KHAN LOOKING AT STILLS ON THE SET OF *MAAN* ("SOUL")

143
POP SINGER JASPINDER NARULA MAKING A VIDEO AT FILM CITY

145
(R) AMITABH BACHCHAN

154
BRIAN AND BETTY JO BURTON

172
SCOTT BLAKE

176/177
THRUST SUPERSONIC CAR ON BLACK ROCK DESERT, NEVADA

178
(LOWER RIGHT) *SPIRIT OF AMERICA* IN BREEDLOVE'S SHOP IN RIO VISTA, CA

179
(LOWER LEFT) INSPECTING *SPIRIT OF AMERICA* IN QUONSET HUT ON BLACK ROCK DESERT

179
(LOWER RIGHT) ONE OF *THRUST*'S ROLLS-ROYCE SPEY 205 JET ENGINES

180
(LOWER RIGHT) RICHARD NOBLE MONITORING *THRUST*'S RETURN TO THE GARAGE UNDER TOW

181
(LOWER RIGHT) THE SLATE-FLAT EXPANSE OF THE BLACK ROCK DESERT

182
(LOWER LEFT) *THRUST* DRIVER ANDY GREEN

182
(LOWER RIGHT) *SPIRIT OF AMERICA* IN RIO VISTA, CA

184
(LOWER LEFT) *THRUST*'S IN-LINE REAR WHEELS

184
(LOWER RIGHT) CRAIG BREEDLOVE TESTING OXYGEN EQUIPMENT

186/187
COURSE MARKERS ON THE BLACK ROCK DESERT

COPYRIGHT © 2000 BY DOUG AITKEN AND DEAN KUIPERS

ALL RIGHTS RESERVED. NO PART OF THIS BOOK MAY BE REPRODUCED OR TRANSMITTED IN ANY FORM OR BY ANY MEANS, ELECTRONIC OR MECHANICAL, INCLUDING PHOTOCOPYING, RECORDING, OR BY ANY INFORMATION STORAGE AND RETRIEVAL SYSTEM, WITHOUT PERMISSION IN WRITING FROM THE PUBLISHER.

PUBLISHED BY CROWN PUBLISHERS, NEW YORK, NEW YORK
MEMBER OF THE CROWN PUBLISHING GROUP.

RANDOM HOUSE, INC. NEW YORK, TORONTO, LONDON, SYDNEY, AUCKLAND
WWW.RANDOMHOUSE.COM

CROWN IS A TRADEMARK AND THE CROWN COLOPHON IS A REGISTERED TRADEMARK OF RANDOM HOUSE, INC.
PRINTED IN CHINA

LIBRARY OF CONGRESS CATALOGING-IN-PUBLICATION DATA
KUIPERS, DEAN.
    I AM A BULLET: SCENES FROM AN ACCELERATING CULTURE / TEXT BY DEAN KUIPERS; AND PHOTOGRAPHS BY
        DOUG AITKEN.
    1. TIME—MISCELLANEA. 2. SPEED—MISCELLANEA. 3. CULTURE—MISCELLANEA. I. TITLE.
    BD638.K78   2000
    306—DC21   99-41286
                   CIP

ISBN 0-609-60409-0

10 9 8 7 6 5 4 3 2 1

FIRST EDITION